Shakespeare *Recycled*

Shakespeare *Recycled*

The Making of Historical Drama

Graham Holderness

Professor of Humanities
Hatfield Polytechnic

HARVESTER
WHEATSHEAF

New York   London   Toronto   Sydney   Tokyo   Singapore

First published 1992 by
Harvester Wheatsheaf,
66 Wood Lane End, Hemel Hempstead,
Hertfordshire, HP2 4RG
A division of
Simon & Schuster International Group

Typeset in 10½/12pt Perpetua and Times
by Keyboard Services, Luton

Printed and bound in Great Britain by
Billing & Sons Ltd, Worcester

British Library Cataloguing in Publication Data

Holderness, Graham
    Shakespeare recycled: The making of historical
    drama.
    I. Title
    822.3

    ISBN 0–7450–1116–0
    ISBN 0–7450–1117–9 (pbk)

---

1 2 3 4 5   96 95 94 93 92

For
Susan, Elaine
and
Stephen Holderness

Contents

Acknowledgements

Passages of the present book have appeared previously in various forms, both prior and subsequent to the publication of *Shakespeare's History* (Dublin: Gill and Macmillan, 1985).

Various parts of Chapter One appeared in '*Der Widerspenstigen Zähmung:* "Eine Art Historie"', *Shakespeare Jahrbuch*, 124 (1988), pp. 101–8; 'The Albatross and the Swan: Two Productions at Stratford', *New Theatre Quarterly*, 14 (May 1988); and in *Yearbook of English Studies*, vol. 85, part 1 (1989), pp. 141–4.

Parts of Chapter Two originally appeared in 'Shakespeare's History: *Richard II*', *Literature and History* (1980), pp. 2–24, and were reprinted in '*Richard II*', in *Shakespearean Criticism*, 6 (Detroit, MI: Gale Research, 1987), pp. 414–21.

Parts of Chapter Three originally appeared as '"A woman's war": Femininity in *Richard II*', in *Critical Essays on 'Richard II'*, Bryan Loughrey and Linda Cookson (eds) (Harlow: Longman, 1989), pp. 53–65, and were reprinted in '"A woman's war": a feminist reading of *Richard II*', in *Shakespeare Left and Right*, edited by Ivo Kamps (New York: Routledge, Chapman and Hall, 1991).

Parts of Chapter Seven were originally published as 'Agincourt 1944: Readings in the Shakespeare Myth', *Literature and History*, 10:1 (1984), pp. 24–45, and reprinted in 'Readings in the Shakespeare Myth', in *Popular Fictions: Essays in Literature and History*, Peter Humm, Paul Stigant and Peter Widdowson (eds) (London: Methuen, 1986), pp. 173–95, and in 'Agincourt 1944: Olivier's *Henry V*', in *Shakespearean Criticism*, 14 (Detroit, MI: Gale Research, 1991). Other sections of that chapter first appeared as '"What is my nation?": Shakespeare and National Identities', *Textual Practice*, 5/1 (1991), pp. 80–99.

I am grateful to all editors and publishers involved for permission to reprint the material of this new volume. Gratitude is also due to Jonathan Dollimore and Kiernan Ryan, who helped me reshape this book into its present form.

Graham Holderness   Chiswick, September 1991

History

THIS book is an exercise in the reading of Shakespeare's history plays as history. The need for such an emphasis may well be considered questionable: after all, that group of plays based on the English chronicles was clearly designated 'histories' in the First Folio of 1623, and as 'history plays' they have generally presented (unlike other forms such as comedy and tragedy) few problems of a generic kind. I will however be proposing in the following pages that the accepted definitions of these plays' historical status can be extended so far as to claim that they represent a type of Renaissance historiography.

What emphasis is intended, what theoretical definition proposed, by terming the plays 'historiography'; and how does that classification relate to other possible 'historical' descriptions, some of which would be pretty universally accepted? A convenient theoretical formulation is provided by the *trivium* history, historical evidence and historiography.

The plays would be accepted as *historical evidence* – surviving records and documents attesting to the existence of historical fact – only in a very limited sense: as the record of an Elizabethan intellectual's view of his own society, mediated through fictional reconstructions of that society's past. They could be judged relevant to *history* – the 'aggregate of past events', the chronological sequence of happenings which can be assumed, by a reasonable consensus of historical analysis and judgment, to have occurred – insofar as they adhere to works of historical record and interpretation as sources; the closer the plays approximate to written records, to the chronicles of Halle, Holinshed and other Tudor historians, the nearer they can be judged to approach to actual 'history'. These definitions make good sense in terms of the dominant practices of historiography in modern western societies – essentially literate, empirical, positivist and quasi-scientific – but when applied to Renaissance historical drama, they reveal certain inadequacies. Henry V was a historical character, King Lear a legend (i.e. there is no surviving historical record except tradition to enable us to attribute to Lear a real existence): therefore Shakespeare's *Henry V* is a history play, *King Lear* a fable. If the argument is conducted entirely within the parameters prescribed by modern historical thought, which has its roots in those decades of the seventeenth century immediately following the demise of the historical drama, *some* of Shakespeare's history plays – in common with other works of the period – must be acknowledged a loose and confused mixture of historically authenticated facts and imaginatively-invented fictions. According to the positivistic criteria prescribed by modern historiography, the two categories can be rigidly demarcated, and plays like *Richard II* and *Henry V* can be privileged as possessing a certain authenticity (with suitable allowances made for poetic licence), since they achieve a medium of articulation which observes the distinction between fact and fable, rigorously excluding all legendary and fabulous matter (the victory of Agincourt is 'legend' in a different sense from the ghosts who visit Richard III on the night before Bosworth, or the fiends who support Jeanne d'Arc in *Henry VI Part One*), all folktale and romance situations, all supernatural apparitions; and limiting the elements of historical 'fiction' to an emblematic interlude or a segregated comic sub-plot. From the perspective of modern historiography, the English history plays of Shakespeare would not normally be considered historiography at all. To the new science of history as it developed in the seventeenth century, the plays belong to a world without a proper historiography, to a culture dominated by medieval ideas, mingling legend and fact, myth and reality in a glorious confusion, relying on tradition rather than documentary record and primary source; a world unable, in short, to see the past as anything other than a distorted reflection of its own contemporary present.

In the work of that influential school of historicist criticism which established its basis of cultural power and secured its ideological dominance after the Second World War, and can still be accurately summarised by the name of Tillyard, the historical ideas informing Shakespeare's plays were located within a general world-view dominated by the heritage of medieval Christianity: a philosophical system in which the state, or 'body politic', was never considered relativistically as a particular form of social organisation, developed from and subject to change – but as one of the functions of a universal order, created and supervised by God, and ruled directly by the machinations of divine providence. A state of human society occupied a median position in a cosmic hierarchy (the chain of being) with God and the angels above, and the animal and plant kingdoms below. The structure of a well-ordered state was itself a microcosm of the hierarchical cosmos, containing within itself a chain of being, from the monarch at the head, through the various gradations of social rank down to the lowest orders. The ruler of a body politic possessed power which reflected, but was also subject to, that of God: a king therefore ruled by Divine Right. The natural condition of a state, like the natural condition of the cosmos, was 'order', defined primarily in terms of the maintenance of this rigid hierarchy. Any rupturing of this pattern would produce disorder or 'chaos'; since the state was a component of divine order, such alteration could not be accepted as legitimate social change, but had to be condemned as a disruption of the divine and natural order, to the displeasure of God. The extreme forms of such disruption, such as the deposition of a king and the usurpation of a throne, would constitute a gross violation of order, inevitably punished by the vengeance of God, working through the machinery of providence.

This comprehensive system of Elizabethan thought was developed fully by Tillyard in *The Elizabethan World Picture* (1943), and applied specifically to the functioning of the state within the universal order in *Shakespeare's History Plays* (1944).[1] Here the whole sequence of English chronicle plays becomes a grand illustration of the operation of divine providence in human affairs, with the deposition and murder of Richard II initiating a disruption of the universal order, a century of social chaos and civil war, the punishment of those responsible and their descendants by the exercise of divine wrath – a process ended only by the 'succession' of Henry VII to the English throne. The plays are said to offer a unified historical narrative expressing a politically and morally orthodox monarchist philosophy of history, in which the Tudor dynasty is celebrated as a divinely sanctioned legitimate regime, automatically identifiable with political stability and the good of the commonwealth. Reflecting rather than expressing, since the system had already been developed by the great Tudor historiographers, especially in Edward Halle's *Union of the Two Noble and Illustre Families of Lancaster and York*

(1548); and was embodied in various forms of loyalist political discourse, from government directives like the homilies against rebellion to comprehensive works of political science.

This authoritarian school of criticism, anticipated by L. C. Knights and G. Wilson Knight, and extended by J. Dover Wilson, constructed its model of Elizabethan culture from a highly selective range of sources, arbitrarily privileged and tendentiously assembled. The sources drawn on are either works of government propaganda or of Tudor apology from the more conservative 'organic intellectuals' of the state (Tillyard asserts for instance that the Machiavellian school of Italian humanist thought had no impact on English culture); or convenient details arbitrarily stripped from works which are by no means as reductively orthodox as Tillyard implies. These materials constitute a fair description of the dominant *ideology* of Elizabethan society: in no sense do they represent a complete or even adequate picture of the true complexity and contradictoriness of culture and ideology in this rapidly changing, historically transitional period. In the writings of Tillyard the plays derive their 'historical' character entirely from the very rigid ideological constrictions of their own time: they present the past as a mirror-image of the present; they speak of the history of the late sixteenth century rather than the history of the later middle ages; they are historical evidence rather than historiography.

In the last thirty years this model of Elizabethan culture has been thoroughly displaced. Historical scholarship has demonstrated, by researching more deeply into the cultural and ideological context of Tudor and Elizabethan England, that this 'world-picture', powerful and influential though it may have been, was only *one* dimension of Renaissance ideology, an official or orthodox world-view held, imposed and preached by church and state and by an organic establishment intelligentsia. In practice, Elizabethan culture was as diverse and as contradictory as could be expected of the culture of a rapidly changing and at times turbulent historical period. Not every Elizabethan accepted the state's official ideology: there were Catholics who thought differently from Protestants, Puritans who thought differently from either, and not only about religion; there were apologists for absolute monarchy and opponents of it. This is more than just a way of saying that in any society there is likely to be a wide diversity of opinion about everything: it is rather an insistence that in any society there are connected but separable and conflicting ideologies, dominant, residual and emergent; antagonistic and competing bodies of thought and systems of value, which in their perpetual struggle for political power constitute the complex and contradictory structure of a given historical conjuncture.

In particular these competing ideologies delivered different modes of understanding the past. As long ago as 1957 Irving Ribner wrote:

> What Tillyard says of Shakespeare is largely true, but by limiting the goals of the serious history play within the narrow framework of Halle's particular view, he compresses the wide range of Elizabethan historical drama into entirely too narrow a compass. There were other schools of historiography in Elizabethan England. The providential history of Halle, in fact, represents a tradition which, when Shakespeare was writing, was already in decline.[2]

Since it was however the encyclopaedic chronicles of Halle and Holinshed, with their heritage of medieval providentialism, that Shakespeare tended to use as major sources for his English historical dramas, before considering the importance of other schools of historiography, those sources should be re-examined to determine whether or not they contain historiographical materials of sufficient complexity to engage the interests of an intellectual probably quite uncommitted to antiquated medieval theories of providential disposition; to establish whether the *writing* of history in the period prior to the emergence of the historical drama, though not as yet graduating to the sophistication and objectivity of the 'new historiography', was not more complex in practice than the medieval theories the historians sometimes espoused.

Sixteenth-century England was itself, of course, a period which experienced crises of the monarchy, though no supplanting of the Tudor dynasty. The historical period which, above all others, Tudor historiographers sought to analyze, that stretching from the death of Richard II to the accession of Henry VII (1399–1485) – the period given shape by Halle's *Union* and Shakespeare's two tetralogies – was much more notable for its dynastic changes and civil conflicts. A simple theological theory of history such as that outlined by Tillyard would have been singularly ill-adapted for understanding the battles, real and ideological, of those turbulent times; in fact the Tudor historians were not confined within any such simple and reductive theoretical framework. One writer who has helped to subvert the Tillyardian view is H. A. Kelly,[3] who undertook a massive study of the Tudor historians and their own sources in fifteenth-century chronicles, to reveal some of the complexities underlying the whole Tudor historiographical enterprise. Kelly's main theme is the attempt to disprove that there was any general acceptance of providential theories of history in the Renaissance; and in the course of making this argument he uncovers much of interest and significance about Renaissance historical writing. Kelly shows that roughly three bodies of myth were generated in the period 1399–1485, and transmitted to the humanist historians of the early Renaissance – Polydore Vergil, Halle, Holinshed: a Lancastrian myth, a Yorkist myth (subsuming materials sympathetic to Richard II), and a Tudor myth. When Richard fell, opinions were naturally divided between Ricardian and Lancastrian sympathizers: French chroniclers such as Froissart and Jean Creton wrote of Richard's fall as an unjust tragedy; while Thomas Walsingham gave a Lancastrian account – God punished Richard for the murder of Woodstock, and inspired Henry Bolingbroke's return from banishment. The Lancaster myth is summarised by Kelly:

> The corrupt reign of Richard II was providentially over-thrown by Henry Bolingbroke, his cousin, who was next in line for the crown. God continued to bestow his beneficence upon the new king until the end of his life, and showed his favour even more to his pious son, Henry V, and aided him in maintaining his sovereignty both in England and in France.[4]

The York myth reversed the Lancaster myth: the Lancastrians were usurpers who overthrew the rightful king; they were providentially deprived of their stolen crown by the divinely supported claim of the true heirs, the Yorkists. In the Tudor myth, the Lancastrian line was divinely vindicated and restored in the person of Henry VIII, the Yorkist usurpation punished, but with their royal pretensions appeased – the heiress Elizabeth joined in marriage to the inheritor of the Lancastrian right.

Tudor historians drew on these accounts, often in a judicious and discriminating way, creating their own interpretations from collation of their diversified sources. Polydore Vergil, for example, Halle's primary source, accepted some aspects of both the Lancastrian and

Yorkist myths. He regarded Richard II as imprudent, though not deserving of the fate he encountered; but he did not condemn Henry IV, and regarded Henry V as the recipient of divine grace. Later he suggests that the loss of France after Henry V's death was providential – God was on France's side – and he admires Jeanne d'Arc; though there is no corresponding attack on Henry VI. An intelligent humanist account like Vergil's could choose from a wide range of interpretations and construct a narrative which, despite its attempt to subsume all these details into an overriding providential pattern, contains much awareness and evidence of the ideological conflicts which naturally characterized the period under discussion. This is so even in the chronicle of Halle, which is conventionally regarded as the major source of the providential theory of the history of England from 1399–1485 and of the Tudor myth. Halle in fact was himself extremely sceptical about providential explanations of history. And it is particularly the case in Holinshed, whose encyclopaedic method of compilation gives a very full representation to diverse and contradictory accounts.

Shakespeare's historical sources then were more complex than we often take them to be. Through their compilation of the ideological conflicts inscribed in the fifteenth-century chronicles, they offered to the Elizabethan dramatists a rich and detailed repository of historical evidence, the materials necessary for a more rational and objective understanding of the past.

The materials themselves of course were not enough: every 'understanding' of history is to some degree ideological, and the providential theory embodied in the Tudor myth was particularly adept at incorporating contradictions – no event, however unpredictable or apparently the result of an arbitrary and capricious chance, can resist explanation in terms of an overriding divine will, mediated through the complex machinery of 'fortune' and the 'secondary causes' of human action. A new historiography could not be constructed simply on the basis of a broader and more diverse reservoir of empirical evidence; for such materials to attain a new significance, they had to be incorporated into new theoretical models, new modes of conceptual analysis, new techniques of investigation and new methods of sociological definition.

Several post-Tillyard critics discussing the English history plays have observed that historiography in this period was not a passive reflector of medieval providential theology nor a loyal transmitter of Tudor political commonplace, but a varied and changing activity producing different and competing methods and forms. Providentialism was part of the cultural apparatus of medieval Christian Europe and, with the Reformation and consequent cultural isolation of the Tudor nation-state, lost its predominant position: compared with the theology of Aquinas the providentialism of the Tudor myth was a feeble affair, self-evidently apologetic, in its extreme form of Stuart absolutism ripe for interrogation and challenge by the Puritan idea of providence, which saw the course of history in quite different terms. 'Modern' historiography was established in the early seventeenth century in the writings of Bacon, Stow, Camden and Selden, in the studies of philologists, the curiosity of antiquarians, the passion and patronage of bibliophiles, the conscientiousness of public record-keepers. From these varied roots grew the recognisable shape of secular, empiricist, progressive historiography, later to become 'Whig' history, later still to become visible as itself historically relative, inseparable from the ideological coherence of the bourgeois state. The period of the English Renaissance history play falls precisely between these decisive historical 'breaks', and represents inevitably a transitional period in which different ideas of history competed for dominance. The enormous success of the victorious historiography which emerged dominant after the Restoration should not be allowed to persuade us that it was always the only and inevitable historical method.

The old Christian providentialism continued to exert an influence upon even those writers whose findings increasingly seemed to contradict it, and it provided the Stuarts with the concept of divinely sanctioned monarchy which they developed into a defence of their legitimacy. It was giving way to the influence of Italian humanism, which brought a more secular and sceptical spirit of enquiry to bear on historical issues.[5] Sir Thomas More's *Historie of King Richard the Third* (1513) followed the principles of Leonardo Bruni and his school: unlike Shakepeare's play, based on later sources, it has little to say of the operations of providence. Humanist history could be Christian, providential and apologetic, but its tendency was towards a more rationalist, secularized and positivist historiography. Where the medieval chronicles wrote of universal world history, beginning with the creation, treating indiscriminately historical events and biblical fictions, Italian humanists, on the other hand, wrote histories of their city-states, based on principles derived from classical historiography, observing sharp distinctions between truth and falsehood, rejecting myths of origin and studying historical records, glorifying the prince or oligarchy rather than God. The later Florentine school of Machiavelli and Guicciardini, which made historiography a kind of political science, a method of harnessing history for the purposes of political instruction, also had a tangible impact on English writing, as testified by Bacon's *Historie of the Reign of King Henry the Seventh* (1622).

It has been argued that in Italian humanism, and particularly in the political science of Machiavelli, we can see the shape of a 'new history' emerging in Shakespeare's plays. Contrary to Tillyard's providentialist orthodoxy, critics have argued that in plays like *Richard II* the traditional 'providential' ideas are shown giving way to a new 'political' understanding of history: the breakdown of an order reposing on providence and the emergence of a new regime deploying a flexible political pragmatism.[6] Clearly this distinction has considerable value, and is particularly helpful in providing a more genuinely historical approach to *Richard II*. On the other hand, the thought of the humanists does not by any means represent an accomplished transition from a medieval to a modern historiography. As organic intellectuals of the new Renaissance state, the humanists were concerned with history as a source of moral instruction and political wisdom: with how a prince should rule, how a people should conduct itself, in the light of an intelligent and informed reading of history. This concern with practical utility and contemporary relevance gave humanism common cause with medieval providentialism: both, being committed to learning from history, were forced to assume that past societies were essentially no different from the present. The classical sources used by the humanists, as J. G. A. Pocock observes, 'did not quite reach the point of postulating that there existed, in the past of their own civilisation, tracts of time in which the thoughts and actions of men had been so remote in character from those of the present as to be intelligible only if the entire world in which they had occurred were resurrected, described in detail and used to interpret them'.[7] Pocock further suggests that the humanist enterprise was self-contradictory: their original purpose was to resurrect an ancient world as precisely as possible in order to apply its lessons to the present, but the world they recovered was so utterly unlike their own world that the task of application became increasingly difficult.

Meanwhile, in circumstances apparently remote from the colourful world of the public playhouse, 'modern' history was being created: making use of the advances in philological studies, the growth of book and manuscript collections, the increased efficiency in techniques of record keeping, the 'antiquarians' were developing a science of historiography, approaching the past through empirically verifiable evidence; interested in the past as fact, not as theological pattern, moral instruction or political wisdom. William Camden's patriotic national history *Britannia* (1586), John Stow's *Survey of London* (1598) a middle-class urban history, and John Selden's secularizing *History of Tithes* (1618), which offered a naturalistic explanation of theologically sanctioned customs, can be regarded as landmarks in the growth of the new historiography. In the later sixteenth and early seventeenth centuries, the writing of history was approaching the point where the past would become visible as nothing more or less than the history of man, a naturalistic rather than a providential process, and therefore subject to question and rational analysis; not a mirror-image of the present conflated into a providential process, but a lost world of experience as alien as the most distant foreign country.[8]

This latter point, which brings us to the heart of the argument, has to be approached with some care. It would be foolish to underestimate, in this period or any other, the overpowering force of the universalist idea of human nature. If the Italian humanist could walk with ease and familiarity into the ancient civilisations of Greece and Rome, what Elizabethan Englishman would be capable of recognizing his own national history as in any way remote or foreign to his immediate experience? Camden wrote for the patriotic noble, Stow for the proud London bourgeois, both anxious to establish continuity with their *own* past, not to voyage into strange and uncharted seas of alien history. And yet it was in this very period that European scholars discovered and guessed at the most remarkable and disturbing feature of their history: the fact that, in the centuries between the fall of Rome and their own civilisation there had developed, flourished and decayed a unique and self-contained social formation, with its own peculiar economic and military systems, its own hierarchical social structure, its own individual codes of values and conventions of behaviour: feudalism.

It was in legal theory that this great breakthrough took place in England: in the developments of constitutional and jurisprudential thought characteristic of a period when questions of right and legitimate title, and debates on forms of government, were emerging into prominence and sharpening until they became life-or-death issues in the Civil War. The French humanist school of legal scholars in the sixteenth century attained a highly sophisticated understanding of feudal customs by studying the only written systematization of feudal law, the Lombard *Libri Feudorum*. They succeeded in defining the central relationship of feudalism, and debated whether its origin should be traced back to Roman law or to the customs of Germanic barbarian tribes. A Scots historian, Sir Thomas Craig, who studied law in Paris in the late 1550s, applied the findings of the French scholars to his own country, arguing that feudal law had been established in England at the Norman Conquest, in Scotland a century earlier through an alliance with France, and remained the basis of all property law to the present day. Though he failed to understand the passing of feudalism, Craig was able to recognize that in England the Norman Conquest succeeded in establishing an entirely new social form, wiping away all Anglo-Saxon law and custom. It was this acknowledgment of the possibility of fundamental social change – the realization that a historically-constituted social structure could be created simply by military conquest, and could subsequently wither away leaving a legacy of custom and practice sustained by, but barely intelligible to, subsequent generations – that offered the most radical challenge to the dominant universalist ideas of permanence in human societies. In legal thought those ideas were embodied firmly in the institution of the English common law. Common Law is the law of custom and precedent: not a written body of theoretical doctrines or a systematized structure of legal rules, but an empirical assemblage of practices conceived as immemorial custom. The law was supposed to evolve organically, always changing but always the same, a premise which permitted the lawyer to read back existing law into the remote past, and hold that no radical constitutional change had ever taken place:

> For the *Common Law* of *England* is nothing else but the *Common Custom* of the Realm, and a Custom which hath obtained the force of a Law is always said to be *Jus non scriptum*: for it cannot be made or created either by Charter, or by Parliament, which are Acts reduced to writing, and are always matter of Record: but being only matter of fact, and consisting in use and practice, it can be recorded and registered nowhere but in the memory of the people.[9]

The memory of the people is an unreliable historical record; and the ideologues of the Common Law held absolutely that the Norman Conquest, the one radical discontinuity in the nation's history, did not in fact change the native institutions. The laws of Anglo-Saxon England had been confirmed by William and maintained by his successors: this historical myth (initiated by the Normans themselves) became in the sixteenth century a means of denying the possibility of fundamental social change, in the past or in the future. The common law could of course be used as a parliamentary argument by identifying Parliament with immemorial custom in resistance to the royal prerogative. But defenders of the monarchy employed the same argument: there was certainly an immemorial law, and the king's prerogative was part of it. In the 1640s and 1650s the common-law constitutional position became identified with royalism: the best safeguard of an ancient constitution and an immemorial law was in fact the restoration of an ancient and immemorial monarchy. The progressive forces in the Civil War used the argument in an entirely different way: the Leveller theory of history insisted that the Norman Conquest *had* fundamentally changed the old native customs, by imposing a system of tyranny (the 'Norman yoke') on Anglo-Saxon representative institutions. And while common-law apologists like Sir Edward Coke believed that the law was immemorial:

> What Walwyn, Lilburne and Winstanley said was the very reverse of this. Being engaged in a revolt against the whole existing structure of the common law, they declared that there had indeed been a Conquest; the existing law derived from the tyranny of the Conquerer and partook of the illegitimacy that had characterised his entire rule. Their historicism was not conservative. It was a radical criticism of existing society; the common-law myth stood on its head, as Marx said he had stood Hegel. Both parties indeed looked to the past and laid emphasis on the rights of Englishmen in the past, but what the common lawyers described was the unbroken continuity between past and present, which alone gave justification to the present; while the radicals were talking of a golden age, a lost paradise in which Englishmen had enjoyed liberties that had been taken from them and must be restored.[10]

The great English discoverer of feudalism was Sir Henry Spelman, an antiquarian whose scattered writings were haphazardly published between 1626 and 1721. Spelman's research produced a comprehensive description of feudal relationships, customs and institutions, and also offered a historical view of feudal society as a system introduced into England in the eleventh century and decaying in the fourteenth and fifteenth centuries: once history revealed the existence of freeholders attending Parliament, voluntarily rather than in fulfilment of a statutory obligation to the king, feudal relations were visibly, at that point, a thing of the past.

While it is possible with confidence to ascribe the origins of Shakespeare's historical plays to the Tudor chronicles and the humanist histories, there is no possibility of postulating such a cause-and-effect relation between the new historical ideas and the drama; and to argue that the plays express a seventeenth-century historical consciousness will seem a very unhistorical procedure, inevitably drawing the charge of anachronism. In addition, the diverse cultural spaces occupied by those different activities will seem so remote as to defy identification: what connection could there be between the antiquarian historiographer, laboriously and conscientiously researching the dusty records of the past and preserving them for posterity – and the busy professional dramatist, writing quickly and carelessly for a showy and ephemeral medium of entertainment? But what we call literature is not merely the effect of a cause, and historical drama is not a mere reflection of a discourse which can claim greater authenticity by virtue of its proximity to the 'real' of history. Shakespeare's historical plays are not just *reflections* of a cultural debate: they are *interventions* in that debate, *contributions* to the historiographical effort to reconstruct the past and discover the methods and principles of that reconstruction. They are as much locations of historical controversy as the history books: they are, in themselves and not derivatively, historiography. We cannot establish whether or not Shakespeare was familiar with new currents of historical thought; but we cannot establish, except by inferring from the plays, precisely what 'he' thought about anything. We can only say that 'he' wrote his plays in a critical and transitional epoch of his national history, a few decades before that history was to be put in fundamental question by the greatest historical upheaval since the Norman Conquest; and we can attempt to maintain, by practical demonstration, that the plays can be read as serious attempts to reconstruct and theorize the past – as major initiatives of Renaissance historical thought.

I am proposing, and will be attempting to demonstrate, that these plays embody a conscious understanding of feudal society as a peculiar historical formation, revealing unique cultural characteristics, codes of value, conventions of manners, based on particular structures of political organisation and social relationship. This 'understanding' should not be exaggeratedly *identified* with the discoveries of a historical scientist like Spelman or with the radical speculations of a theoretician like Winstanley: we will find no attempt in Shakespeare to establish the origins of the *feudum*, or to define precisely the links between land tenure and military service; nor will we find any characterization of the post-feudal ruling class as Norman tyrants – they are very definitely English, and Henry V has barely mastered the basics of French grammar. What the plays offer is rather a form of historiography *analogous* to the new science, in that it perceives human problems and experiences to be located within a definable historical form, a society visibly different in fundamental ways from the society of the late sixteenth century. That assertion in itself will require demonstration, since so much criticism insists so firmly on the rudimentary character of Renaissance historiography that we will consider it very unlikely that a thoughtful Elizabethan would have been able to draw any firm historical distinction between the kingship of Edward III and that of Elizabeth; between the punctilious pride of a Renaissance noble and the 'honour' of a feudal knight; between the crusades and the war against Catholicism, the Turk and the Spaniard; between the blood-feud and the duel. I will be attempting to prove in a brief discussion of *Henry V* that, despite the sixteenth century's inheritance of a visible legacy of feudalism, there is no question of the plays' confusing the present with the past, the modern national sovereign of a Renaissance state with the warrior-king of a feudal society.

In defining and describing these three historical methods – the chronicle-compilation with its providential theory and encyclopaedic practice; the didactic political science of humanism; and the 'new history', with its discovery of the pastness of the past – we have not entirely exhausted the diversified currents of English Renaissance historiography. The three 'schools' already mentioned will serve to characterize the historiography of a certain type of history play such as *Richard II*; but the approach to a play like *Henry IV Part One* cannot proceed without acknowledging other, more venerable modes of historical discourse.

Richard II represents a distinct type of historical drama, remarkable for its strict adherence to historical sources: in this respect it resembles Marlowe's *Edward II*, since in both plays action and incident are drawn largely or exclusively from written historiographical materials. However elaborate and innovative the dramatization and poetic stylizing, the events and characters (with a few minor exceptions, such as the gardeners in *Richard II*), follow those authenticated as historically accurate by the chronicles. Such plays derive from and are inextricably involved with a highly *literate* culture: they dramatize what has already been *written*, they speak to those already familiar with the literary discourses of historiography, with Halle and Holinshed. This fact has its implications for the plays' visions of history: they are necessarily deterministic, since they record a finished historical narrative cast into permanence by the fixity of the written word, a chronological sequence of events which admits of no change or fundamental reconstruction. Obviously Marlowe and Shakespeare reshaped their historical materials to create new narrative and dramatic patterns, but they observed, in these plays, a strict adherence to the authoritative word of the written historiographical text. It is natural then that these works should be tragic: in the secularizing Renaissance drama tragic nemesis and historical determinism begin to share a common discourse. In Marlowe's *Edward II*, Shakespeare's *Richard II* and *Henry VI*, images of flight and recapture symbolize the helplessness of the individual confronted by the ineluctable tyranny of history, the inescapable determination of the unalterable past.

The *genre* of the Renaissance history play was, however, considerably more elastic and flexible than the deterministic medium of these literary tragedies. It contains plays in which the style of historiographical drama interacts with older modes, with the conventions of romance and the manners of comedy. In such plays the historical drama reveals itself as very much a popular *genre* often acknowledging by its themes and situations an origin on the public stages of citizen London. It did not recognize the absolute authority of the chronicles, maintaining a freedom to invent actions and situations without precedent, or quite unthinkable, in written history. Its sources were less the written chronicles, more materials from a still largely oral popular culture – ballads, romances, songs and stories incorporating legends, folk-tales, fairy-stories, myths. It represents an older kind of history, still indeed visible in the Tudor chronicles, in which the rich and varied fantasy worlds of myth and legend consort with the new positivism of historical narrative. In historical medleys such as *James IV* and *Edward I*, historical characters mingle with citizens and figures of legend such as Robin Hood and Maid Marian. It was in fact this *genre* which produced the dominant tradition for the dramatic representation of Henry V: a comic tradition, in which the king's 'riotous youth' is used positively as a means of humanizing the monarch. This king is not so much the hero of Agincourt as the good fellow of Eastcheap; not the mirror of all Christian kings, but the prince of carnival. In Dekker's *The Shoemaker's Holiday* (1599), a carnival play based on the London apprentices' Shrove Tuesday Saturnalia, Henry V appears as a 'bully king' who associates freely with citizens and apprentices, dispenses justice and equality, resolves conflict and promotes harmony. The King does not pose as a common man, but acts like one; and Simon Eyre, the 'madcap' Lord Mayor, humorously claims 'princely birth' – an inversion of social roles characteristic of carnival and festive, saturnalian comedy. The main source for the *Henry IV* and *Henry V* plays, the anonymous *Famous Victories of Henry the Fifth*, is mainly in the comic mode.

Anne Barton has discussed in an illuminating article[11] the relation of *Henry V* to the comic history; and called attention to the most striking emblem of this drama's freedom from the determinism of historical event, the motif of the 'king disguised'. Most of the romance and comic histories contain a king who poses as a common man and mingles with a varied company of folk heroes and common citizens, the outlaws of Sherwood Forest or the shoemakers of London. In the tragic history, disguise is a hopeless attempt to evade the inevitable – capture, imprisonment, death: the king's tragic destiny written inexorably into the unchangeable past (see *Henry VI*). In the comic history disguise is a liberation: it dispenses with the distances of class and hierarchy separating the king from his common people, and enables a direct *rapprochement* (usually complicated by comic misunderstanding) between monarch and subject. Anne Barton quotes from Maurice Keen's *The Outlaws of Mediaeval Legend*, which sees the 'informal meeting of commoner and king' as 'the wish-dream of a peasantry harried by a new class of officials, an impersonal bureaucracy against which the ordinary man seemed to have no redress':

They only knew that the king was the ultimate repository of a law whose justice they acknowledged, and they saw treason against him as a betrayal of their allegiance to God himself. If they could only get past his corrupt officers, whose abuse of the trust reposed in them amounted to treason in itself, and bring their case before the king, they believed that right would be done. Their unshakeable faith in the king's own justice was the most tragic of the misconceptions of the mediaeval peasantry, and the ballad-makers and their audiences shared it to the full.[12]

The motif of the disguised king certainly originates from that historical conjuncture: but the image of a king humanized, crossing barriers of hierarchy and class to mingle freely with his subjects in mutual affection and concord, seems almost endemic to the ideology of monarchy itself: it has its modern counterpart in that popular curiosity about the lives of the royal family, which mingles a gratified welcome at their revealed humanity with a malicious and cynical contempt at their descending to the level of their own 'subjects'. But there is also a strong egalitarian impulse behind this wish to confront the ruler directly, person to person – to be able to explain the abuses, demonstrate the social evils which the monarch would surely redress if only he could be made aware. A tragic misconception, certainly, but scarcely a futile one: it was the programme of the Peasants' Revolt of 1381, the ambition of the Blanketeers' March of 1816, the slogan of the 1930s Hunger Marches and of the 'Right to Work' marches of the 1980s.

It is misleading to explain such a mixed form in terms of a single ideology; the style is more a receptacle for varied and possibly even antagonistic ideologies to interact. Perhaps the primary ideological function of such drama was to endorse monarchy – to propose that the rigidity of hierarchical social relations concealed the true equality of king and subject, ruler and ruled. But the romance mode of such plays could also function quite differently: by posing an ideal commonwealth in romantic-comic terms, a play could differentiate sharply between its own self-evidently fantastic world and the reality its fantasy denied. Anne Barton attaches the plays too firmly to that peasant ideology (which could scarcely have had much currency in the London of the 1590s); and consequently underestimates those potentialities of the comic romance which Shakespeare exploited most strikingly in *Henry IV*:

By 1599, the comical history was a consciously reactionary, an
outdated dramatic mode . . .[13]

In fact Barton does not acknowledge the comic history *genre* to be
active in Shakespeare's plays at all. Rather, she differentiates sharply
between the comical history and Shakespeare's essentially *tragic*
history, showing that in *Henry V* the king attempts to implement the
rapprochement of monarch and subject but fails, for he is caught in
an insoluble contradiction between the king's *personal* and his
public natures. The later play *The True and Honourable History of
Sir John Oldcastle*, by contrast, turns Shakespeare's tragic history
back into comic romance:

As it was defined by Shakespeare, the tragical history became a
serious, and politically somewhat incendiary, examination into
the nature of kingship.[14]

This differentiation of ideological functions between the separate
categories of historiographical drama is unsatisfactory. The tragic
history, with its submission to the deterministic authority of written
historiography, certainly represents a new secular positivism associated with the priorities of the Tudor state, reflecting the new
humanistic status of history and of the written word. But it would be
unwise to categorize every cultural development of that state as
necessarily 'progressive'. The Tudor construction of a positivistic
historiography, initiated by Henry VII, was certainly an instrumental factor in the consolidation of the Tudor state apparatus, and it
was also a method of imposing new and increasingly sharp ideological constraints on the human understanding of the past: history
became necessity, and the outcome of necessity the Tudor dynasty.
The determinism of the tragic history foreclosed on the liberty of
the comic history play; evidently Shakespeare recognized this process, since he moved from the pure chronicle-play style to a drama
constructed on a confrontation of chronicle and popular-comic
historical discourses. In *Henry IV*, it is actually the popular tradition
which points to a progressive, egalitarian and democratic tendency:
an oppositional energy which is gradually narrowed, controlled and
ultimately destroyed by the necessitarianism of chronicle drama.
    The comic history, then, is a mixed mode, without the stylistic
consistency of the chronicle play. It is fantastic and utopian rather

than realistic and historically accurate. It is a popular form, which makes free use of the conventions of drama, and thereby provides a space of freedom from event, from the necessity of a complete history; thus a historical character can be liberated from his historical destiny, can play roles not dictated to him by the written authority of history. It is festive and saturnalian in character – the mighty are put down from their seats, and those of low degree exalted. The plays are written and performed as popular entertainment: they make much use of song, dance, popular pastime and holiday custom. They are a contradictory fusion of chronicle and carnival.

Henry IV is a 'mixed' type of drama not only in Coleridge's sense of the fusion of comedy with history; but in its *rapprochement* of popular and patrician discourses. Broadly speaking, the central figure of the chronicle-history dimension is the king himself, and the central preoccupation is an extension of the historical narrative commenced in *Richard II*. The popular-comic-history element is dominated by the figure of Falstaff, centre of an oppositional play of comic energies. Prince Hal straddles the two dimensions and seeks reconciliation between them, a reconciliation achieved at the end of *Henry IV Part One*, and broken at the conclusion to *Part Two*.

Shakespeare's plays of English history are chronicles of feudalism: they offer empirical reconstruction and theoretical analysis of a social formation firmly located in the past, and distinctly severed from the contemporary world. In this historiographical reconstruction, which focuses on the decline of feudalism in the fourteenth and fifteenth centuries, society is seen as a historical formation built on certain fundamental contradictions, and incapable of resolving or overcoming them within the framework of political and ideological determinants provided by the historical basis itself. As the vision of feudal society is historically specific, the disclosure of contradictions cannot be defined as reversion to medieval pessimism or a compliance with Machiavellian pragmatism: if a conception of the past admits the possibility of fundamental social change, the contradictions of a particular historical formation cannot be identified with 'the human condition'; and an acknowledgment of distance between past and present confirms that a society's contradictions can be resolved or negated simply by the fact of radical and irreversible social change.

In the sixteenth century this recognition of historical relativity was a progressive development: the consciousness of a new society awakening to the fact of past transformation, the possibility of future change. Inevitably, however, the progressive quality of this discovery was equally relative to the limitations and contradictions of the emergent social formation, the nascent capitalist state. A few years after Shakespeare's death the transitional society of the Tudor state was overthrown by a bourgeois revolution, which required for its ideological constitution a historiography based on the principle of change. The bourgeois revolution accomplished, the alliance between old and new ruling classes required a conservative historiography, to secure ideological stability by insisting on the gradualist, evolutionary nature of social change: the revolutionary historiography of Milton and Winstanley was smoothly incorporated into the moderate empiricism of 'Whig' history.

Shakespeare's direct analysis of feudalism in *Richard II* seems to be accomplished within the context of this 'new' historiography: both the providential and the pragmatic views of history are strategically manipulated within the framework of a theory conscious of the relativity of both. The historical approach is progressive insofar as it locates its problems in a self-contained society of the past, neither idealized nor regretted but objectively analyzed and evaluated. But the play is also potentially reactionary, since its combination of tragic form and literate, deterministic historiography can too easily collapse into a resigned pessimism where 'mutability', without its parent principle of universal order, becomes an appropriate metaphor for the 'human condition'. Perhaps it was a growing dissatisfaction with the tragic determinism of the literary chronicle-drama that induced Shakespeare to bring into play a force capable of challenging it, a popular and comic mode of historical drama which challenges deterministic historiography with the utopian purity of an inflexible and unqualified demand for freedom. The new historiography was in fact emergent bourgeois historiography, and in *Henry IV Part One* an older popular culture is invoked to interrogate the terms on which that historiography was constructing the present as well as the past.

Chapter One

Appropriations

All criticism of the histories emanates from E. M. W. Tillyard's
pioneering work, *Shakespeare's History Plays* (1944). Whether one
agrees or disagrees with it, Tillyard's has become the traditional
interpretation of the history plays.[1]

As David M. Bergeran suggests, virtually all modern critical accounts
of Shakespeare's historical drama in one way or another take their
bearings from Tillyard. That continual orientation back towards
so early a source of interpretation (unparalleled in the critical
histories of other Shakespearean *genres*), that persistent refocus-
ing of Tillyard that seems to have survived the various revolu-
tions in literary criticism and theory, presents an unusual cultural
relationship. Tillyard's survival as a point of reference is all the
more striking given that his work (together with other related
studies of Shakespeare and of the history plays deriving from
that same period) is so firmly rooted in precisely the kinds of
conservative, nationalistic and authoritarian ideology contemporary criticism has sought comprehensively and systematically to
challenge.

In Tillyard's study the sequence of plays from *Richard II* to *Henry
V*, were constituted as a central chapter in the great nationalistic
'epic' of England (an American critic subsequently even found a
name for this epic narrative – the *Henriad*.[2] The plays are
interpreted as a linked and integrated series, revealing a broad and
complex panorama of national life, unified and balanced into a
coherent aesthetic 'order' mirroring the political order of the Elizabethan state. Tillyard's study thus reproduces the plays as parables
of political order, or as what contemporary criticism would prefer to
call 'strategies of legitimation', cultural forms by means of which the
dominant ideology of the Tudor state validated its own moral and

political power, through the voluntary intervention and commitment of a loyal and talented subject, Shakespeare.

Tillyard's version of the history plays as loyal celebrations of Tudor power, functioning within the context of a general ideology in which that power was conceived as an element of an inclusive natural order, became a strong and powerful critical position dominating discussion of the plays for many years. Essentially similar approaches to these plays were put forward in the 1940s by Lily B. Campbell in *Shakespeare's Histories: Mirrors of Elizabethan Policy* (1947), and by G. Wilson Knight in *The Olive and the Sword* (1944). They were then promulgated more widely to different publics by J. Dover Wilson through the popular revised 'complete works', the *New Shakespeare* (1953), and by critics associated with Leavis's journal *Scrutiny* such as D. A. Traversi in *Shakespeare from 'Richard II' to 'Henry V'* (1957).[3] Whatever diversities of argument and approach differentiate these interventions one from another, they all derive from a common problematic: the ideological crisis of British nationalism precipitated by the events of the 1930s and 1940s: the Depression, the crisis of Empire and particularly of course the Second World War. What these critics said of 'order' in Elizabethan England can easily be read at this distance as a coded address to immediate problems of political authority in their contemporary Britain. As my later discussion of war-time patriotic appropriations of Shakespeare (such as those of Wilson Knight and Laurence Olivier: see Chapter Seven below) will demonstrate, some of these interventions were quite explicit about their propagandist application of Shakespeare's historical drama to the requirements of an urgent contemporary crisis. Tillyard's book (published, like Wilson Knight's patriotic essay and Olivier's film of *Henry V*, in 1944) is no less a work of nationalistic appropriation because its polemical immediacy is disguised as historical scholarship.

Tillyard, Wilson Knight and Dover Wilson all found in Shakespeare's history plays a ruling ideology of order because that is precisely what they wanted to find. Their real ideological commitment (suppressed and implicit in Tillyard, frequently overt and declamatory in Wilson Knight and Dover Wilson) was only indirectly to the order of a vanished historical state, and directly to the political and ideological problems of Britain in the late 1930s and 1940s.

Tillyard's study, despite sharing a common subject, common preoccupations and – ultimately – a common ideology, differs signally from the work of the other two critics in displaying an apparent innocence of contemporary engagement. The study is purely a discourse of academic scholarship, giving the impression that a characteristic and central activity of English culture has been quietly proceeding, unravaged by the fierce reality of world history. While Wilson Knight and Dover Wilson were reconstructing Shakespeare to point his relevance to the nation's crisis, Tillyard, with a gesture of academic indifference to contemporary events, was patiently clearing the earth of history from the roots of English culture, re-establishing a continuity with the Elizabethan age unbroken by crisis, war and threatened invasion.

Tillyard's major argument is that *order* was the dominant Eliza-bethan belief. Even the teaching of so influential a thinker as Machia-velli, with his view that 'disorder was the natural state of man', meant little to Shakespeare's contemporaries:

> Such a way of thinking was abhorrent to the Elizabethans, (as indeed it always has been and is now to the majority), who pre-ferred to think of order as the norm to which disorder, though lamentably common, was yet the exception.[4]

This ideology (which, we notice, is still in Tillyard's view a 'majority' opinion) was Shakespeare's:

> In his most violent representations of chaos Shakespeare never tries to persuade that it is the norm: however long and violent is its sway, it is unnatural; and in the end order and the natural law will reassert themselves[5] . . . it is not likely that anyone will question my conclusion that Shakespeare's Histories, with their constant pictures of disorder cannot be understood without assuming a larger principle of order in the background. . . . In the total sequence of his plays dealing with the subject-matter of Hall he expressed successfully a universally held and still com-prehensible scheme of history: a scheme fundamentally religious, by which events evolve under a law of justice and under the ruling of God's Providence, and of which Elizabeth's England was the acknowledged outcome.[6]

Tillyard asserts what appear to be historical facts about a long-vanished age: there is little to suggest that his concern with 'order' –

an unspecified and politically ambiguous vision of society – belongs as much to war-time Britain as to Elizabethan England. He never betrays any suggestion that his universal political moral might have relevance to his own time. The nearest Tillyard comes to an acknowledgment of the claims of contemporary history is a species of ambiguous aside: discussing the tradition of sentimentalizing Falstaff, he attributes it to Victorian military optimism:

> The sense of security created in nineteenth century England by the predominance of the British navy induced men to rate that very security too cheaply and to exalt the instinct of rebellion above its legitimate station. They forgot the threat of disorder which was ever present with the Elizabethans. Schooled by recent events we should have no difficulty now in taking Falstaff as the Elizabethans took him.[7]

The word 'schooled' matches the ambiguous portentousness of the academic mannerism: participation in history is a matter of education in moral and political wisdom. What Tillyard means by 'recent events' it is scarcely possible to know. 'Rebellion' could refer to the ascension and territorial expansion of fascism. Or it may more probably refer to the paramount necessity for maintaining order and national unity in face of the threat of foreign conquest. 'We' in 1944, in other words, have as much reason to value order, national unity, a strong but humane monarchy, as did the Elizabethans and Shakespeare.

Such an aside is however a flaw in the seamless unity of Tillyard's ideology, which masks its essential conservatism in an impenetrable disguise of academic scholarship. The object we are required to contemplate is not Tillyard thinking about *his* England but Shakespeare thinking about his:

> *Henry IV* shows a stable society and it is crowded, like no other play of Shakespeare, with pictures of life as it was lived in the age of Elizabeth. . . . Those who, like myself, believe that Shakespeare had a massively reflective as well as a brilliantly opportunistic brain will expect these matters of Elizabethan life to serve more than one end and will not be surprised if through them he expresses his own feelings about his fatherland. It is also perfectly natural that Shakespeare should have chosen this particular

point in the total stretch of history he covered, as suited to this
expression. Henry V was traditionally not only the perfect king,
but a king after the Englishman's heart; one who added the quality
of good mixer to the specifically regal virtues. The picture of
England would be connected with the typical English monarch.[8]

The concept of Renaissance England as a well-ordered state is however infused with a sentimental attachment to the 'everyday' life of
England dramatized in *Henry IV Part Two*: into Tillyard's discourse
penetrates an emotional tone which declares, unmistakably, that
Shakespeare's 'fatherland' is also his. This 'epic' drama offers a
comprehensive cross-section of English life, linking the monarchy
with the essential, unchanging rhythm of traditional rural society.
The emphasis on the enduring quality of traditional social patterns is
confirmed by Tillyard's quoting of Hardy's 'In Time of the Breaking
of Nations':

> Yet this will go onward the same
> Though Dynasties pass.

> . . . From first to last Shakespeare was loyal to the country life.
> He took it for granted as the norm, as the background before
> which the more formal or spectacular events were transacted.[9]

Or in the words of the popular song: 'There'll always be an England . . .'. The argument and the quotation deliver us back into an
organic, immutable 'English' society: that golden age which, though
vanished, can yet linger and survive, unravaged by the fierce historical crisis of the present.

The remarkable logical slide from a description of Renaissance
ideology to the celebration of an apparently immutable social and
cultural entity called 'England' is Tillyard's most effective ideological strategy: it is, in fact, the quality which ensured that of all
the cultural interventions of this period, Tillyard's piece of formal
criticism would survive as the seminal, determinant text. Without
making any explicit acknowledgment of the fact that the England of
the Second World War is as much an object of address as that of the
sixteenth century, Tillyard invokes and affirms values which were
being assiduously – and much more openly – cultivated in the
culture as a whole.

The general Elizabethan philosophy of 'order' is regarded here as the basic structure of all fifteenth/sixteenth-century historiographical writing: the metaphysical dialectic of 'order' and 'disorder' was observed in the process of English history, and explained in terms of the ruling idea of providence. The deposition and murder of Richard II was seen as a violation of natural order: the perpetrators of it earned the punishment of divine vengeance, which was also visited generally on the nation as a whole. This pattern Tillyard detected in the chronicles of Holinshed and Halle, the historical narratives of Daniel and *The Mirror for Magistrates*, in the whole *genre* of the Elizabethan history play, and in Shakespeare.

The ideological structure which emerges from this application is what Tillyard (and after him generations of A-level candidates) agree to call 'the theme of England' – a preoccupation derived from the Morality play, in which 'Respublica', the state, can occupy a central position as character or even hero. Shakespeare's 'theme of England' is in one sense historical – a vision of the providential pattern implicit in the development of a historical process from Richard II to Henry VII – but in a larger sense it is what Tillyard calls 'epic' – a dramatization of the whole texture and experience of English life, lived between the reality of 'disorder' (dynastic struggle, rebellion, civil war) and the potentiality of 'order' (a static and hierarchical but well-governed state). Just as the great 'order' of the cosmos supervises and contains its internal 'disorder', so the upheavals of English society between 1399 and 1485 are constrained within a grand conception of the 'order' which the nation really represents:

> The theme of Respublica, now given a new turn and treating not merely the future but the very nature of England, what I am calling the epic theme, is subtly contrived . . . the theme of England grows naturally till its full compass is reached when Henry V, the perfect English king, comes to the throne. If we were in doubt about the Prince's decision, we should not have the mental repose necessary for appreciating a static picture of England: we should be obsessed, as we are in *Henry VI*, with the events of civil war; and the troubles of Henry IV would quench our interest in the drone of the Lincolnshire bagpipes or the price of stock at Stamford Fair.[10]

Inspired . . . by his own genius, he combined with the grim didactic exposition of the fortunes of England during her terrible ordeal of civil war his epic version of what England was.[11]

The indispensable key to political 'order' is the sovereign – as God's deputy the king must accept high responsibilities, and the man must be fitted to the office. Tillyard regards the two parts of *Henry IV* as in one sense an account of Prince Hal's training for office. The Prince is Shakespeare's ideal portrayal of the 'kingly type': a well-governed personality who confronts 'disorder' (in the form of Falstaff) only to understand and reject it; and who thereby equips himself to govern and embody the 'order' of the state:

> The Prince as depicted in *Henry IV* . . . is a man of large powers, Olympian loftiness, and high sophistication who has acquired a thorough knowledge of human nature both in himself and in others. He is Shakespeare's studied picture of the kingly type . . .[12]

Tillyard has nothing to reproach the Prince with: his behaviour is always exemplary, a model of what history requires of him. One illustration of this scheme of princely education is the scene in which Hal mocks and manipulates Francis the drawer:

> Why should the Prince, after Francis has given him his heart . . . join with Poins to put him through a brutal piece of horseplay? . . . The answer is first that the Prince wanted to see just how little brain Francis had and puts him to the test, and secondly that in matters of humanity we must not judge Shakespeare by standards of twentieth century humanitarianism. . . . Further we must remember the principle of degree. . . . The subhuman element in the population must have been considerable in Shakespeare's day; that it should be treated almost like beasts was taken for granted.[13]

Tillyard draws a clear distinction here between Renaissance attitudes and the standards of 'twentieth century humanitarianism': a qualification which would, if consistently applied, break the tacit link between his celebration of Elizabethan 'order' and the implicit conservatism of the book's ideology. Tillyard, however, dissociates himself from that 'humanitarianism', not only in his attempt at an imaginative penetration into the psychology of a historically remote civilisation, but in his casual use of a phrase like 'subhuman' – which seems to belong more to the fastidious class-bound vision of a twentieth-century Cambridge critic, than to the author of *King Lear*.

Tillyard does not think highly of *Henry V*. He believes the character to be quite inconsistent with the Prince Hal of *Henry IV*, and the play itself to be forced and mechanical. A shying-away from more robust forms of patriotism is characteristic of Tillyard: writing at a time when the epic heroism of the past could easily be affirmed (as it was in Olivier's film) as living in the present, the scholar relegates it to an inferior status: the play about the nature of 'England' is more important than the play about the military victories of a warrior-king. Tillyard's business was not with winning the war but with reconstituting the national culture in expectation of an Allied victory.

The distinctive quality of Tillyard's work is its denial of contemporary history, its apparently timeless innocence of political orientation. Where others declared that Britain in her hour of need could turn to Shakespeare, Tillyard quietly affirmed that Shakespeare has always been, is and always will be 'England'. The effectiveness of the enterprise can be measured by the fact that assent to that proposition can seem like recognition of the long familiar. Shakespeare has 'always' been the national poet, identifiable with the greatest of our cultural achievements, and with the greatest age of our history: what could seem more 'natural' than to invoke his presence in a time of national peril? Such familiarizing, with its absence of any explicit avowal of a determinant historical context, was pecularly well-adapted to the task of establishing an image of 'Shakespeare's England' which would serve as an ideological power of social cohesion in Churchill's Britain. The scholarly imagination, revisiting a vanished past, severs the history it addresses from the exigencies of the present; and thus insidiously operates on the reader who, aware only of the attention focused on Shakespeare, is quite unaware of how a specific image of Britain is being implicitly celebrated and affirmed.

Many people felt during the Second World War that they were fighting for a new society of democracy, peace and justice: that the ordeal of the war could be made tolerable by assurance that the old society of poverty, inequality, unemployment, could never return. Tillyard offered his readers a different reason for fighting and enduring: to defend the society which existed once, still remains (implicitly) the 'natural' form of political order, and is visible in the works of Shakespeare. In the Labour victory of 1945, it seemed that the old world lay in ruins and was decisively rejected by the people. E. M. W. Tillyard's *Shakespeare's History Plays* was reprinted in 1948, 1951, 1956, 1959, 1961, 1964, 1969 and 1974.

Nonetheless, Tillyard's study remains the critical text which above all others framed and shaped the subsequent and continuing debate over the history plays largely because, as Alan Sinfield and Jonathan Dollimore have pointed out,[14] he positioned the plays firmly within a context in which the terms history, historical evidence, historiography, must be regarded as indispensible theoretical factors in the activity of interpretation. Tillyard's approach was based on a 'historicist' methodology quite distinct from the traditional forms of 'literary history' that preceded him. Literary history presented the history of literature as an independent realm of art and thought, a sequence of great writers producing major works which then constituted the literary 'tradition'. Historicist approaches such as those of G. W. F. Hegel (1770–1831) or Thomas Carlyle (1795–1881) substituted a broader, more inclusive totality of cultural development, the 'history' of which literature was an essential component. Here 'literature' became identified as the 'voice' or 'spirit' of an age or a society. Tillyard's work embodied a Hegelian analysis of literature as the expression of a common spirit of the age. In some ways Tillyard's study must be acknowledged as revolutionary (just as Marx acknowledged the revolutionary significance of Hegel[15]), since both the critical orthodoxy it established and the counter-currents it provoked assume the historical as a basic premise, and therefore open up the debate for some of the characteristic concerns of contemporary criticism.

In this sense Tillyard's *method* was in its cultural moment radical and controversial, and was opposed almost immediately by critical positions which looked backward to other traditional certainties, as well as forward to more recent critical interventions. What Tillyard was proposing was a particular relationship between the writer and ideology, which proved quite unacceptable to critics committed to a more traditional notion of art as free from the constructions of ideology or the determinants of history. Such critics as Irving

Ribner, A. P. Rossiter, Robert Ornstein, accepted the historicism of Tillyard's position, but denied his contention that Shakespeare held and expressed the orthodox thought of his time.[16] Such an affirmation of ideological complicity with a dominant system of thought challenged the traditional post-romantic concept of the writer as a free imagination, liberal of sympathy and pluralist in ideas. This line of opposition to Tillyard displayed a characteristic double movement: restoring the status of the author as a free and independent witness to the historical processes and ideas addressed in his work; and insisting on a more rigorous and complex historical methodology on the part of the critic.

In particular, the argument of Robert Ornstein's *A Kingdom for a Stage* (1972) took the positions of Ribner and Rossiter a stage further. Both Tillyard and Lily B. Campbell claimed that Shakespeare's historical vision was identical to that of Edward Halle, which in turn reflected the orthodox Tudor political position of the homilies against disobedience and rebellion. Ornstein questions all the terms of this proposed ideological relationship, arguing that Halle's position was not that attributed to him by Tillyard and Campbell; that Shakespeare's historical dramas seem closer to the more empiricist historical writing of Holinshed; and that in any case the dramatist used a wide range of sources, with widely differing ideological origins and political inflections. Surveying the process of history with the imaginative liberty and ideological independence of the 'artist', Shakespeare discovered at work an altogether more Machiavellian process, in which 'politics is the art of accommodation and survival'.[17]

Shakespeare emerges from this account, and from parallel studies by Wilbur Sanders and Moody E. Prior,[18] in the guise of a free and independent citizen of the republic of letters, a modern Renaissance man fully cognizant of the most advanced philosophical currents of the age. Shakespeare also appears in these accounts as a prototype of the modern liberal-humanist intellectual, sceptical and disenchanted, preferring curiosity to conviction, disengagement to political commitment. Where British critics of the 1940s were concerned to reproduce a Shakespeare capable of resolving the ideological tensions of the national culture, their American colleagues of a decade or so later fashioned a Shakespeare more closely attuned to their intellectual needs, a free-thinking liberal judiciously suspicious of all ideology (Ornstein's book contains many references, for example, to the reactionary nature of American Cold War culture).

The emphasis on humanist historiography as a means of interpreting Shakespeare's history plays, though a definite advance on the providentialist orthodoxy, has led critics into a complicity with those ideologues of the Italian Renaissance and their English apostles. The history plays have often been discussed in terms of an extremely abstract definition of 'politics', conceived not as the specific discourses and practices of power in a particular historical moment, but as a Machiavellian system located in the universal shabbiness of political practices throughout the ages. In criticism of the late 1960s and 1970s, the providential organicism of post-war reconstruction gave way (especially in American academic circles) to a sceptical and pessimistic existentialism, prone to reduce politics to a series of dirty tricks characteristic of the degenerate but unchanging nature of abstract 'society'. A curious effect of this cultural matrix, to some extent negating its intensified historicity, is to elide the contradictions between the medieval and Renaissance worlds: medieval pessimism and humanist pragmatism, adopting an equally cynical view of human life as fundamentally unchanging and unchangeable, are made to share a common discourse. In both philosophies, change occurs relative to a larger stability – the universal power of God or the unchanging imperfection of man. In both, little significance or value can be attached to many human actions, for the willed and conscious actions of men are overdetermed by a predetermined fate or the subtle power of the ruler. *The Lost Garden* (1978) by John Wilders begins by rejecting both the orthodox view of the plays as patterns of divine providence, and the counter-orthodoxy which constitutes the plays as humanistic treatises teaching the secular lessons of history to rulers and peoples. They embody, rather, 'the expression of a consistently-held view of the human condition as one in which the solution of one problem creates problems of another kind, in which men thrive or suffer in ways which do not correspond to any ideal principles of justice, and choices are forced upon them, not between right and wrong, but between various courses of action all more or less unsatisfactory'. This theory of 'the human condition' was achieved by conflating the pessimism of Boethius and St Augustine with the sceptical pragmatism of Machiavelli; the result could be incorporated into the theological doctrine of the Fall of Man. 'Shakespeare portrays history as a struggle by succeeding generations of men to establish ideal worlds which are beyond their power to create . . . portraying in social and political terms the theological idea of a "fallen" humanity'.[19]

In the course of the 1970s and 1980s a whole range of new critical approaches to Shakespeare's history plays emerged, capable of a much more comprehensive and systematic exposure and demystification of the ideological character of Tillyard's thesis. Prominent among them was a 'new historicism' which offered to reconstitute the chronicle plays in different and politically oppositional ways. 'New Historicism', a critical movement originating in America and strongly influenced by the work of the radical psychological theorist Michel Foucault, and the Marxist theoretician Louis Althusser,[20] started from the same point as Tillyard, with a will to grasp the relationships between literature and the larger cultural totality of 'history'. Where the old historicism relied on a basically empiricist form of historical research, confident in its capacity to excavate and define the events of the past, New Historicism drew on post-structuralist theory, and accepted 'history' only as a contemporary activity of narrating or representing the past. It follows from this that New Historicism dismisses the claims of traditional scholarship to objectivity and disinterestedness: historians reconstruct the past in the light of their own ideological preoccupations and constraints. New Historicism rejects the conception of unified historical periods (such as the 'England of Elizabeth'), replacing what it regards as a propagandist myth by the alternative notion of different, contradictory and discontinuous 'histories' experienced by the various groups within a society; so the history of the Elizabethan aristocracy is not the same as that of the Elizabethan peasantry, and the history of women cannot be subsumed into the history of men. Lastly, for New Historicism there can be no privileging of 'literature' as an ahistorical body of achievement standing out from a historical 'background'. All writing is equally historical, and the texts conventionally designated as 'literature' need therefore to be read in relation to other texts not so prioritized.

These theoretical principles produced entirely different historical methods from those employed either by Tillyard or his critics. New Historicism began to examine Renaissance drama as a functional 'discourse' in which the ideological conflicts and material power-struggles of the age would be fought out in more or less overt forms. If history is always a contemporary narrative, then what Tillyard saw as the intellectual spirit of an age becomes merely that story the Tudor government wished to have told about its own rise to power and continuing dominance; and it becomes legitimate for a modern critic to refashion that story otherwise, to disclose a different range of meanings and values. If the notion of historical totality needs to be replaced by the alternative concept of a fragmentary and discontinuous series of historical differences, then the drama should be able to speak of diverse and contradictory ideologies. If the kinds of writing traditionally separated off as 'literature' need to be restored to their intertextual relations with other kinds of writing, then new methods of inquiry and explication become appropriate.

These methods can be seen at their most characteristic in the work of the founder of New Historicism, Stephen Greenblatt.[21] Greenblatt's method takes its starting-point from an interdisciplinary convergence of literary and historical methodologies. The traditionally constitutive structures of literary understanding – the author, the canon, the organic text – are deconstructed, and dramatic texts returned to the historical culture from which they emanated. The traditionally indispensable techniques of literary investigation – verbal analysis, qualitative identification, evaluation – are largely abandoned in favour of an intertextual juxtapositioning of authorized literary works with the products of 'non-literary' discourses. Thus in an influential essay on the history plays Greenblatt read the second tetralogy in relation to Thomas Harriot's *A Brief and True Report of the New Found Land of Virginia* (1588), in order to demonstrate that both the drama and the contemporary political document embody the same ideological structure.[22]

Throughout Greenblatt's essays, other plays and other texts, together with contemporary beliefs and cultural customs, social practices and institutional structures, are continually thrown into an exciting and liberating interplay of discourses, as the critic traces the continuous flow and circulation of ideological forms and political interventions throughout the complex body of Renaissance society. The isolation of Shakespeare as deified author, and the strict perimeters of demarcation between Shakespearean texts and other forms of writing, are convincingly broken down, and Renaissance culture opened up to new methods of literary and historical analysis. The ultimate objective of that analysis is the sphere of the political: through verbal and structural investigation of a range of rhetorical strategies, the critic discloses the conditions of cultural, ideological and political power, and the dramatic texts become sites for the negotiation and authorization, interrogation and subversion, containment and recuperation of the forms of Renaissance power.

Thus literature can be seen to enact a type of political discourse. Yet whenever in New Historicist readings literature seems to voice subversive or alternative attitudes or emotions, these are always contained within the dominant ideology: the provocation, challenging and defeat of subversion is in fact one of the means by which a dominant ideology secures its power. Leonard Tennenhouse, in another important New Historicist essay on the second tetralogy, relates the chronicle plays of the 1590s to other *genres* such as the court masque, and finds in both a common ideological structure: the idealization of state authority. In Shakespeare's history plays, he argues, political power is seen to depend not on legitimacy but on legitimation, on the capacity of the contender to seize and appropriate the signs of authority: 'Power is an inversion of legitimate authority which gains possession, as such, of the means of self-legitimation . . .'[23] The methods employed by 'old' and 'new' historicisms could hardly be more distinct. For Tillyard, order and misrule were simply real forces present in the moral and political world of Elizabethan England. Shakespeare's achievement was to designate and distinguish them as ethical categories, and to articulate a model of their appropriate relationship. Tennenhouse regards the plays as constituent elements of a cultural formation in which state power was producing the images of its own legitimacy, and provoking the oppositional energies against which it could define its own licit authority. Here the critic's own political evaluation of the plays is committed to an oppositional exposure of such strategies of legitimation. Old and new historicisms however, despite their obvious antagonisms, appear to be in agreement that the relationship between dominant and subversive ideologies within the plays is implicitly an orthodox or conservative one. In general, American New Historicism has preferred to reproduce a model of historical culture in which dissent is always already suppressed, subversion always previously contained, and opposition always strategically anticipated, controlled and defeated. This particular political interpretation of the past, in which struggle, resistance, contradiction serve only to reproduce and confirm the power of a dominant state apparatus and a hegemonic ideology, implies in the present a form of political quietism, in which there is a clear role for the intellectual, but no acknowledgement of any other agency of democratic or progressive change. This characteristic of New Historicism has in the past decade become a target for the more politically-engaged forms of post-structuralist criticism such as British cultural materialism.

While New Historicism is by definition concerned directly with matters of historical theory, and finds in historical drama a natural object of interest and analysis, other new theoretical approaches to literature, which have invested less attention in the history plays, nonetheless provide important elements of the contemporary theoretical context, and exert distinct theoretical pressures on the approaches used in the present book. I shall discuss two of them here: deconstruction and feminism. Deconstruction questions many of the terms upon which most traditional practices of literary criticism depend, since they all belong to the 'logocentric' universe of Western philosophical discourse, with its continual insistence on establishing meaning by constructing arbitrary 'centres'. Notions such as the text, language, the reader, are all revealed by deconstruction to be ideological strategies concerned with maintaining an illusion of presence by postulating a coherent centre – the inherent meaning of the text, the structure of language, the subjectivity of the reader. In particular the traditional premise, shared by many critical schools and theoretical approaches, that the literary or dramatic text contains inherent meaning and is capable of delivering up such meaning to the activity of analysis, is rejected by some deconstructionists in favour of the assertion that the category of 'the text' has no real existence. This view can be seen in Tony Bennet's application of the theories of Jacques Derrida: while traditional criticism assumes the objectivity of its object, deconstructionist criticism holds this assumption to be essentially meaningless, since there is no authentic text to recover, only a series of ideological reproductions to analyze:

> Ultimately, there is no such thing as 'the text'. There is no pure text, no fixed and final form of the text which conceals a hidden truth which has but to be penetrated for criticism to retire, its task completed. There is no once-and-for-all, final truth about the text which criticism is forever in the process of acquiring. The text always and only exists in a variety of historically concrete forms.[24]

Here Bennett rejects the idealist metaphysic of the text in favour
of a historically variable 'text' existing only in its various readings. Subsequently in an influential essay called 'Text and History'
Bennett developed this position further, invoking Jacques Derrida
who argues that a piece of writing can only function as literature if it
possesses that infinitely flexible capacity for arbitrary reproduction,
that 'iterability':

> This 'iterability', Derrida goes on to argue, liberates the text
> from any possible enclosing context, be it the context of the
> originating moment of inscription favoured by interpretative
> criticism or the context of the semiotic code favoured by struc-
> turalism. The very structure of the written text is such that it
> carries with it a force that breaks with its context; and, indeed,
> with each of the contexts in which it may be successively
> inscribed during the course of its history. It cannot be limited by
> or to the context of the originating moment of its production,
> anchored in the intentionality of its author, because 'the sign
> possesses the characteristic of being readable even if the moment
> of its production is irrevocably lost and even if I do not know
> what its alleged author-scriptor consciously intended to say at the
> moment he wrote it'.[25]

The attention of the student of literature should therefore be deflected from textual study towards 'what might be called "the living life
of the text"; the history of its iterability, of the diverse meanings
which it supports and of the plural effects to which it gives rise in the
light of the variant contexts within which it is inscribed as it is
incessantly re-read and re-written.'
Even where this argument is wholly accepted, a persuasive case
can still be made for not throwing out the baby of the text with the
ideologically contaminated bathwater of traditional criticism. In a
materialist criticism the study of literature is conceived as a *practice*,
an assemblage of cultural activities, generated and supervised by
certain educational institutions. If that activity and those institutions are not perceived with clarity and analyzed with political
definition, radical cultural work becomes blindly complicit with the
ideological processes it seeks to understand and master. On the
other hand, if literature is a practice, and if the object is to speak
intelligibly to those engaged in that practice, it is acutely necessary

to intervene directly into the concrete activity at some meaningful point of access. The ideological reproduction of Shakespeare will continue with far stronger impetus, far greater resourcefulness, far suppler flexibility than the theoretical analysis of that reproduction provided by a materialist criticism: because the former has the power and adaptability of a dominant cultural apparatus. Opposition to that structure can best be focused by a dialectical strategy of simultaneous internal and external, practical and theoretical intervention: where 'reading', the practical analysis of an objective phenomenon (appropriately qualified by the awareness that one is developing *potentialities* of an object which can always offer alternative positions of intelligibility), can be strengthened by a clear-sighted description and evaluation of examples of such alternative readings and their ideological effects.

This pragmatic and strategic approach to criticism and teaching is widely advocated on the left and clearly it has much to recommend it.[26] But I would also want to challenge the persuasive view that literary texts have *no* inherent qualities and have therefore infinite plurality of meaning. The basic philosophical premise of this theory is of course irrefutable: a text only exists, only produces meaning, when it is subjected to the operations of reading, criticism, reproduction. Both meaning and value are produced only by certain operations of human intelligence working on the text: they are, self-evidently, historically variable. But if texts had no inherent qualities, literary criticism would be a much more efficiently organized conspiracy than it actually is: a solid tacit agreement, unbreached for centuries, to restrict readings to a particular series of problems, subjects, themes; achieved not by focusing on the limited area of meaning illuminated by the text, but by an astonishingly expert exercise of arbitrary cultural power. The text itself, I am suggesting, has a kind of authority, dependent certainly on its being situated within a certain context of discourse, but also inscribed into it by the specific conditions of its historical genesis. That authority is a matter of *meaning* rather than of *value*; and it needs to be sharply discriminated from the *authoritarianism* of those established orthodoxies such as that of Tillyard which act coercively in criticism and education, policing the perimeters of literary-critical discourse. But all readings, whatever their ideological tendencies, must observe the disciplined frame of reference, must inhabit the constrained area of meaning given by the text, if they are to remain in any way

committed to the text as a category. Peter Stallybrass, discussing
Macbeth in a manner designed (in Walter Benjamin's phrase) to
'brush history against the grain', and drawing on Bakhtin, Benjamin,
Fredric Jameson, Macherey and Robert Weimann, adheres nevertheless very firmly to a constellation of deeply ingrained topics –
Stuart patronage, witches, and the tension between courtly and
popular cultures.[27] This is no criticism of his approach, which is
admirable, but at no point does this typically radical analysis escape
that limited area of interests prescribed by the authority of the text.
Stallybrass begins not just with the play, but with important political
questions of the present; it would be perfectly possible to begin with
other urgent contemporary issues, and thus manipulate the text into
an alternative frame of reference: the morality of political assassina-
tion, or nationalism. The text would answer to those questions.
Other external modes of address would require ingenuity on the
critic's part, but could conceivably be made to intersect with the
text's range of preoccupations: abortion, baby-battering, cookery.
But if we sought to mobilize the text for a discussion of unemployment, pit closures, poverty, the wages struggle, there would be
no answer: the identity of the text would deny, would refuse to
authorize, the relevance of those issues to its imagined world.

   This is not, I hope, a *reductio ad absurdum* of the deconstructionist position, but a practical application of its theoretical assertions.
Seeking to dispose for ever of the pure autonomous text, this
methodology approximates in practice to the very metaphysical
idealism it opposes. In deconstruction the text is free, expropriated
from its author's intentions, liberated from the historical determinants operating on its original production, stripped even of the
apparently accessible public meanings inscribed in its language and
form. The text is free – to be arbitrarily manipulated and strategically
mobilized by any cause and in any direction. This boundless plurality
of the text is simply a fetishizing of the historically concrete: a
metaphysical faith in a theoretical ultimate which is never, in
practice, explored or charted. To reserve the space of infinity while
never in practice occupying more than a limited part of it would be
called, in any other sphere of discourse, religion.[28]

   To deny the literary text the freedom guaranteed to it by the
polysemic plurality of deconstructionism, and to argue for some
conception of intrinsic identity or authority inherent in it (though
the *inherence* can only be inferred from empirical observation of the

practice of reading, an activity determined by considerations other than the character of the text) is a dangerous procedure; but the methodology I am advocating is in no sense a return to the objective text of orthodox criticism. To insist that a text belongs to a history of reception in important ways separable from the conditions of its production, in no way diminishes the significance of that moment of production: the text is a part of history as it is produced and as it is consumed. The latter assertion would hardly be contested by orthodox criticism, though there is room for considerable dispute about how a text's 'historical' character should properly be disclosed. Deconstructionists on the other hand, grudgingly acknowledging the relevance of this initial history, deny its *primacy* as a determinant:

> The position which a text occupies within the relations of ideological class struggle at its originating moment of production is . . . no necessary indication of the positions which it may subsequently come to occupy in different historical and political contexts . . . the specific constellation of determinations characterising the originating moment of a text's production may be regarded as of unique significance. But these are in no sense ontologically privileged in relation to the subsequent determinations which bear upon the text's history.[29]

While agreeing with Bennett that 'marxist criticism has sought to historicise literary phenomena only one-sidedly', I would confer much more significance on the specific character of the originating moment of production as a historical determinant shaping both the text and its subsequent history of reproduction. The latter history can tell us how a drama like Shakespeare's becomes constituted as a central symbol of artistic and national culture, and what social forces have required of it that ideological function; it cannot however demonstrate why in particular *Shakespeare's* drama should have been chosen, except in terms of some well-organized conspiracy arbitrarily selecting one writer for installation at the peak of the cultural hierarchy. Since it cannot be shown that literary texts contain immanent *aesthetic* values, are there not particular *historical* reasons why the drama of Shakespeare should have been chosen for the purpose? I shall be arguing in the following pages that the specific historical conditions attending the genesis of Shakespeare's drama inscribed into it patterns of meaning determining the materiality of the texts, and the subsequent history of their reproduction as a central focus of British national culture. To attempt an analysis of those conditions is to recover the literary text, not as a self-contained repository of meaning, but as a specified arena in which particular struggles for meaning (ultimately, though not necessarily immediately, political struggles) once took place, and can therefore be taken up again. Not any and every meaning, but those meanings and values which fall within the text's circumscribed range of significances:

> Literature or fiction is not a knowledge, but it is not only a site where knowledge is produced. It is also the location of a range of knowledges. . . .
>
> While on the one hand meaning is never single, eternally inscribed in the words on the page, on the other hand readings do not spring unilaterally out of the subjectivities (or the ideologies) of readers. The text is not an empty space, filled with meaning from outside itself, any more than it is the transcription of an authorial intention, filled with meaning from outside language. As a signifying practice, writing always offers raw material for the production of meanings . . .[30]

Beginning with oppositional rereadings and reinterpretations of literary texts, feminism has gone on, together with other forms of post-structuralist criticism, to require of its readers a radical critique of the whole concept of 'literature', and of the institutions which support literature as a cultural activity. For feminists these institutions are male-dominated, both in terms of the actual power in the hands of the men who run them, and in terms of the 'patriarchal' ideologies the institutions presuppose and foster. The feminist intellectual who identifies such 'patriarchal' ideologies in Renaissance literature is not only writing about a history marked by masculine dominance and the subjection of women; she is also writing out of a cultural situation in which contemporary structures of oppression and institutionalized inequality bear directly upon her. Her utterance is therefore inevitably polemical, tendentious, political.

There are within feminist studies of Shakespeare a range of

interpretive approaches and theoretical positions. Feminist critics have reread Shakespeare's texts with a new kind of attention to the female characters in the plays, producing what is termed an 'images of women' criticism. This approach has been used to argue that the presentation of women in Shakespeare is generally positive and supportive, even proto-feminist;[31] and also that the plays represent women negatively, within a framework of patriarchal ideology.[32] Other feminist work has drawn on the social history of women, marriage and the family in the Renaissance, debating the role of Shakespeare's drama within a process of general change.[33] Much American feminist criticism has based its explorations in psycho-analytical theories of gender and sexuality, interpreting the texts as paradigms of masculine anxiety and female subjection. Some of the most advanced and difficult feminist work has developed along this line, synthesizing psychoanalysis with deconstructionist studies in language.[34]

In general feminist critics have, for fairly obvious reasons, declined to address Shakespeare's historical drama, finding the *genres* of tragedy, comedy, romance and 'problem play' answering much more directly to their particular concerns.[35] In the work of those feminist critics who have written on the history plays can be found an enduring sense of incompatibility between the Renaissance his-tory play and the priorities of feminist analysis, which has deflected such critics from that dramatic *genre*, and which has its theoretical counterpart in current disagreements between feminism and other new theoretical perspectives such as New Historicism and cultural materialism.[36] If indeed, as Linda Bamber first suggested, the kind of gendered vision produced by historical drama effectively expels the female as a significant dramatic presence, then the much more pronounced interest displayed by feminist criticism in tragedy, comedy and romance would be strategically intelligible.

Certain feminist approaches, such as those based in a binary polarisation of gender (such as Marilyn French's *Shakespeare's Division of Experience*, 1982) and some of those based in psycho-analytic theory, have been opposed by other critics who have con-sistently resisted any divorce between feminist theory and historical knowledge – especially Catherine Belsey, Kate McLuskie, Lisa Jardine and Juliet Dusinberre.[37] Their application of a 'materialist feminism' seems to me to suggest ways in which the appropriate analytical methods and political preoccupations of feminism can be drawn productively into historical studies, facilitating substantial and enabling shifts of perspective as well as an attention to fundamental matters of equality and justice.

The historical–materialist approach of the present book, though founded in a long tradition of marxist philosophy and marxist literary criticism, and moreover committed to certain methods of inquiry and demonstration which might in the intellectual universe of post-structuralism seem 'traditional', has developed in close relation to these new theoretical perspectives as well as in a combative relation with the conservative historicism of the Tillyard school. Its primary concern is with matters that belong to the marxist understanding of history: with questions of ideology, with social and economic development, with the nature of the state, with problems of power and resistance, struggle and oppression. In keeping with New Historicism, however, it is also concerned with history as textuality, specifically with the writing of history in the Renaissance; and conceives the relationship between historical drama and formal historical writing as an intertextual relation, with each mode of writing operating at a different point in the same discursive field. Its approach also differs from the governing methodologies of New Historicism, in that it does not see Shakespeare's history plays as operating ultimately in ideological complicity with the ruling interests of their times. Although the plays are sites of cultural struggle across which ideological contradictions intersect and engage in contestation, they are capable, both in criticism and performance, of offering a sceptical, demystified grasp of power. As conscious acts of historiography these plays are also powerful imaginative agents of resistance and renewal.

From deconstructionist criticism *Shakespeare Recycled* has drawn the recognition that no cultural text can be properly analyzed only by reference to an originating moment of production. If the 'after-life' of a text is in a sense the only kind of life it ever has, then analysis must concern itself not only with the contextual and contingent history bearing upon the originating moment of a text's production, but also with the subsequent history of that text's strategic mobilization and ideological incorporation by different cultural forces in different social formations. I have argued that these two contexts are related more organically than deconstruction allows. The historical genesis of a literary (or dramatic) discourse inscribes into its structural form different possibilities of meaning. These possibilities are not arbitrary or infinite, but neither are they simply inherent in the text itself, or generated purely by the interaction of text and reader's sensibility. As they are manipulated, appropriated and practically applied in criticism and theoretical analysis, in performance and adaptation; as they are installed and reconstituted into canons, traditions and hierarchies by the practices of academic and educational institutions; as they are used and exploited to serve various different and conflicting ideological ends; they become unquestionably, in the broadest sense, political.

Politics is about understanding society and making choices. Politics requires knowledge, analysis, conviction and practical commitment; but none of these is politically meaningful without judgment: the taking of sides. A political criticism should then be a question of judging the political meanings literature generates, evaluating the political potentialities of specific works, and discriminating between reactionary and progressive forms of criticism. Post-structuralist theories have, however, been so effective in exposing the ideological function of evaluation in literary criticism, that criticism on the left has grown intensely sceptical about aesthetic evaluations of any kind. Since texts are infinitely 'iterable', the act of making meaning with them contains in itself no value that is not political: one 'reading' of a text is neither better nor worse than any other except in terms of its position *vis-à-vis* an established, preconceived criterion of political values. If my reading of *Richard II* is better than Tillyard's or Traversi's, it is only, in deconstructionist terms, because it has a progressive political purpose. I cannot *demonstrate* that my ideological appropriation has more truth, accuracy or plausibility than Dover Wilson's, since my criticism too is a matter of logistics: I can only expose his reading as reactionary and offer mine as politically progressive: 'The claim is not that . . . such a reading of literary texts, is more accurate, but only that it is more radical'.[38]

Of course one primary motive of deconstructionist criticism is to force a confession from orthodox criticism: the necessary task of exposing as politically motivated that which denies its own relation to politics. Once that has been accomplished, the issue can be shifted away from aesthetic discussion to political debate. But such a procedure leaves inviting opportunities unexplored: if it can be shown that there *are* relationships of *value* between aesthetic and political discourses; if a reactionary or liberal-humanist appropriation of a text can be revealed as demonstrably inferior, less truthful, less accurate, less convincing than a progressive and materialist reading, then it becomes possible to engage with orthodox criticism on a broader front, to take issue in concrete as well as theoretical terms with those cultural and ideological forces a marxist criticism must oppose.

The peril inherent in this procedure is again that possibility of reversion to an unprovable objectivity of the text: less truthful in relation to what criteria? It seems to me one of the formidable recommendations of a historical criticism that it can avoid the seductive circularity of the endlessly fetishizable text. A historical criticism is simply a method which recognizes the historical nature of literature. Such an acknowledgment will perhaps be declared uncontroversial, but we still do not have a firmly established historical criticism: one which analyzes cultural discourses in the light of historical knowledge and historical theory; traces the social determinants inscribed in a literary work's aesthetic form and discloses the complex interplay of historical meanings its discourse sets in motion; recognizes literature as a specific cultural practice constituting a political intervention into some ideological problematic; and pursues a literary work's history as an established *locus* of the struggle for particular significances, an arena constantly inhabited by competing ideologies locked in a perpetual contest for meaning. Such criticism recognizes the dialectical relations between aesthetic form, ideological matrix, historical conjuncture and history of reproduction, and returns us to the possibility of *evaluating* both literature and criticism, simply because it can claim greater sensitivity than other orthodox and conventional modes of criticism to the true nature of 'literature' as a cultural and ideological praxis, always historically specific, relative and variable. A historical criticism acknowledges the dialectical *rapprochement* of literary form (whether it be called discourse or rhetoric) and historical context: a conjuncture which Jeremy Hawthorne once defined, in a still useful formulation, as the paradox of 'identity' and 'relationship'.[39] Both contexts are historical, both are definitions of a work's reality: its identity is a matter of history, and its history the history of its identity.

The elements of feminist theory that appear in the following pages derive necessarily from existing feminist work on the history plays. Two of the pioneers of feminist Shakespeare criticism, Linda

Bamber and Coppélia Kahn, in their respective discussions of the history plays, offered interestingly divergent accounts of the relations between femininity, masculinity and history.[40] For Bamber, there can be no dialectical relation here between femininity and history, since history is a grand narrative of male achievement, a 'masculine–historical struggle for power', a 'military–political adventure', which specifically denies any significant space to 'feminine Otherness'.[41] Those contrasting images of apparently powerful and aggressive women – such as Joan of Arc or Queen Margaret – which can be found in the earlier historical cycle, *Henry VI* to *Richard III*, do not resolve this problem, since they may more appropriately be considered as male impersonators who unsex themselves in order to ape the violence and cruelty of men: though they participate in history, they do not participate in history *as women*.

Bamber therefore posits 'a female principle apart from history',[42] a positive image of feminine Otherness which can issue, albeit from a position of acknowledged impotence, a challenge to the priorities of masculine *his*tory. Richard's Queen Isabel is described for example as 'queen of an alternative realm' in which the female principle is 'fully differentiated from the masculine Self'[43]; and it is only as such that the imagery of woman can hope to assimilate any degree of power: 'Only as the Other are women in Shakespeare consistently the equals of men. Only in opposition to the hero and the world of men, only as representatives of alternative experience do the women characters matter to Shakespeare's drama as much as the men'.[44] Since the *genre* of the historical drama could not contain a full expansion of this female principle, which would subvert its very *raison d'être*, feminine Otherness has to wait for the *genre* of tragedy to provide it with an occupiable space. The relationship between 'femininity' and 'history' is thus constructed in Linda Bamber's argument as a binary opposition of mutually incompatible contraries.

Coppélia Kahn's treatment of the history plays in her book *Man's Estate* (1981) discovers an alternative to this resigned acknowledgment of female occlusion: she is not primarily concerned with the representation of women, but rather with dramatic explorations of masculine ideology: 'the patriarchal world of Shakespeare's history plays is emphatically masculine. Its few women are relatively insignificant, and a man's identity is determined by his relationship to his father, son or brother'.[45] Kahn's theoretical approach thus enables a direct address to the dramatized historical context as a patriarchal structure, the ideological site of a crisis of masculine identity.

Employing both Bamber's focus on representations of the female, and Kahn's analysis of the patriarchal mentality, it seems to me possible to link the historical concerns of my argument with some of the basic preoccupations of feminist theory and criticism. Despite the obvious occlusion of female activity from the history plays (though more from the second tetralogy than from the first) in favour of the almost exclusively masculine preserves of politics and war, it remains possible to excavate a female sub-text from within the ostensibly patriarchal structure of these plays.

I have defined the governing method of this book as an application to literary, theatrical and cultural analysis of historical materialism. 'Historical materialism' is of course a phrase drawn from marxist philosophy; and though marxism is clearly one of the constitutive roots of contemporary theoretically-informed criticism, recent intellectual debates and global political developments render some cautious and circumspect discussion of 'marxism' imperative. In its purest (many would say rather its 'crudest') form marxism is a political science entailing a political commitment: a philosophy that requires an unswerving dedication to the destruction of the capitalist state and economy, and the establishing, if necessary by violent means, of a proletarian communist state. In practice marxism has never represented a single ideology or a single party: there have been many types of 'marxist' political organisation, and very different types of society have emerged from 'marxist' political action. Marxism is today associated particularly with the communist regimes of Eastern Europe, authoritarian states that have recently turned away from centralized communist structures, not without enormous difficulties, but to the evident relief of their peoples. In intellectual terms however marxism has exercised a powerful and complex influence, capable of considerable development and transformation. In Britain in the late 1960s and 1970s many intellectuals working in literary and cultural studies would have called themselves marxists, and were involved in marxist political organisations. Now marxism is less a political creed than a philosophy, a sociology, and a method of cultural analysis. In American intellectual circles this has been more generally the case all along, as Stephen Greenblatt has observed:

It is possible in the United States to describe oneself and to be perceived as a Marxist literary critic without believing in the class struggle as the principle motor force in history; without believing in the theory of surplus value; without believing in the determining power of economic base over ideological superstructure; without believing in the inevitability, let alone the imminence, of capitalism's collapse.[46]

Although the philosophical concepts of determinism and inevitability have been unquestioned imperatives only in the crudest forms of what Marx called 'mechanical materialism', it is very difficult (certainly from this side of the Atlantic, where marxist political science and marxist cultural theory have much stronger and more visible intellectual roots) to conceive of a marxist politics without class-struggle, a marxist economics without the concept of surplus value – to accept, in short, as 'marxism' an intellectual position emptied of all the principal tenets of marxist philosophy. In contemporary British criticism marxism is more likely to be acknowledged – along with poststructuralism or deconstruction, feminism and psychoanalysis – as a seminal influence, and the marxist element in cultural work likely to be more clearly in evidence. It is possible that this difference is more apparent than real, and is due rather to the strongly overt anti-communism of American culture, which probably makes it professionally more difficult there for an intellectual to acknowledge the marxist inheritance.[47] The work of Leonard Tennenhouse, with its rigorous analysis of power-relations and ideological contradiction in Renaissance society, displays the traces of its marxist antecedents with relative clarity; and some degree of marxist permeation can be detected even in more refined instances of scholarly discourse. It is nonetheless clear that British materialist criticism, such as the 'cultural materialism' established by Jonathan Dollimore and Alan Sinfield (the title itself derived directly from Raymond Williams,[48] but ultimately from Marx's 'historical' or 'dialectical' materialism) is more evidently and openly marxist than its American counterpart New Historicism.

One of the key contemporary debates in political philosophy is that between Marxism and theories of 'postmodernism'. One of marxism's acknowledged intellectual achievements was that of exposing and demystifying some of the great ideological illusions by which human societies justify their structures of oppression and inequality. Marxism exposes the liberal idea of progress, the pretensions of religion, the masking of economic exploitation as a 'natural' condition, the disguising of capitalism's violence as 'orderly' and 'peaceful'. Postmodern theory, particularly in the work of Jean-François Lyotard,[49] takes this process a stage further, to a point where marxism itself is exposed along with progress, religion, nature, as yet another grand illusion constructed and sustained in the interests of arbitrary political power. Lyotard identifies all these ideologies as 'grand narratives' which are in themselves inevitably oppressive, since they conceal the real diversity, contradiction, difference of social and cultural experience. Where marxist historicism conceives of 'history' as a real process of development with measurable laws, with an identifiable origin and a projected outcome, 'history', for Lyotard, is a fiction designed to confer a spurious unity on a complex process of discontinuous and differential development.

Catherine Belsey has interestingly revalued the work of Tillyard and addressed the problems posed for marxism in the light of postmodern theory.[50] Postmodernism renders any confidence in the objective reality of the past impossible. The kind of historicism represented by Tillyard, which acknowledged the historical as part of a national cultural life signified by the notion of 'English history', is usually thought of as an assertion of nationalistic confidence. Belsey proposes that Tillyard's historical myth should be regarded rather as an expression of growing anxiety about the crisis of the postmodern world, in which the optimism behind the enlightenment values of liberal capitalism – progress, equality, political liberty – began to seem newly empty. She traces an early consciousness of this epistemological scepticism in the theoretical work of Saussure; locates its defining crisis in the immediate aftermath of the Second World War; and identifies its emergence into full theoretical consciousness in postmodernism. Belsey thus traces a distinct line from Saussure to Lyotard, with *The Postmodern Condition* introduced as the logical culmination of a century's work, dethroning the last of the metanarrative signifiers, History. After Lyotard, there can be no belief in a single historical trajectory.

Most marxist cultural theorists demonstrate considerable unease at this wholesale disposal of the certainties of history.[51] Belsey however finds it possible to accommodate a revised marxism to the theoretical subversions of postmodernism. Marx's theory of the 'modes of production', which offered a model of social development as a periodic sequence of economic systems, each destroying its predecessor, with the ultimately inevitable overthrow of capitalism by socialism, is now visible as a myth, one of the fictitious metanarratives exploded by Lyotard. Belsey welcomes this revision of marxism, arguing that Marx's theory of the 'relations of production', a method of analyzing dispositions of economic and political power within a social formation, is far more important for contemporary cultural and political theory. Lyotard defined the essence of the postmodern condition as a general 'resistance to metanarratives', a turning away from grand master-narratives and towards what he called 'petit recits', partial and fragmentary constructions of specific experience with no global, totalizing aspiration to tell the whole story, or to speak for all. Belsey finds such an inflection towards 'petit recits' in the work of Marx himself (her example is Marx's analysis of the 1848 revolution in France, *The Eighteenth Brumaire of Louis Bonaparte*[52]): fragmentary explorations into history which discover no grand narratives, no heroic quests, only voyages of ruthless conquest and suppression. This convergence of Marx and postmodern theory produces a marxism that is no longer a totalizing metanarrative, but a scientific method of analysis capable of recognizing contradiction, political intervention, difference.

Although I would resist the degree of concession to postmodern theory offered by Belsey, I accept the need to register this theoretical problem. If my work has a stronger sense of relationship with a 'tradition' of British marxism, it is largely because the post-Althusserian marxist philosophy of the 1970s – in its wholesale revision of earlier variants of marxism; its transformation of terms such as ideology, base and superstructure, humanism; its capacity to enter into dialectical relations with linguistic, psychoanalytic, and feminist theories – anticipated many of the objections of postmodernism. The revisionist marxism declared by Belsey as a defence against postmodernism is not so very different from the marxism we inherited at the end of the 1960s, in which it was certainly not an item of belief that the proletarian revolution was inevitable. Classic marxist texts such as *The Communist Manifesto*, with their 'master-narrative' describing successive phases of economic development, and adumbrating the final overthrow of capitalism by socialism, were not read as metaphysical prophecy, but rather as political exhortation. The marxist philosophy of history, and the marxist

methods of economic and political analysis, were means of understanding the developments of the past: which could then be applied
to specific tasks of political action which would, if successful, realize
the political development of the future.

British marxism in that crucial period was very much a philosophy
in crisis and change: a Stalinist deformation already destabilized by
the assault of Althusserian philosophy, and its interaction with a
Hegelian humanist variation of marxism developed in resistance to
Althusser. Politically it contained and retained a version of the
'Popular Front' strategy of a broad-based alliance of anti-capitalist
groups. The key problem was, and still is, whether marxist philosophy could ever hope to offer a macronarrative complex enough to
incorporate this pluralism, without either excluding or oppressing
particular groups which would wish to be part of the progressive
movement, but not on terms which would marginalize their own
interests; or becoming so attenuated as to disappear altogether as a
totalizing force. This project remains feasible only if the *analytical*
content of marxist politics – specific analysis of concrete historical
situations, and applied political strategies designed to realize ultimate objectives – is accepted as more important than the *theoretical*
content of marxist philosophy.

What we can carry forward from that earlier tradition of *praxis*,
contemporary engagement and direct commitment, into a greatly
strengthened and theoretically-developed historical materialism,
are certain methods of political analysis and cultural intervention.
We can draw on the 'empiricist' leanings of an earlier form of marxism, to reintroduce methods of concrete historical and cultural
analysis (fears of empiricism seem naive in the context of the New
Right's formidable rejection of the empiricist method in favour of a
radical and stridently ideological critique). We can focus our attention much more firmly on contemporary cultural conditions, con-
solidating and developing a continuous analysis of immediately
contemporary forms of cultural construction; building on work that
has been extensively proposed but only fitfully achieved. And we
can derive from that marxist philosophy, as a model for any kind of
political, economic or cultural analysis, the fundamental unity of
theory and practice.

Chapter Two

Chivalry and Kingship: Richard II

RICHARD II is distinguished sharply from the other histories by its peculiar *style* – what Tillyard[1] called the 'extreme formality' of its shape and pattern, the elaborately ceremonial and ritualistic character of its action, and the very heightened and overtly lyrical style of Richard's tragedy. These peculiarities make the play in some ways a self-contained and self-referential dramatic poem; even though it is clearly incorporated into a series by the *Henry IV* plays, its individual treatment of history remains distinctive. And yet no other historical drama of Shakespeare's has proved more difficult to understand and interpret without the aid of external authorities.

Richard II seems to depend to an unusual degree on what the Arden editor calls 'open questions' – unsolved or even unexplored problems of incident or character.[2] These questions usually present themselves as inconsistencies of plot or characterization: they are in fact questions about the play's understanding of history. They include such things as the apparent changes in Richard's character, the silences in Bolingbroke's, Richard's decision to stop the duel between Bolingbroke and Mowbray, and a question with which *I* shall be particularly concerned – how should the reader understand and respond to the murder of Thomas of Woodstock, Duke of Gloucester? Woodstock's death underlies the conflict of the first act, and indeed haunts the whole play. Every reader finds it necessary to take an attitude towards his death, and the most common interpretation is that Richard *did* have Gloucester murdered by Mowbray (which is in Holinshed's *Chronicles*);[3] and that the murder smears the Crown with a taint of crime and sin which all but disqualifies the king from any pretensions to unquestioned monarchical authority (which is certainly *not* in Holinshed).

The 'internal' evidence bearing on such questions is not always self-explanatory; hence scholars and critics are particularly prone to interrogating 'external' evidence in search of satisfactory answers – a hypothetical 'old play', the anonymous play *Woodstock*, Edward Halle's *Union of the Two Noble Houses*, the general framework of Tudor historical philosophy. Those who have sought to explain the play formalistically usually conclude that it is disorganized and incoherent.

A context *is* necessary to explain not only the play's internal problems, but its general shape and style; and I propose to argue that the necessary context is in fact a *historical* one. I believe Shakespeare had, as context, an understanding of medieval history much more complex and detailed than is generally acknowledged – a sense of history which is present in the play and accessible by literary critical methods, and the materials of which were readily available in those historical works which we know Shakespeare used as sources. I have discussed the relative probabilities of other suggested sources elsewhere: the principal source, Holinshed's *Chronicles*, is here an adequate basis for my argument.

Holinshed interpreted the Middle Ages with real understanding; although the ideological forces shaping Tudor and Elizabethan history bore upon his writing, they did so with less pressure and constriction than on, say, Halle or *The Mirror for Magistrates*. Shakespeare, whose interest in history was not merely a search for dramatic 'source-material', read Holinshed with understanding; and his appropriation of Holinshed's materials produced in *Richard II* a historical vision significantly different from either the orthodox conceptions of Tudor history, or Holinshed's intelligent version of that history. These are the three areas which need to be defined, distinguished, and the distances between them measured: the commonplace of Tudor history, Holinshed's complex understanding of the substance of that history, and Shakespeare's production in *Richard II* of a unique and specific piece of Renaissance historiography.

The conventional understanding of the 'history' dramatized by this play is well known; it is thought to portray a medieval society (that which John of Gaunt looks back on), which was a harmonious, organic community, dominated by kings, bound together by order, hierarchy, degree – an order which is mismanaged by Richard, and therefore falls prey to the civil conflict which deposes him. But the nature of that old society guaranteed that Richard's deposition could not be a mere change of regime; Bolingbroke's usurpation destroyed a traditional, divinely-ordained and divinely-sanctioned monarchy, and thereby destroyed the old medieval 'order' irrevocably. The break ushers in civil war, which divides the realm until the Tudor reconciliation.

If, as I am proposing, Shakespeare developed his own understanding of history from his historical sources – rather than simply interpreting the past by the concepts and images of Tudor political and historical philosophy – then he would have known the Middle Ages *not* as a period dominated by order, legitimacy and the undisputed sovereignty of a monarchy sanctioned by Divine Right, but as a turbulent period dominated by a great and fundamental conflict, fought out again and again and rarely suppressed, between the power of the Crown, and the power of the feudal barons.

Holinshed relates in considerable detail the constitutional struggles between monarchy and nobility which led ultimately to Richard's deposition, and which modern historians regard as the decisive political developments of this transitional late-medieval reign. We can enter Holinshed's narrative conveniently in 1386.[5] In that year Richard advanced two close friends, Aubrey de Vere and Michael de la Pole, to high office – they became respectively Duke of Ireland and Lord Chancellor. These men did not have the approval of the powerful group known variously as the Magnates, the Lancastrian party, the Baronial Opposition; and these nobles secured the support of the Commons in a bid to accuse de la Pole of treason. That tactic, that pattern, will become a familiar one, up to its final conclusive appearance in Bolingbroke's challenge to Mowbray. The baronial opposition engaged in a power-struggle against the king and his policies, using the 'favourites' as pawns; at this point the nobility strengthened their grasp over the reins of power. The sovereignty of Parliament was affirmed by lords and commons; thirteen lords were chosen 'to have oversight under the King of the whole government of the realm'. Holinshed reports here rumours of a plot between Richard and his supporters to dispose of Arundel, Warwick, Derby and Nottingham. The opposition faction has here taken shape: the five opposition leaders who came to be known as the appellants (or Lords Appellant) are here identified as a group: their leader, Thomas of Woodstock, Duke of Gloucester (brother to Lancaster and York); Thomas, Earl of Arundel; the Earl of Warwick; and the other two, here obscured by their titles, but easily recognizable by their policy – Henry Bolingbroke, son to the Duke of Lancaster, here Earl of Derby, later Earl of Hereford; and Thomas Mowbray, here Earl of Nottingham, later Earl of Norfolk.[6]

In 1388 came Richard's response to the events of 1386; modern historians have called this his 'First Tyranny'. A Parliament was packed with justices who declared the proceedings of 1386 illegal and treasonable. Events led to the inevitable military clash, and to a defeat for the monarchy; the king's forces were beaten at the Battle of Radcot Bridge by the Earl of Derby; Richard was besieged in the Tower of London. The lords continued to affirm their basic policy (which is also the essence of the Mowbray-Bolingbroke conflict) – that they bring their powers to defend king and realm against 'evil counsellors'. Lords and commons jointly demanded that Richard should come to Westminster; when he refused, they threatened to 'choose another king'.

The Baronial Opposition was now supreme. The 'Wonderful Parliament' (1388) declared the previous parliament illegal; the Appellants (now acting as a 'gang of five') accused the 'favourites' of treason; the king's failed to appear and were banished. Several of the king's men were executed, and Richard was forced to swear an oath to abide by the rule of the barons – a restoration of the reciprocal 'fealty' of the days of Magna Carta.[7]

The struggle continued until 1396. In 1397 Gloucester, Arundel, Warwick and Derby plotted to murder Richard; Mowbray, who was initially privy to this conspiracy, informed the king. Warwick and Arundel were arrested and indicted, Mowbray being one of the accusers. Arundel was beheaded. Warwick was exiled. Gloucester was murdered at Calais, because Richard feared to risk a public trial and execution. The gang of five was thus reduced to one: Bolingbroke.[8]

In 1397, Richard consolidated his power by means of a Parliament which taxed heavily, disinherited estates, made huge borrowings and devised the 'blank charters'; and sought new oaths of allegiance from those alleged to have supported the Appellants. Richard, says Holinshed, had become a tyrant. 'He began to rule by will more than by reason, threatening death to each that obeid not his inordinate desires.' The Crown became increasingly unpopular. Bolingbroke, the only surviving Appellant, became the focal point and leader of popular discontent. Re-enacting the Appellant policy for the last time, in 1398 he accused Thomas Mowbray of treason.[9]

This is the point where Shakespeare chose to begin his play: the appeal of treason by Bolingbroke against Mowbray. The choice of incident testifies both to dramatic skill *and* to depth and complexity of historical sense. The quarrel between the earls is an appropriate inception for the action of *Richard II*, as all the succeeding events can be seen to flow from it. But this incident also links the play indissolubly to precedent history, as Shakespeare read it in Holinshed: the appeal is the climax of that conflict between monarchy and feudalism which had been actively fought out throughout Richard's reign. The last remaining Appellant accuses the King's favourite of treason, ostensibly in defence of King and realm; the central accusation concerns the murder of the King's greatest enemy, leader of the Baronial Opposition, Thomas of Woodstock, Duke of Gloucester. The appeal is the latest and last in a long succession of similar bids for power by the opposition faction of powerful feudal lords.

It is important to see the characters in this kind of context, and forming this kind of pattern: Mowbray the erstwhile Appellant turned king's favourite; Bolingbroke the last surviving representative of the Appellant faction, now the leader of popular discontent with the policies of the Crown; Richard recognizing instinctively the full implicit significance of Bolingbroke's challenge.

Critics such as Tillyard and Traversi have spoken of the 'high formality' and 'courtly ceremony' of these proceedings, recognizing that the elaborate formal style is Shakespeare's attempt to create a specifically 'medieval' atmosphere and tone. Both these critics see this formal order as the expression of kingship:

> The conspirators, working as such, do not share the ceremonial style used to represent Richard and his court . . . we have in fact the contrast not only of two characters but of two ways of life . . . the world of medieval refinement . . . is threatened and in the end superseded by the more familiar world of the present.[10]

> The high formality . . . reflects a kingship which combines legitimacy with the assertion of a sanction ultimately divine . . . the legitimate but inadequate conception of feudal loyalty represented by Richard against the advance of a formidable but unsanctioned political energy.[11]

The king himself is regarded as the source of this specifically 'medieval' culture, which is dramatized here to show what medieval society was at the moment of its undermining by the more 'modern' forces of political ambition, power-politics and Machiavellianism. To these critics feudal law and chivalry mean, quite simply, 'order' and 'kings'.

It is advisable to be exact about this 'formality', these 'ceremonies', and to define precisely what they are. Neither Tillyard nor Traversi seems particularly conscious of the fact that the appeal of treason and the consequent trial by battle are stages of a legal process, conducted in the Court of Chivalry, according to definite procedures which Shakespeare appears to have known and understood. The sense of legal procedures being followed in this initial meeting of the earls is absent from any of the sources: it is Shakespeare's invention, and it shows the King adhering to procedures which (though odd indeed from the point of view of modern law, and clearly enough distinguishable from Elizabethan justice) according to feudal law are conducted throughout with perfect propriety.

The king, the fount of justice, presides over this legal process: legally his authority is absolute; in practice (in the drama as in actual history), his control is somewhat tenuous. In the first scene he restricts himself carefully to the role of mediating authority, 'chairman'. But the scene resolves itself into an assertion by the barons of a code of values which is actually antagonistic to royal power, *hostile* to Richard's authority as sovereign; and the ceremony and pageantry of the proceedings are *connected more closely* with *that* code of values, than with the courtly culture of the crown. It is in recognition of this fact that Richard seeks to remain ostensibly neutral (a position which symbolizes very precisely the predicament of a king in a still largely feudal society). The conflict which ultimately leads to the king's deposition is not a conflict between old and new, between absolute medieval monarchy and new Machiavellian power-politics. It is a conflict between the king's sovereignty and the ancient code of chivalry, which is here firmly located in the older and more primitive tribal and family code of blood-vengeance. Richard initially acquiesces in this code (as medieval kings tended perforce to do), although it is actually independent of royal authority. But like the later medieval European kings who tried to stamp out trial by battle (by the introduction of Roman law codes in the thirteenth century[12]) Richard subsequently attempts to affirm a policy of royal absolutism, which insists on the king's prerogative overriding the procedures of chivalric law. Richard's political response to this constant clamouring for power on the part of the feudal lords, is to impose a policy of *absolutism*.

Throughout the first scene Richard's behaviour is absolutely proper, formal, legal, impartial, and a sense of order does actually flow from his presence. It is invoked in his first words, by which he summons his most powerful subject: ceremonial exchanges of formal address express the specific quality of personal relationship between the most powerful members of the ruling class – the subordination of noble to monarch – and thereby invoke and describe the specific structure of power within their society:

> Old John of Gaunt, time-honoured Lancaster,
> Hast thou, *according to thy oath and band*
> Brought hither Harry Herford thy bold son . . .
> . . . I have, *my liege*
> (I, i, 1–7; my italics)

The king carefully characterizes himself as president, not judge; claiming to be an institution standing over and above the conflicting interests of the combatants – he *is* the law, the state, justice. He is there to see that justice is observed, and to counsel agreement; but he does not seek – at this stage – to intervene or suppress the rights enjoyed by the lords under feudal law, even though his own position (as we see later) is very remote from the feudal conception of justice.

Bolingbroke and Mowbray both offer formal expressions of allegiance, which Richard accepts with prudent reservation. Bolingbroke's speech of appeal (I, i, 30–46) can be recognized clearly as a continuation of the policy of Baronial Opposition: he *is* attacking the king, but is very careful to establish (as the Baronial Opposition always had) that his challenge is not to the king's authority, which is above reproach, but against the 'evil counsellor':

> In the devotion of a subject's love,
> Tend'ring the precious safety of my prince . . .
> . . . Since the more fair and crystal is the sky,
> The uglier seem the clouds that in it fly.
> (I, i, 31–2; 41–2)

Under medieval law the appeal of treason (gradually replaced by the procedure of impeachment in Parliament) was an individual accusation which did not have to be proved or defended – if the accused denied the charges, the appeal went straight to trial by battle.[13] As Bolingbroke implies, the only 'proof' necessary is that

of his 'right drawn sword'. Mowbray further clarifies this antiquated
legal process by setting aside discussion and reason, and offering in
their place a central image around which the play's first act could be
said to revolve – that of *blood*. The quarrel is one of 'bloods',
hot, angry, impatient. But the hot blood is also knightly blood, the
honourable blood of noble men; the quarrel can therefore be
properly resolved by chivalric blood-battle (i, i, 47–60).

Bolingbroke snatches at the blood-image as quickly as he throws
down his gage; and in a striking declaration *disclaims* the king's
kinship (i, i, 70–1), rejects his royal connection, and invokes 'the
rites of knighthood' (75). He is therefore the first to suggest that the
obligations of chivalry and those of royal allegiance can enter into
conflict. Mowbray replies in the same chivalric language –

> I'll answer thee in any fair degree
> Or chivalrous design of knightly trial . . .
>   (i, i, 80–1)

– all reference to the king has disappeared.

Bolingbroke then makes his accusations against Mowbray. The
charges of embezzlement and conspiracy are vague and uninterest-
ing: but they would actually have more place in a charge of treason
than the third accusation – the real substance of Bolingbroke's
attack on Mowbray – that Mowbray was instrumental in the clan-
destine execution of the king's greatest and most ambitious enemy,
Thomas of Woodstock, Duke of Gloucester:

> . . . That he did plot the Duke of Gloster's death,
> Suggest his soon-believing adversaries,
> And consequently, like a traitor coward,
> Sluic'd out his innocent soul through streams of blood,
> Which blood, like sacrificing Abel's, cries
> Even from the tongueless caverns of the earth
> To me for justice and rough chastisement;
>   (i, i, 100–6)

The glittering veil of the Baron's chivalric language trembles a little
here, and behind it we perceive the shape of something more
primitive – the motive of blood-vengeance for a slaughtered kinsman. For Bolingbroke there is no disparity at all between chivalry

and blood-vengeance – the one is the means to the other; justice can be 'proved' by force of arms. But a different texture of language encourages the reader to separate the two different concepts: Bolingbroke's 'rough chastisement' is surely a cruder, more primitive thing than the abstract concept of 'justice'.

The code of chivalry enables Bolingbroke to regard *himself* as a responsible administrator of justice, because blood-vengeance of kin and justice are for him synonymous; he is speaking the language of an ancient code of feudal values. He believes that his 'glorious descent' (I, i, 107) (which is exactly the same as Richard's) gives *him* greater responsibility for prosecuting the law than the king himself. With Holinshed's history as context, we can appreciate the full seriousness of this assertion, which is a direct baronial challenge to the power of the throne; and appreciate also the justice of Richard's sarcastic remarks, which put Bolingbroke firmly in his place:

> How high a pitch his resolution soars! . . .
> . . . Were he my brother, nay, my kingdom's heir,
> As he is *but my father's brother's son* . . .
> (I, i, 109; 116–17; my italics)

In the same speech Richard asserts that the ties of blood and kin do not have the same significance to him as they do to Bolingbroke; his 'sacred blood' is absolved from such partialities; all are equal before his 'sceptre's awe', the dignity of his sovereign authority. Royal absolutism and feudal kinship are placed in sharp opposition.

Critics have found Mowbray's self-defence (I, i, 124–151) suspiciously evasive. It *is* evasive, as he is to some extent covering up for the king; but legally he does not need to prove his innocence by evidence or argument, but only to deny the charges and accept the offer of combat. It is not at all clear whether he acknowledges Gloucester's death as a crime, saying only that he 'neglected his sworn duty in that case'.

Throughout Richard remains inactive, but it would be wrong to interpret this inactivity as weakness. The king is confronted with a powerful baronial offensive, articulating itself in chivalric terms. The power-struggle is fought out within the ideology of chivalry, which gives the king a tenuous control, but is actually based more firmly on feudal power and values than on the sovereignty of the Crown. Richard tries initially to reason with them, to secure agreement and compromise – a solution which, like the subsequent affirmation of absolutism, cuts across the structure of feudal values.

Such compromise, however, is impossible. A spirit of reason and compromise, acceptable also to the royalist baron Gaunt, who co-operates in the attempt at reconciliation, meets the stubborn, intractable values of chivalry which now break away completely from the structure of monarchic authority which had striven to control and contain them, subdue them to a royalist social pattern:

Bol. Myself I throw, dread sovereign, at thy foot;
       My life thou shalt command, but not my shame:
       The one my duty owes, but my fair name,
       Despite of death, that lives upon my grave,
       To dark dishonour's use thou shalt not have.
       I am disgrac'd, impeached, and baffled here,
       Pierc'd to the soul with slander's venom'd speare, . . .
       [*Baffled*: the rendering infamous of a recreant knight by public ridicule].

Mow. Mine honour is my life, both grow in one,
       Take honour from me, and my life is done . . .

Bol. O God defend my soul from such deep sin!
       Shall I seem crest-fall'n in my father's sight?
       Or with pale beggar-fear impeach my height
       Before this out-dared dastard? Ere my tongue
       Shall wound my honour with such feeble wrong,
       Or sound so base a parle, my teeth shall tear
       The slavish motive of recanting fear . . .
                                        (i, i, 165–195)

The piling-up of chivalric language here is remarkable, and it is virtually all Shakespeare's invention. It is used to show that in this conflict king's man and opposition baron have both broken away from royal authority, into the realm of knighthood. Honour has become more absolute than allegiance; loyalty to kin has superseded duty to sovereign; chivalric personal dignity has exceeded civil obligation. Monarchy has failed to control the power of feudalism.

The second scene continues to develop the main themes of the first, and establishes clearly the centrality and significance of Gloucester's death. Gaunt continues his son's use of the 'blood' image, in a similar way: his blood-kinship to Gloucester places the obligation of blood-vengeance upon him also – the 'murdered' kinsman's blood cries out to the brother as it had to the nephew. But Gaunt's instinct of blood-vengeance is subdued to a clear conception of loyalty to a divinely-ordained sovereign. (It is perhaps worth noting that this is the first mention of such an idea; Richard himself does not invoke it until half-way through act III).

The Duchess, Woodstock's widow, speaks – as her nephew speaks – an older, more primitive language: sovereignty has no hold over her imagination, which is possessed by the imagery of blood-kin and blood-vengeance. The highly personal utterance of the widow (Woodstock's 'next of kin') places the strongest of personal pressures on Gaunt: to revenge your own blood is a form of personal survival; to decline revenge, a form of personal self-destruction. The old woman, like Bolingbroke, identifies justice with chivalric law, synthesizes the language of blood-vengeance with that of chivalric justice:

> O sit my husband's wrongs on Herford's spear,
> That it may enter butcher Mowbray's breast!
> . . . And throw the rider headlong in the lists
> A caitive recreant to my cousin Herford!
>
> (I, ii, 47–53)

Gaunt makes no concession here: he stands by his concept of Divine Right and royal prerogative – 'God's is the quarrel' – and even suggests that the murder of Gloucester may not have been 'wrongful':

> . . . for God's substitute,
> His deputy anointed in His sight,
> Hath caused his death; the which *if wrongfully*,
> Let heaven revenge . . .
>
> (I, ii, 37–40; my italics)

Gaunt believes firmly in the necessary subjugation of feudal rights to royal prerogative. In the next scene however (the Combat) we find Gaunt using the widow's language; and it becomes apparent that one of the purposes of I, ii, is to dramatize the conflicting pressures operating on Gaunt just as strongly as they operate on his brother York. Bolingbroke again invokes his noble lineage, this time as 'blood':

> Oh thou, the earthly author of my blood,
> Whose youthful spirit in me regenerate
> Doth with a twofold vigour lift me up
> To reach at victory above my head . . .
>
> (I, iii, 69–72)

Stirred by this appeal, Gaunt's loyalism is shaken:

> God in thy good cause make thee prosperous,
> Be swift like lightning in the execution,
> And let thy blows, doubly redoubled,
> Fall like amazing thunder on the casque
> Of thy adverse pernicious enemy!
> Rouse up thy youthful blood, be valiant and live.
>
> (78–83)

Gaunt encourages the 'youthful blood' of the chivalric spirit, and identifies it with justice. The imagery of thunder and lightning confers on Bolingbroke extraordinary power as the instrument of divine and natural justice. Gaunt has here adopted the language of chivalry, blood, kin and justice which we have learned from his son and from the Duchess. He remains, of course, divided: his ambivalence is made clear later when he agrees in Council with Richard's decision to banish the earls, but distinguishes between his *personal* and his *political* allegiances.

Richard's decision to stop the combat is another open question for which various explanations have been offered, and various motives supplied.[14] Richard's speech at I iii, 138 is an impressive homily against civil war and the disorganizing militaristic feudalism which has precipitated that danger. It also gives us a sense of Richard's own image of his kingdom. Running through the speech is an underlying pattern of images, creating a strong positive sense of the realm as it should be:

> Our kingdom's earth . . . : plough'd up . . . our peace, sweet
> infant, . . . till twice five summers have enrich'd our fields . . .
>
> (I, iii, 125–143)

The pastoral imagery of rural peace, fecundity, new life, is violated by the language of bloodshed, civil wounds, swords; the assertive arrogance of feudal pride; 'the grating shock of wrathful iron arms'. If feudalism has become a real threat to the stability and harmony of the realm, then Richard is clearly attempting not just to banish two quarrelling earls, but to dismantle the very structures of feudal power.[15]

Though absolutist, Richard's solution combines authority with diplomatic concession: the unequal banishments tacitly acknowledge Mowbray's guilt, and endeavour to appease the Lancastrian interest. They, however, are far from satisfied. Bolingbroke's words:

> The sun that warms you here, shall shine on me,
> And those his golden beams to you here lent
> Shall point on me and gild my banishment.
>
> (145–8)

– playing as they do on the royal associations of the sun-image – cannot be less than a veiled threat; and Gaunt's response is one of grudging discontent. Bolingbroke's irony about the extent of royal power (213–15) is turned by Gaunt into a definition of its limits. The king is not as powerful as he imagines: and this assertion shapes the advice he gives his son:

> Think not the King did banish thee
> But thou the King
>
> (279–80)

He exhorts his son to *cancel*, imaginatively, the king's power; to consider *himself* as sovereign. Bolingbroke makes it plain that such fantasy fulfilments are not for him – nothing less than reality will do:

> O, who can hold a fire in his hand
> By thinking on the frosty Caucasus?
> Or cloy the hungry edge of appetite
> By bare imagination of a feast?
> Or wallow naked in December snow
> By thinking on fantastic summer's heat?
>
> (294–9)

That materialist philosophy, applied to Gaunt's advice, produces nothing less than rebellion and the deposition of the king.

Gaunt and York, the older generation of barons, are both loyal but now reluctant supporters of the Crown. Gaunt's famous speech (given a disproportionate weight and authority by the royalist patriotism it has so usefully served) is clearly one of the strongest incentives to accept the conventional ideas of 'medieval kingship'. His language is uncompromisingly royalist: the realm is (or rather has been – the speech is an elegy) properly defined in terms of its monarchy, its history distinguished by the quality of its kings. Gaunt, unlike Bolingbroke, identifies kingship and chivalry, and looks back nostalgically to a time when England united the two. That identification, and the role Gaunt adopts towards Richard (that of sage counsellor), imply a kingdom in which a careful and diplomatic balancing of forces synthesized Crown and nobility into a united 'Happy breed of men' – a situation which prevailed in the reign of Edward III. The appropriate image for this marriage of Crown and aristocracy, of Christian monarchy and 'true chivalry', is that of the crusade.[16] Though Gaunt's language is that of royalism and Divine Right, he is certainly no absolutist: his Golden Age is that of a feudalism given cohesion and structure by the central authority of a king bound to his subjects by the reciprocal bonds of fealty.

The climax of Gaunt's speech draws the attack on Richard's economic policies[17] into a powerful image of the dissolution of traditional social bonds: England, formerly united in itself and against other nations is now bound together by economic contracts:

> England, bound in with the triumphant sea
> . . . is now bound in with shame,
> With inky blots and rotten parchment bonds.
>   (II, i, 61–4)

Gaunt's elegy is no panegyric of absolutism: it is a lament for the dissolution of a society in which king and nobility were organically bound together into a strong and unified nation – the King is now a mere 'landlord'. The unnatural quality (from the baronial point of view) of these developments is focused by a reiteration of the charge about Gloucester's murder: an offence against kin, a stain of dishonour on the family of Edward III, a cause of division within the patrician order. This also serves to remind us that the immediate cause (in dramatic terms) of Gaunt's discontent is the banishment of his son.

The Duke of York presents a different point of view, and I think it is important to understand and to acknowledge the seriousness of his position. York's ideas are usually compromised by attention to his very obvious self-division – on stage the role is usually played as that of a fussy and indecisive senior civil servant. But we have seen the same self-division in Gaunt as well, resolved only by his death; York has to live with the difficulty of carrying his divided allegiance into the new conditions:

> Oh my liege,
> Pardon me, if you please; if not, I pleas'd
> Not to be pardoned, am content withal.
> Seek you to seize and gripe into your hands
> The royalties and rights of banished Herford?
> Is not Gaunt dead? and doth not Herford live? . . .
> Take Herford's rights away, and take from time
> His charters, and his customary rights;
> Let not tomorrow then ensue today:
> Be not thyself. For how art thou a king
> But by fair sequence and succession?
>
> (II, i, 187–208)

The spirit underlying this speech is that of Magna Carta. Richard is demanding *obedience* rather than *fealty*: fealty being a reciprocal relationship which guarantees the lord certain constitutional rights in exchange for his service and loyalty.[19] Fealty binds subjects *and* ruler: Bolingbroke's homage to Richard is no mere subjection but the entry into a reciprocal social bond. York's image of society is that of a social contract: the king, by violating the contract, inevitably raises the spectre of rebellion even in the most 'well-disposed' hearts. There is even a touch in York's speech of the early medieval view that rebellion could be justified against a monarch who violated his own side of the 'fealty' contract. York's self-division is clearly expressed again in II, ii:

> . . . Both are my kinsmen:
> Th'one is my sovereign, whom both my oath

And duty bids defend; th'other again
Is my kinsman, whom the King hath wrong'd,
Whom conscience and my kindred bids to right.

(ii, ii, 111–15)

York recognizes here two equally valid but conflicting conceptions of justice and duty, a historical contradiction. Richard, who has made it plain that he regards the Lancastrians in general as enemies – ('Right, you say true; as Herford's love, so his; As theirs, so mine; and all be as it is,' ii, i, 145–6) – deals with York's sliding loyalty by a characteristic political gamble: appointing him Protector in his absence.

By the end of this scene rebellion is a reality. Northumberland makes it plain here, despite his covert and non-committal speech, that he is proposing to rescue the Crown from its present incumbent, to reclaim the throne on behalf of the nobility. The barons are preparing to replace the dynastically legitimate king with one of their own choice and approval.

The royalist and baronial ideologies are brought into direct collision in the meeting between York and the newly-returned Bolingbroke (ii, iii.). Within the language of royalism ('Cam'st thou because the anointed king is hence?') Bolingbroke's actions receive their automatic valuation as 'gross rebellion and detested treason'. Bolingbroke's case, however, is also reasonable and valid, within its limits – he restricts his thinking to feudal terms, and does not imagine or conceptualize the consequences of his pushing at the balance of power. He appeals (as he had previously appealed to Gaunt) to those sympathies York had already displayed in his nostalgic invocations of the great days of the Black Prince and John of Gaunt; he asserts that he is a baron, and is claiming baronial rights; he connects York with his brother, whose 'rights and royalties' have been expropriated and given away to 'upstart unthrifts' (Richard's favourites); he uses York's own argument –

If that my cousin King be King in England,
It must be granted I am Duke of Lancaster.

(ii, iii, 122–3)

– and clinches the argument by appealing to justice, and his right to 'challenge law'.

York cannot deny the justice of the case, although he cannot see rebellion as an appropriate means of securing justice; and he also detects a larger purpose underlying the conspiracy:

> Well, well, I see the issue of these arms.
>
> (ii, iii, 151)

This is perhaps confirmed by Bolingbroke's decision to seek out the 'caterpillars'; though that too is compatible with traditional baronial policy, (and was enacted, Shakespeare knew from Holinshed, in 1388). York wavers into neutrality, but is already half-way to joining the revolution. He is 'loath to break our country's laws' but is unable to resolve the historical contradiction – the paradox of *two* laws, each in its way valid and absolute, but incompatible and mutually exclusive.

By this stage the political and military battles are really over: and in the speech of Salisbury in ii, iv, we hear the first stirrings of the language and imagery of royal tragedy, Divine Right and apocalyptic prophecy which will dominate the rest of the play.

Act iii opens with Bolingbroke in a commanding position (though not necessarily any nearer to the throne than the barons had been in 1388, when the king's supporters were executed by Parliament). His speech defines very precisely his specific relationship with England: it is the solid, proprietary language of a nobleman talking about his estate, it contrasts with Gaunt's impersonal conception of the realm as a feudal nation and even more sharply with Richard's image of England, as it is revealed in the next scene. Like the charges against Mowbray, those against the favourites are no more than a gesture towards public justice: and just as those charges collapsed into the fundamental accusation of Gloucester's murder, so the allegations of treason carry very little weight by comparison with the *personal* injury sustained by Bolingbroke himself – *that* part of the speech carries an accent of personal grudge and recrimination, the response to an offence against the aristocratic class:

> Myself – a prince by fortune of my birth,
> Near to the King in blood, and near in love,
> Till you did make him misinterpret me –
> Have stoop'd my neck under your injuries,
> And sigh'd my English breath in foreign clouds,

Eating the bitter bread of banishment,
Whilst you have fed upon my signories,
Dispark'd my parks and fell'd my forest woods,
From my own windows torn my household coat,
Rac'd out my imprese, leaving me no sign,
Save men's opinions and my living blood,
To show the world I am a gentleman . . .

(III, i, 16–27)

[*Signories*: estates. *Imprese*: a heraldic device]

The 'caterpillars' have fed on Bolingbroke's *property*, his *estates*, concepts defined very precisely by his clear, concrete images of parks, forests, emblazoned windows, coats-of-arms, personal heraldic symbols – the concrete social identity of a 'gentleman'. Bolingbroke's consciousness is still that of a rebellious baron rather than the incipient king although in fact he has already pushed the policy of opposition beyond the point of balance; the whole realm of England is about to become the baron's property.

That solid, possessive sense of England as private property contrasts sharply with Richard's feelings about his kingdom on his return from Ireland, in the next scene (III, ii.). For the first time, Richard's speech moves towards the language and imagery of Divine Right – though there is no explicit affirmation of this doctrine for almost forty lines. In the preceding lines we see a fantastic reduction of Divine right to a kind of childish superstition as the strong and bitter masculinity of Bolingbroke's relation to his estate gives way to Richard's intimate, sentimental, physical cherishing of 'my kingdom'. The conjuration is that of a child, who invokes the supernatural to combat the apparent omnipotence of parents – it is the voice of an imagination already beginning to experience defeat.

A sentimental poetic fancy peoples the realm with 'familiars', sympathetic creatures who will resist Bolingbroke's assault. Having failed in his ruling of society, Richard seeks to imagine a kingdom of nature, in which everything is subject to his will, everything naturally loyal to his sovereignty. We hardly need the Bishop of Carlisle to inform us that the 'power' of Divine Right, and the kind of power that can rule a state, have become separated from one another.

For it is here, at the point where his defeat is imminent, that Richard's mind begins to split king and man, divine power and practical authority. 'Divine Right' is not seriously offered by the play as an unquestionably valid understanding of Plantagenet England: it is shown as a historical myth, emerging with its full imaginative force and splendour in the alienation of Richard's consciousness as it responds to specific conditions of military and political defeat.

If we listen sympathetically to the practical, commonsense advice of his followers, it is easy to assume that Richard is experiencing a simple failure of the will, an indication of his personal weakness and unfitness for royal office. But he is no longer interested in the practical 'means of succour and redress'. His kingship has been faced with a situation which could be resolved only by conciliation or absolutism. Choosing the latter course, Richard has appeared throughout as the absolutist monarch in the legal, economic and political spheres. The baronial rebellion makes conciliation impossible, and absolutism impracticable: so Richard's imagination begins to seek out new kingdoms to dominate with the absolute power of his will. The kingdom of nature succumbs to his fantasy and the whole cosmos is subdued to his power in the imagery of Divine Right.

The state itself ready to fall into Bolingbroke's hands, Richard's imagination is released to a vivid realization of the difference between effective power and 'mere' legitimacy; between the power of the man and the authority of the royal office; between the man who can rule a state and the king who has only the charisma of 'Divine Right'. He feels that he has reached death, and has nothing to bequeath to his heirs, no property in the realm. The only substance of his kingship is now the experience of royal tragedy. The only thing he can bequeath is his own tragic myth: 'sad stories of the deaths of kings'. This speech is a penetrating tragic insight into the hollowness of 'Power' without power – the imagery of hollowness runs from the hollow grave, to the hollow crown, to the 'wall of flesh' encircling the mortal life, which seems as impregnable as a castle, but contains only a vulnerable, isolated life –

> . . . and with a little pin
> Bores through his castle wall, and farewell king!
>   (III, ii, 169–70)

'Tradition, form and ceremonious duty' are indices of real power; remove them, and the king is a vulnerable man:

... subjected thus
How can you say to me, I am a king?
(III, ii, 176–7)

If the king's body is mortal, then sovereignty is a mere pageant, a stage performance ('a little scene, To monarchise') and Death is the real sovereign of the royal court, the 'antic' who parodies and mocks all seriousness. This awareness of royal tragedy (which comes to Hamlet and Lear) is actually the Divine Right of Kings inverted. The earlier speech had affirmed that the king needs only the personal charisma of his royal identity; this speech is the inversion of that position – without effective power the king himself is nothing. It is characteristic of *Richard II* that the full splendour of the concept of divine monarchy is dramatized as the process of its destruction. The play does not simply endorse or affirm a historical myth, but dramatizes a specific situation: Richard is consciously creating himself in the role of tragic king, consciously dramatizing his own historical myth.

Richard continues this powerful performance in IV, i, by playing on the idea of 'service', comparing himself to Christ and his erstwhile followers to Judas; and by invoking the conventional ceremonies of kingship, now 'inverted' with powerful effect.[20] He makes the giving of the crown, the abdication, the divesting of royal power, the ceremony with the mirror, all contribute to the effect of this 'woeful pageant'. In V, i, he again dramatizes his experience as a tragedy to be told in 'lamentable tale'; and on the journey to London, according to York's theatrical analogy, he 'upstages' the much more popular star-actor who precedes his entry.

The final culmination of Richard's absolutism is his isolation in prison (V, v). The prison is a world without people, a kingdom without subjects, which he can fill with his own personality: he can be both ruler and ruled. At last Richard's imagination and will are supreme – now his kingdom has been reduced to the confines of his own mind.

It is clear, then, that the 'history' of the play is much more complex than the conventional accounts allow. Shakespeare grasps very firmly and clearly the central contradiction of early medieval society: the struggle between royal authority and feudal power. He sees the deposition of Richard II, not as the overturning of a traditional order by new, ruthless political forces, but as the consequence of an attempt by a later medieval monarch to impose on feudal power an absolutist solution. The victorious forces are not new but old: feudal reaction rather than political revolution. The society we see dissolving had been an effective unity and balance of royal prerogative and feudal rights – both parties in the conflict have pushed their interests to the point of inevitable rupture.

This argument does not seek to invalidate the concept of divinely sanctioned kingship, which is clearly central to the play; but to suggest a different view of its *status*. The play does not tell us that this conception represents Shakespeare's understanding of the structure and quality of medieval society before the deposition of Richard II. On the contrary, the precedent past, the 'pre-history' of the present' is dramatized as a social contract held together by the mutual agreement of powerful forces. The older generation of barons, sons of Edward III, *are* committed (though in different ways) to the concept of monarchy; but they see this operating *only* within a conception of commonwealth, a union of Crown and nobility, and independence or absolutism on the part of the King distresses them deeply. Richard himself does not describe his rule as sanctioned by Divine Right until his defeat is well under way.

The idea of Divine Right is actually presented in the play as a historical myth (a mystifying fiction, but a real and powerful form of human consciousness) which develops and emerges from the defeat of the monarchy. Richard dramatizes that myth as the monarchy itself dissolves; he affirms it most powerfully as his power disappears; and as his effective rule declines, his tragic myth exerts ever more powerful pressures on the imaginations of those responsible for his defeat. It is a matter of critical commonplace that Richard is not only a tragic role on the stage, but a 'tragic actor' like Charles I in Marvell's poem, conscious of the role he is playing; and that he is not only a mouthpiece for tragic poetry, but a poet, comprising his own 'lamentable tale'. We can now add to these a third role: Richard is also a historian, constructing and creating the myth of his own tragic history.

Once created, that myth becomes a powerful ideology, and the play reveals it to be precisely that. Like the ideology of monarchic feudalism, which was both organic order *and* battleground of historical forces, the myth of Richard's tragedy (in its twin form of martyr king and deposed tyrant) continues to haunt the civil conflicts of his successors, who are thus, in T. S. Eliot's words, 'united in the strife which divided them'; *and* determines the shape and form of the ultimate reconciliation. When Richmond at the end of *Richard III* unites the red rose and the white, his action is subsumed into the powerful mythology created by his predecessor, 'that sweet lovely rose' Richard II.

Chapter Three

Patriarchy and Gender:
Richard II

IN the course of that elaborate exchange of formal speeches which constitutes the opening scene of *Richard II*, Mowbray offers a useful commentary on the relations between gender and history, between masculine and feminine identities:

> Let not my cold words here accuse my zeal.
> 'Tis not the trial of a woman's war,
> The bitter clamour of two eager tongues,
> Can arbitrate this cause betwixt us twain.
> The blood is hot that must be cooled for this.
>   (I, i, 47–51)

It is hard to imagine a more precise or more decisive definition of an absolute and irreconcilable difference between the sexes. Fighting, an active and positive enterprise, is done with the 'blood' and the body, and it can be done only by men. The only kind of fighting Mowbray can imagine women being involved in is a scolding squabble between 'two eager tongues'. The energy and vigour that characterize masculine militarism are absent from the latter activity: the woman's words are 'cold', while the warrior's blood is 'hot'. There is even a latent accusation of constitutional cowardice on the part of women, who are far more 'eager' to engage in the cold clamour of a verbal quarrel than they would be to undertake the physical challenge of a real battle. The patent substance of Mowbray's words is of course an accusation against Bolingbroke, tantamount to a charge of effeminacy: he (Mowbray) is too manly to join in this humiliating conflict of words, and cannot wait to get onto the field where the real 'trial' can begin.

It should seem odd from our modern conceptions of law and justice that the value of words and of argument to a legal process should be so discredited. But that of course is the nature of a chivalric trial by combat. Both Mowbray's misogyny and his superstitious reliance on physical force as a means of securing justice are clearly, to us (and were, in my view, to the historical consciousness that found its way into Shakespeare's plays[1]) visible as anachronisms; dated, old-fashioned, antiquated beliefs, belonging to a particular historical society. Mowbray's words are dramatically located into that post-feudal society of the late fourteenth century in which, according to the dominant systems of belief, men were warriors and women a protected species.

This disclosure of masculine identity has its counterpart in the representation of female character. Towards the end of the key scene, II, i, King Richard marks his departure from the stage by speaking, almost as an afterthought, to his queen, Isabella:

> Come on, our Queen; tomorrow must we part.
> Be merry; for our time of stay is short.
> $$(\text{I, i, 222–3})$$

A reader of the printed play-text (as distinct from the spectator of a performance) could be forgiven for wondering, at least momentarily, where this queen came from. In the course of the 150 or so lines during which she occupies the stage, she speaks only one line, and is neither spoken nor referred to. For a reader it is almost necessary to look back to the stage-direction which announces the arrival of the king (at line 68) to see that the queen enters with the king and a group of nobles. The reader of the play (whose attention is necessarily focused on those characters who manifest their presence in speech) encounters a virtually silent, self-effacing character, who is also ignored by everyone else in the room, virtually as an absence, a non-existence. In a stage production, of course, things are different: the text calls for the queen to be physically, visibly present among the king's entourage, and her passive presence could actually be made quite significant: the female body is as eloquent a theatrical sign as the presence secured through verbalization. But when deciding what to do with the queen, actors and directors are left entirely to their own devices, reliant on the resources of their own imaginations: for the verbal text itself has almost nothing to say about the strange quiet presence of Queen Isabella.

Act II, scene i involves eleven characters, only one of whom – the queen – is female. That disproportionate marginalization of the female population is typical of this play as a whole. Only five female characters appear in a cast of over thirty identified parts (not counting various supernumery servants, attendants, soldiers, who are also overwhelmingly male): these are the Duchess of Gloucester, who appears only in I, ii (her death is then reported at II, ii, 97); the Duchess of York, who appears only in V, ii; and the queen, who appears in three scenes – II, ii; III, iv; V, i – in addition to her gestural presence in II, i.

 Now a number of common-sense arguments naturally present themselves to suggest that there is really nothing remarkable in this. There is never more than a handful of female parts in any of Shakespeare's plays; a fact obviously connected with the Elizabethan practice of using boys to play the roles of women. Elizabethan history plays were drawn from historical writings which did not particularly emphasize the presence or agency of women in history: history was largely thought of as an account of the actions of men. Lastly, this particular historical drama deals with the kinds of political and military crisis which necessarily excluded women from active participation: political struggles, trials by combat, military campaigns. Those active and enterprising heroines who appear in other Shakespeare plays seem to belong to a later age when a formidable 'queen' showed herself capable (in a sense) of fighting her own battles, such as that against the Spanish Armada; and they appear naturally sympathetic to our own later age in which the principle of female equality is, though hardly universally attained, at least widely established, in western societies, within codes of law and social convention. That exclusion of women from the decisive and determinant activities of a society is something we would, from the perspective of modern ideas, decry: but it is a historical injustice for which we can hardly blame Shakespeare. In the historical story of the deposition of Richard II, he found no remarkable or influential women: so that absence was duly and dutifully reflected in the play.

A moment's consideration will reveal that all these apparently 'common-sense' arguments are suspect. It is a fact that only a small number of female roles is to be found in Elizabethan plays. But the women characters who occupy those roles usually have a disproportionate influence within the world of the play: Viola, Rosalind, Portia; Cordelia, Desdemona, Lady Macbeth. It is even often the case that they show strengths and abilities, kinds of determination and resourcefulness, not displayed at all by their menfolk. As we witness Portia dominating and winning Antonio's trial in *The Merchant of Venice*, or Cordelia leading an army in *King Lear*, or Lady Macbeth returning to the murdered Duncan's chamber, we are unlikely to derive from Shakespeare's plays any simple notion of women as 'the weaker sex'. This is certainly not the case in *Richard II*, where the queen is a pathetic melancholy spectator of her husband's downfall.

As we have seen, the Elizabethan dramatist's relationship with his historical sources was not a passive and automatic subservience. When Shakespeare dramatized other periods of history in which women are described as having some kind of prominence, he gave them more assertive roles in his plays – Joan of Arc and Queen Margaret in the *Henry VI* plays are obvious examples. After *Richard II* Shakespeare started to interpolate fictional comic sub-plots into the 'factual' material of the chronicle drama, thus providing more space for the participation of women: in the *Henry IV* plays, women like the Hostess and Doll Tearsheet have active and important (if distinctly 'low-life') roles to play. It was quite open to him to make more of Queen Isabella than the historical sources themselves warranted. In fact he did, since the young woman who appears in the play to express her unfocused melancholy, to complain of her husband's declining fortunes, and to lament his tragic overthrow, has no real historical authority at all: Isabella was a child of ten when these events occurred. Her passive role in the play is then, we might say, historically appropriate; her dramatic characterization is all Shakespeare's invention.

The third argument from 'common-sense', that the particular historical character of this action excludes the active agency of women in a particularly decisive and intractable way, has rather more force than the other two. It is one thing to invent an interesting dramatic character for Isabella; but if women did not (outside romances like Spenser's *The Faerie Queen*), take part in chivalric combats, Shakespeare could hardly clap his queen in armour and let her fight the king's battles for him. But that exclusion of women from the central and constitutive activities of a society can either be accepted as a natural condition, or foregrounded and interrogated as an arbitrary structure of patriarchal authority, a carefully-engineered inequality in the disposition of power.

It seems to me possible that the marginalization of women in a play like *Richard II* is not simply the symptomatic expression of an unconscious misogyny, or a passive reflection of pre-determined historical conditions. It is rather a historical reality of the past, grasped by the specific mode of historical consciousness active in the play, a reality which the play in turn foregrounds, interrogates and criticizes. Women may not be much in evidence in the play, but feminity is. Let us take a closer look at the scene with which we began (ii, i), the scene of Isabella's strangely absent presence. As I noted above, Isabella appears there in a scene populated otherwise entirely by men. The problems and issues debated in the scene are specifically 'masculine' preserves: politics, war, economics, law, property. Throughout the scene what the characters say about their specific situation carries with it wider dimensions of reference, so that other groups of people are continually being alluded to and moving into temporary focus. Again, these are all groups of men. Young men, sick men, dying men, living men, flattering courtiers, lawyers, Englishmen ('this happy breed'), Frenchmen, Irishmen, fathers, grandfathers, brothers, sons, uncles, kings, knights, commons, nobles, ancestors, 'men of war'. It would be hard to imagine a world more thoroughly cleared of any sign of the female gender.

Yet if we look a little closer, vestigial traces of feminity begin to surface: the repressed returns. John of Gaunt sings the praises of that 'happy breed of men' (ii, i, 45) who under the strong government of warrior kings like Edward III had excelled in the conquest of other nations. Englishmen are famous for their strength, their military successes, their masculinity. But to describe a category of men, however unimpeachably manly, as a 'breed', is to draw attention to the fact that somehow they must have been 'bred', and that therefore members of the female sex must have played in the process something more than a marginal role. Gaunt also talks about 'birth' (ii, i, 52), though he is there, perhaps, talking less about the biological process by which children are delivered than about the male-dominated dynastic system of lineage. More distinctively revealing are his references to England as a 'nurse' and as a 'teeming womb of royal kings' (ii, i, 51), metaphors which draw attention to the specifically female capacities of gestation and suckling. As Gaunt's celebration of the achievements of the English aristocracy extends to include the crusades, he actually finds space to mention a woman's name:

> This nurse, this teeming womb of royal kings,
> Feared by their breed, and famous by their birth,
> Renowned for their deeds as far from home
> For Christian service and true chivalry
> As is the sepulchre in stubborn Jewry
> Of the world's ransom, blessed Mary's son . . .
>
> (II, i, 51–6)

The allusion to the Virgin Mary is perhaps representative of Gaunt's view of women. Whatever cults of worship may attach to Mary, her primary significance is the fact that she gave birth to a remarkable man, Jesus. In Gaunt's feudal and aristocratic perspective, women appear as the passive vehicles by means of which the patriarchal seed is procreated, the patrilinear dynasty secured. Even the femininity of his metaphorical 'England' is ultimately spurious: since that maternal symbol is so completely a construction of the kings and warriors who have served their country in loyalty, fidelity and truth. Nonetheless, however strenuous Gaunt's efforts to suppress the reality of the female, it continues to appear, if only in the interstices of his metaphorical language. You cannot really talk about nurses, and wombs, and birth, and breeding, without bringing into play a feminine dimension of meaning. Once that meaning occupies a space inside the imaginative universe of the play, it proves remarkably hard to expel.

I will now examine the part played in the drama by its three female characters. All three are present in the play not in their own right, or because they have any distinctive individual contribution to make to the play's action: but in terms of their relationships with men. They are all, primarily and even exclusively, wives and mothers. The Duchess of Gloucester is there to lament and preserve the memory of her murdered husband. The Duchess of York is there to plead, successfully, for the life of Aumerle, her son. Queen Isabella has literally nothing to do in the play except to feel sadness and pity for her husband.

The Duchess of Gloucester, as we have already seen, seems to represent a potentiality for female assertiveness, which is nonetheless deflected and turned to self-destructive grief and melancholy. In her view the murder of her husband was a dreadful crime, since it was not only an unlawful killing, not only an offence committed against a kinsman, but a violation of the royal family itself. Where

Richard sees royalty as inhering in his own person, the Duchess conceives of it as a shared possession dispersed across the family of Edward III, and rooted in each of his seven sons. In killing Gloucester Richard has struck at the very root of the aristocratic kinship system itself.

But the Duchess's very strength and courage are self-denying, self-annihilating, since the noble family she idealizes, the dynasty of Edward III, consists entirely of men; the role of women in the composition of this dynasty is silently effaced, and they have no place or position in the family tree. The royal 'blood' that privileges and sacralizes the aristocratic family is a peculiarly masculine substance: it can be spilt by murder, or redeemed by blood-revenge, but it possesses none of the capacities biologically associated with blood in the female body. Christian patience is scornfully dismissed as the natural subjection of the common, the 'mean' man; for the aristocratic subject, *noblesse oblige*, and principal among those duties is the responsibility for avenging the death of a murdered kinsman.

The Duchess seeks to persuade Gaunt to take revenge against Richard; but Gaunt is committed to preserving the security of the crown, however much he may disapprove of the particular king who wears it. The Duchess's hopes of revenge focus therefore on the possibility of Bolingbroke's emerging victorious from the combat with Mowbray. If Bolingbroke were to kill Mowbray, then a kinsman of Gloucester's would have succeeded in killing his murderer, and in casting a guilty shadow over the instigator of the murder, Richard himself. Revenge would be satisfied, her dead husband's ghost appeased.

> O, sit my husband's wrongs on Hereford's spear,
> That it may enter butcher Mowbray's breast!
> Or if misfortune miss the first career,
> Be Mowbray's sins so heavy in his bosom
> That they may break his foaming courser's back
> And throw the rider headlong in the lists,
> A caitiff recreant to my cousin Hereford!
>   (I, ii, 47–53)

Such militant violence of language proves the Duchess capable of that hot-blooded martial vigour defined by Mowbray as the peculiar prerogative of the male sex. But however strong her feelings, and however forceful their expression, this is still 'the trial of a woman's war': for the Duchess is prevented by the impotence of her gender from acting upon her impulses towards revenge and restitution. She can only ask men to act for her, or support their struggles from the side-lines like a superannuated cheer-leader. Her feminity is negated twice over, first in her espousal of masculine feelings and values that repress the female, and second in the social pro-hibitions restraining her from taking any personal role in the activities she deems essential if her personal honour – which is defined entirely in terms of the honour of the men to whom she is related – is to be effectively defended. Her energies of principle and pride thus frustrated, they turn inwards with a damaging impact upon her vital self-esteem – 'Grief boundeth where it falls' (I, ii, 58) – and produce the emptiness and inconsolable sorrow that destroy her:

> Desolate, desolate will I hence and die.
> The last leave of thee takes my weeping eye.
> (I, ii, 73–4)

Sadness and melancholy are the natural fate of women in this play. Our introduction to Queen Isabella is to a mood of unfocused sadness, a grief without cause, which yet proves to be a prophetic monitor of imminent calamity. Isabella naturally uses the imagery of pregnancy and birth, but displaces such possibilities from her own body, envisaging the birth of nothing but misfortune:

> Some unborn sorrow ripe in fortune's womb
> Is coming towards me . . .
> (II, ii, 10–11)

Silent in her husband's presence, when left alone on Richard's departure to Ireland, the queen is released to self-expression: but her only experience is that of self-abnegation, since she is possessed by a vague melancholy which seems both a disproportionate response to her lord's absence, and an ominous foreboding of his impending tragedy. When Green brings the news of Bolingbroke's return from banishment, that phantom pregnancy is delivered of its burden of sorrow:

So, Green, thou art the midwife to my woe,
And Bolingbroke my sorrow's dismal heir.
Now hath my soul brought forth her prodigy,
And I, a gasping new-delivered mother,
Have woe to woe, sorrow to sorrow joined.
(II, ii, 62–6)

Isabella's 'inward soul' (II, ii, 11 and 28), a concept of female sub-jectivity valorized by Linda Bamber as a vessel of female otherness[2], actually contains nothing of her own: only grief for the absence or future suffering of another. To describe this experience of unfocused sorrow awaiting a cause to which it may be attached, the queen uses the imagery of pregnancy and birth. Isabella means that her prophetic sadness joins with her real sorrow to give her a double 'woe'; but also that as a 'mother' whose symbolic confinement delivers her of a tragic destiny, she also suffers twice – from the pain of childbirth, and from the pain of discovering her 'child' to be the 'prodigy' of Bolingbroke's usurpation. Isabella's language specific-ally draws attention to the way in which women in this play are condemned to suffering by the patriarchalism of the aristocratic dynasty: their only function in this masculine world is that of bear-ing sons for their powerful husbands; so that even in the success-ful achievements of their biological function, their own lives are negated. The more illustrious and legendary the lives of their husbands and sons, the more completely are they themselves eclipsed from the significant structure of the family. Isabella's lot is particularly hard, since she will not bear Richard's children (the historical Isabella was a child of ten when these events occurred): her 'dismal heir' (II, ii, 63) is the succession of Bolingbroke. Deprived by fate of what is seen as the only kind of power women can possess – the capacity to produce powerful men – Isabella's life seems un-speakably and inconsolably sad. In place of the child she will not bear, the Gardener plants in elegaic remembrance of her sorrow a 'bank of rue':

Rue even for ruth here shortly shall be seen
In the remembrance of a weeping Queen.
(III, iv, 106–7)

In the queen's last scene (v, i) where she takes leave of the deposed

king, Isabella laments Richard's fall, and in doing so she acknowledges the blossom of her own life to be 'withered':

> But soft, but see, or rather do not see,
> My fair rose wither.
>
> (v, i, 7–8)

Again, her function is literally marginal: to stand by the roadside
and observe the 'woeful pageant' of the king's disgrace. Here, however, Isabella makes her one display of strength, manifesting that
potentiality for resistance already seen in the Duchess of Gloucester:

> The lion dying thrusteth forth his paw
> And wounds the earth, if nothing else, with rage
> To be o'erpowered. And wilt thou pupil-like
> Take the correction, mildly kiss the rod . . .?
>
> (v, i, 29–32)

But again, whatever reserves of strength and defiance the woman
has, she cannot act for herself: she can only ask men to act for her.
Richard's response to this encouragement is to declare that he is,
in effect, already dead, and the queen already ('Good sometime
Queen', v, i, 37) a widow.

The only other female character in the play, the Duchess of York,
offers what is in effect a contrasting success story, precisely because
she accepts and embraces the subjected and marginal role of women.
Her significance is that she is mother to Aumerle, the close
companion and supporter of Richard who joins the Abbot of Westminster's conspiracy against the life of Henry. She is a mother, now
past the age of child-bearing; the prospect of losing her son would
rob her of her very existence, reduce her to the shadowy unreality of
the childless Isabella:

> Is not my teeming date drunk up with time:
> And wilt thou pluck my fair son from mine age?
> And rob me of a happy mother's name?
>
> (v, ii, 91–3)

In her appeal to her husband to save their son, the Duchess brings
out the contradictions of this ideology of patriarchal maternity. Her

suffering in childbirth to deliver Aumerle predisposes her to a pity
her husband cannot feel:

> Hadst thou groaned for him as I have done
> Thou wouldst be more pitiful.
> (v, ii, 103–4)

Although she does not question the patriarchal principle that a
woman's only proper profession is that of bearing sons, the Duchess
does at least suggest that feminity may have its own peculiar experiences and values, in some ways quite separate from the world of
masculine ideology. But this potential affirmation of feminity is soon
eclipsed, since in order to save Aumerle the Duchess has to plead
with men, and to argue on their terms. She tries to persuade York
that Aumerle resembles only him, not her or any of her relatives:

> He is as like thee as a man may be;
> Not like to me, nor any of my kin . . .
> (v, ii, 109–10)

To save her son the Duchess is not only prepared to humiliate
herself – 'For ever will I walk upon my knees' (v, iii, 92) – but even
to sacrifice from her boy the personal traces of her maternal inheritance: only as the exclusive property of his father will Aumerle
appear to be worth saving. Though she resists her husband, who is
determined to incriminate his son, the Duchess can do so only
by appealing to a greater, symbolic father, who represents the
paternalistic principle of divinity ('God the father') in mortal form,
the king: 'A god on earth art thou!' (v, iii, 135). The intervention of
a woman into political events seems, as far as King Henry himself is
concerned, to render the situation ridiculous: to shift the *genre* of
events from history or tragedy to farce:

> Our scene is altered from a serious thing,
> And now chang'd to 'The Beggar and the King'.
> (v, iii, 77–8)

The play's representation of its female character shows quite clearly
that in this male-dominated society women are consistently margin-
alized and subjected to a passive social role: they are the instruments

and vehicles of masculine power, possessing no effective or positive social identity of their own. This severe limitation on the active presence of women, which is so unusual in Shakespeare's plays, seems to me an aspect of the play's historical vision. This is the unenviable lot of women in a feudal, patriarchal and chivalric society: they may be romanticized as mothers or idealized as lovers, but in themselves they are nothing – they derive their significance only from their relationships with husbands, brothers, sons. It is not a representation of the natural lot of women, or a depiction of women as they existed in Shakespeare's England, where the most powerful member of society was, after all, a woman. The condition of female self-abnegation, discovered within that dramatized fifteenth-century social formation, provokes in the sixteenth-century play a consistent and comprehensive response of pity and compassion (like the Gardener's planting, in elegaic remembrance of Isabella's sorrow, of a bank of the herb rue, symbol of sadness and regret); an anachronistic solicitude which is then read back into the theatrical simulation of a fifteenth-century world. And when in II, ii Bushy attempts to comfort and console the queen's nameless grief, he unwittingly discloses the strange and insubstantial existence allowed to women by this feudal and patriarchal society. In an elaborate conceit, Bushy argues that grief and sorrow multiply themselves into numerous 'shadows', so that when observed from an angle, like perspective paintings, they appear greater than their real substance. The queen's sadness at her lord's departure is thus exaggerated into a disproportionate anxiety. But how then is the sufferer supposed to distinguish shadow from substance, reality from illusion? If Isabella looks correctly at the real conditions of her life, she will see 'naught but shadows/Of what is not' (II, ii, 23–4). Thus we see the woman's life de-realized by the very pity that is offered as her consolation.

The play reveals clearly that in this kind of patriarchal society, dominated by powerful men and their concerns, women have a purely marginal function. It cannot convincingly be argued that the play simply presents that condition as natural and unremarkable, since the women in the play are the objects of a powerful sense of pity. Of course it is easier to offer pity than to secure justice: and it could be argued that Shakespeare's own ideology is as patriarchal as John of Gaunt's, since the play cannot imagine women as anything other than the instruments of men and the bearers and protectors of male children: the saddest thing that can be said of a woman is that she has no children. Some feminist critics might argue that this kind of pity is a more dangerous enemy to the cause of female emancipation than open injustice, since, though it appears to have the interests of women at heart, it still cannot conceive of women as anything other than the passive instruments of masculine oppression or compassion.

My own conviction is that the play can be read as demonstrative of a deep-seated structural injustice in the way this society positions women. If we read the play historically, we can see that it goes further than the utterance of mere compassion for the unfulfilled lives of its female characters. It reveals quite clearly that as long as women are positioned in society in the way they are here, there can be no realization or fulfilment of female existence. Whether a woman has children or is denied them, whether her husband is successful or a failure, the woman's own life remains empty and sterile. In v, iii Bolingbroke, now Henry IV, reveals for the first time that he has a son: the young Prince Henry who will not appear in this play, but whose personal and political development will be the principal subject of the remaining plays in this historical sequence. There is nowhere in this play or any of the others any indication that Bolingbroke must have had a wife, Prince Henry a mother. He is his father's son.

Is the kind of reading I have offered here purely a strategic ideological appropriation? Does it interpret *Richard II* against the grain of the play's own ideological tendencies, using it simply as a mirror capable of reflecting back the critic's own preoccupations and concerns? In the most obvious sense, a reading undertaken from a feminist perspective cannot but be ideological, in the sense of partisan, tendentious, politically committed – otherwise the 'ism' of feminism would have no significance. But if our feminist reading takes the form not of an essentialist universalization, but of a materialist practice, then the critic's activity of reconstruction comes up against something resistant to a radical indeterminacy of the text, or the uninhibited play of textual signifiers: it confronts, in a word, the historical. In the continual dialogue between present and past that we call history, the past can only ever be alive in the present; but it is still the past that we encounter, to be known through its historical difference.

The past in question is one that we know from those modern historiographical attempts at reconstructing the social practices and institutions which inscribed within the Renaissance drama its potentialities for releasing gender-political discourse. From the historiography of Christopher Hill, Lawrence Stone and others, we derive an understanding of the period as characterized by large-scale and far-reaching changes in the institutions of marriage and the family, changes active throughout the Tudor period, and accelerated and consolidated by the rise of Puritanism and the Revolution. Christopher Hill speaks of a 'sexual revolution' which eventually replaced property marriage by 'a monogamous partnership in the affairs of the family';[3] Lawrence Stone has argued for the view that in this period an older dynastic and familial concept of marriage as a property and kinship relationship was beginning to give way to 'companionate marriage' and to the 'nuclear family'.[4]

Though few would seriously argue that the period saw widespread female emanicipation (and Stone believes that Puritan marriages actually enhanced rather than diminished patriarchal power) it is evident that there was, as Catherine Belsey puts it, 'a contest for the meaning of the family in the sixteenth and seventeenth centuries which unfixed the existing system of differences'.[5] Such 'unfixing' of traditional stereotypes and social roles is naturally of interest to feminism: Juliet Dusinberre emphasizes the Puritan revaluation of marriage – 'replacing the legal union of the arranged marriage with a union born of the spirit' as a significant factor in the development of female independence, a principal emphasis of the new conception of 'companionate marriage' being the importance of free choice for the partners, as against the old system of parental arrangement: the voluntary emotional contract of a couple becoming more important than the legal and financial contract engaged in by the parents.[6] This in turn produced a new version of patriarchy, which emphasized reciprocal obligation and mutual respect, and which had to recognize – as Charles I discovered to his cost – the possibility of a false fatherhood from which it was legitimate to withhold consent. We are familiar enough with the frequent expressions in Elizabethan culture of that orthodox vision of social hierarchy and state power, in which the subordination of subject to prince, child to parent, wife to husband and citizen to magistrate, was a fundamental principle of civic order. Yet the logical end of Puritanism was a radical questioning of state authority, which in turn created the further possibility of questioning patriarchy: in 1641 the Leveller

Mrs Chidley argued that just as a magistrate had no rights to control a man's conscience, so in turn that man had no right to control his own wife's.

We are also encouraged by New Historicism to accept that Shakespeare's plays, despite their evident complexity and apparent intellectual independence, may still be shown ultimately to speak for the dominant ideologies of state power and patriarchal authority. Criticism has become perhaps in this respect too exclusively concerned to identify the political and cultural powers Renaissance theatre can be conjectured to have spoken *for*: at the price of neglecting the fundamental truth that all art – particularly the art of the Renaisance theatre – is a dialogue between producers and audience, and that these plays spoke *to* that audience as well as *for* certain powerful vested interests in society. Thus the fundamentally anti-democratic bias characterizing the historicist criticism of the Tillyard school has by no means been expunged from newer kinds of historical criticism: we have to be very wary of the assumption that quoting the letter of state propaganda or the dominant aesthetic language is an adequate way of describing the cultural life of a people. Arguments from demography and reception theory are of course notoriously more difficult to construct than arguments from centralized authority and cultural power. The agents of patriarchal authority in church and state recorded their views on the nature of marriage and the necessary subordination of women: while most of Shakespeare's audience went to their graves in silence.

If sixteenth century patriarchy was an unstable ideological system, a site of contestation and struggle, then it was capable of producing a drama in which the historical contradictions entailed in the construction of gender could be foregrounded and interrogated. Furthermore if, as I have already argued, sixteenth century intellectuals had access to a historical consciousness, and to forms of historiographical discourse, in which the past was becoming visible as past, intelligible as difference rather than continuity, the possibility would arise of projecting the reactionary oppressiveness of Elizabethan patriarchy into a remote historical period where its routine marginalization of women could be clearly apprehended as a functioning system of injustice, a global apparatus of systematic, structural inequality. Feminist interpretation of Renaissance drama can therefore claim, as my reading of *Richard II* attempts to show, that its procedures are valid methods of finding something 'in' these texts, as well as political strategies for relocating the texts into a necessary contemporary debate. Our immediate concern should be to construct a history of feminity, as well as to accomplish a feminization of history.

Chapter Four

Past and Present:
Henry IV, Henry V

Henry IV Part One begins with the image of the crusade, a characteristic Lancastrian symbol of social unity and harmony in the pursuit of piety and violence. The king's opening speech talks of peace and war: but it is war that now constitutes the inescapable condition of existence for the state of England, and for the Lancastrian dynasty. The subsequent achievement of Henry V as king is not to bring or restore *peace*, but to succeed in externalizing conflict, exporting war, as the only practicable alternative to bitter internal conflict, civil war. In doing this, he is directly following his father's advice, given in a speech which links all four plays of the tetralogy, connecting events from the deposition of Richard II to Henry V's invasion of France:

> God knows, my son,
> By what by-paths and indirect crook'd ways
> I met this crown, and I myself well know
> How troublesome it sat upon my head.
> To thee it shall descend with better quiet,
> Better opinion, better confirmation,
> For all the soil of the achievement goes
> With me into the earth. It seem'd in me
> But as an honour snatch'd with boisterous hand,
> And I had many living to upbraid
> My gain of it by their assistances,
> Which daily grew to quarrel and to bloodshed,
> Wounding supposed peace. All these bold fears
> Thou seest with peril I have answered;
> For all my reign hath been but as a scene
> Acting that argument. And now my death
> Changes the mood, for what in me was purchas'd

Falls upon thee in a more fairer sort;
So thou the garland wear'st successively.
Yet though thou stand'st more sure than I could do,
Thou art not firm enough, since griefs are green;
And all my friends, which thou must make thy friends,
Have but their stings and teeth newly ta'en out;
By whose fell working I was first advanced,
And by whose power I well might lodge a fear
To be again displac'd; which to avoid,
I cut them off, and had a purpose now
To lead out many to the Holy Land,
Lest rest and lying still might make them look
Too near unto my state. Therefore, my Harry,
Be it thy course to busy giddy minds
With foreign quarrels, that action hence borne out
May waste the memory of former days.

                                    (*2HIV*, IV, v, 183–215)

This speech defines the true nature of Henry's 'crusade', the subject of the opening speech of *Henry IV, Part One*. All Henry's reign has been, he reflects, 'but as a scene Acting that argument' of civil war. Henry's clear-sighted political analysis acknowledges that conflict, disputed succession, friction within the realm, follow naturally and inevitably from the deposition of Richard II; natural and inevitable, in Henry's view, *not* as a consequence of any providential pattern of metaphysical consequences but as the operation of certain inevitable laws of history. Conflict cannot be prevented or cured; it can only be suppressed, or controlled by *policy* to allow time for the Lancastrian succession to take root. Henry's Christian crusade and his son's imperialist conquest of France are both described, in the same breath, as a means of externalizing conflict and channelling subversive discontent into harmless – or even socially beneficial – directions. 'Action hence borne out' – whether such action is a religious crusade or a shamelessly naked war of conquest – will serve, Henry states, to 'waste the memory of former days'; and create, out of a feudal rebellion, an apparently just and fair dynastic succession.

Henry's language demonstrates what we would call in twentieth-century terms a clear understanding of the importance of *ideology*

in ruling a state full of internal disharmony and civil conflict. This is
the essential substance of his opening speech:

> So shaken as we are, so wan with care,
> Find we a time for frighted peace to pant,
> And breathe short-winded accents of new broils
> To be commenc'd in stronds afar remote:
> No more the thirsty entrance of this soil
> Shall daub her lips with her own children's blood,
> No more shall trenching war channel her fields,
> Nor bruise her flow'rets with the armed hoofs
> Of hostile paces: those opposed eyes,
> Which, like the meteors of a troubled heaven,
> All of one nature, of one substance bred,
> Did lately meet in the intestine shock
> And furious close of civil butchery,
> Shall now, in mutual well-beseeming ranks,
> March all one way, and be no more opposed
> Against acquaintance, kindred and allies.
> The edge of war, like an ill-sheathed knife,
> No more shall cut his master.
>   (*1HIV*, I, i, 1–18)

The breathing-space Henry refers to is in fact only an opportunity to
'pant' and 'breathe short-winded accents of new broils'. *Peace* is
actually nothing more than a brief rest between wars; war is clearly,
the king's language testifies, an inescapable condition of his state.
And yet his speech is full of images of peace and unity, images which
echo directly the speech of Richard II, delivered when he banished
the quarrelling Earls, Mowbray and Bolingbroke, from his kingdom:

> For that our kingdom's earth should not be soiled
> With that dear blood which it hath fostered;
> And for our eyes do hate the dire aspect
> Of civil wounds plough'd up with neighbours swords,
> And for we think the eagle-winged pride
> Of sky-aspiring and ambitious thoughts
> With rival-hating envy, set on you
> To wake our peace, which in our country's cradle
> Draws the sweet infant breath of gentle sleep . . .
>   (*RII*, I, iii, 125–133)

Richard's speech itself was clearly, in its context, ideological – his imagery of 'earth, plough'd up . . . peace, sweet infant . . . till twice five summers have enrich'd our fields' . . . was an attempt to conceal the real state of the kingdom within a medium of courtly pastoral. In the Garden-scene of that play we are given a very different vision of pastoral which undermines Richard's language. But as Richard was attempting at that point to *banish* the quarrelling feudal lords – a much more effective attempt to export the causes of conflict than anything Henry IV can do – he could at least invoke the imagery of peace with more conviction and authority than his successor. Henry's invocation of the language and imagery of peace then is ironical in its effects: war is no longer an accidental condition of the state but its permanent condition; to stop the knife from cutting its master, it is necessary to bear it against some other victim.

Just as the invocation of peace is ironical in its effect, so too is that of the crusade:

. . . Therefore friends,
As far as to the sepulchre of Christ –
Whose soldier now, under whose blessed cross
We are impressed and engaged to fight –
Forthwith a power of English shall we levy,
Whose arms were moulded in their mother's womb
To chase these pagans in those Holy fields
Over whose acres walk'd those blessed feet
Which fourteen hundred years ago were nail'd
For our advantage on the bitter cross.
                                        (*1HIV*, i, i, 18–27)

Henry again echoes a passage from *Richard II*: this time John of Gaunt's speech in ii, i.:

This nurse, this teeming womb of royal kings,
Fear'd by their breed, and famous by their birth,
Renowned for their deeds as far from home,
For Christian service and true chivalry,
As is the sepulchre in stubborn Jewry
Of the world's ransom, blessed Mary's son.
                                        (*RII*, ii, i. 51–6)

Gaunt was there invoking the heroic past, the great days of Edward III, when a chivalric king and a loyal, Christian nobility were united into an organic society for which the appropriate image is the crusade: the *feudal* idea of a harmonious social order in which kings and barons were bound by the Christian faith and reciprocal social bonds of feudal loyalty into a united 'happy breed of men'. Gaunt's speech was itself a nostalgic, melancholy invocation of a vanished world; Henry IV's re-echoing of its pathetic historical nostalgia, appearing in the new context of the baronial struggle and its aftermath, can only appear as irony. The crusade, of course, will never take place, and at this point Henry hardly seems to regret it, entering as swiftly and eagerly as he does into measures against the real conflicts of the state, the Scottish and Welsh rebellions and the defection of the Percies. But the image of the crusade is an ideology in the full sense: it is not a mere policy which Henry uses to blind his subjects: it is for him a real form of historical consciousness, a pressingly personal and urgent conviction and desire. But the play clarifies and measures very precisely the distance between this 'ideology' and the 'real historical conditions' it seeks to resolve.

The play turns immediately from the ideological language of Henry's opening speech to a rapid summary of the real historical forces which threaten the internal stability of the state – Mortimer's failure to suppress Glendower, the rebellion of the Scots, and Henry Percy's refusal to deliver his prisoners to the king. This incident is the primary source of the action of *Henry IV Part One* just as Bolingbroke's challenge to Mowbray initiates the action of *Richard II*. Faced with the resistance of his erstwhile supporters the Percies, Henry finds himself occupying precisely the same position as Richard was when confronted with the baronial challenge for power. And the dispute over the prisoners is an incident which parallels precisely the combat in *Richard II*: it points to the same social contradictions as that combat, the contradiction between royal authority and feudal power. The feudal law of arms specified that prisoners could be kept and ransomed by the man who took them: unless they were of very high rank or of royal blood. Hence Hotspur is prepared to hand over the Earl of Fife, a prince of the blood royal. But Henry insists on taking *all* the prisoners: an assertion of royal prerogative parallel to Richard's stopping of the combat. Henry is *pushing* his barons in the same way as Richard pushed his. The barons themselves, in making an issue about the fate of Mortimer – who had been proclaimed by Richard as legitimate heir to the throne – echo Bolingbroke's making an issue of the Earl of Gloucester's death: in both cases the tension between royal and feudal power is being pushed to breaking-point. Nothing much has changed, except the personalities.

The rest of the scene makes these points explicitly. Westmoreland's account of the conflict between Douglas and Hotspur is a very genuine and accurate statement of the essentially *contradictory* nature of the experiences confronting Henry:

> For more uneven and unwelcome news
> Came from the north, and thus did it import:
> On Holy-rood day, the gallant Hotspur there,
> Young Harry Percy, and brave Archibald,
> The ever valiant and approved Scot,
> At Holmedon met, where they did spend
> A sad and bloody hour;
> As by discharge of their artillery,
> And shape of likelihood, the news was told;
> For he that brought them, in the very heat
> And pride of their contention did take horse,
> Uncertain of the issue any way.
>   (*1HIV*, I, i, 50–61)

Just as Mowbray and Bolingbroke could challenge one another *and* oppose the king, and yet remain convinced that their actions were sanctioned by chivalric values – that both were acting out of *honour*; so here the rebel (Douglas) is 'brave', 'ever valiant', and 'approved'; while Hotspur, at this point the loyal baron faithfully discharging his obligation of military service to the king, is 'gallant'. Westmoreland expresses a moral and political confusion here reminiscent of the baronial opposition in *Richard II* – e.g. IV, i. where a Parliamentary debate becomes a mere competition of chivalric challenge. The state which Henry IV is trying to rule is full of lords whose general outlook on life – the chivalric values of bravery, honour, valour, military prowess – necessitates their perpetuating a ceaseless conflict against one another and against the king. Westmoreland's statement that 'in the very heat and pride of their contention' the issue remained 'uncertain any way', seems to be a strikingly accurate description of the real contradictions of this society. The king, however, has other ideas; he listens to Westmoreland's speech, but then shows that he already *knows* the outcome of the battle of Holmedon, to illustrate which he produces Sir Walter Blunt. He imposes on Westmoreland's complex account a simplifying version, reducing uncertainty and ambiguity to the simplicity of ideology – 'smooth and welcome news'. Hotspur has won: the king praises his achievement, again in chivalric language:

> And is not this an honourable spoil?
> A gallant prize?
>
> (73–4)

Westmoreland replies in the same vein:

> A conquest for a prince to boast of.
>
> (76)

The exchange of chivalric terms seems to prompt the king to reflections on the contrast between the valiant hero of the hour, Hotspur, and his own son Harry. The contradictions within the king's viewpoint, which he is constantly seeking to suppress and conceal, emerge clearly here.

> Yea, there thou mak'st me sad, and mak'st me sin
> In envy that my lord Northumberland
> Should be the father to so blest a son;
> A son who is the theme of honour's tongue,
> Amongst a grove the very straightest plant,
> Who is sweet Fortune's minion, and her pride;
> Whilst I by looking on the praise of him
> See riot and dishonour stain the brow
> Of my young Harry . . .
> But let him from my thoughts. What think you, coz,
> Of this young Percy's pride? The prisoners
> Which he in this adventure hath surprised
> To his own use he keeps, and sends me word
> I shall have none but Mordake, Earl of Fife.
>
> (77–85; 90–4)

The king's admiration for the chivalric virtue of the young hero – the 'pride' of Fortune – co-exists incongruously with a disapproval of that same 'pride' when it challenges his own royal authority. Henry can still admire the chivalric pride of a Hotspur even when that pride causes him to 'bristle up The crest of youth' against his own dignity and power; and disapproves strongly of his own son's indulgence in 'riot and dishonour'. As the play goes on to show, the Prince is fully capable of acquiring honour and displaying valour of the chivalric kind when the need arises.

Ironically his achievement as king will still be bound very firmly within the conventions of chivalry, the essentially *feudal* ideology he inherits from his father; his attempt to reconcile the contradictions between monarchy and chivalry by reproducing, in a substantially enriched and revivified form, his father's combination of Machiavellian kingship and chivalric feeling, will result, not in the achievement of a well-ordered state, but only in a triumph on the battlefield. Meanwhile, the distance between the Earl of Hereford, the Bolingbroke who was 'the most valiant gentleman in England', and the Henry IV whom Hotspur describes as a 'vile politician', is not a mere matter of *opinion*, but a description of antithetical qualities which it is Henry V's destiny to synthesize and temporarily resolve.

That distance is also measured in the play by the apparent contrast between the king (as 'vile politician') and Hotspur (as 'the theme of honour's tongue'). Hotspur can speak in the language of a serious and convinced rebellious baron; in I, iii. his statements echo those his father Northumberland made against another king in *Richard II*:

> O pardon me, that I descend so low,
> To show the line and the predicament
> Wherein you range under this subtle King!
> Shall it for shame be spoken in these days,
> Or fill up chronicles in times to come,
> That men of your nobility and power
> Did gage them both in an unjust behalf
> (As both of you, God pardon it, have done)
> To put down Richard, that sweet lovely rose,
> And plant this thorn, this canker Bolingbroke?
> And shall it in more shame be further spoken,
> That you are fool'd, discarded, and shook off

By him for whom these shames ye underwent?
No, yet time serves wherein you may redeem
Your banished honours, and restore yourselves
Into the good thoughts of the world again . . .
(*1HIV*, I, iii. 165–80; cf. *RII*, II, i.)

But shortly after this a more characteristic kind of language emerges, which shows just how little interest Hotspur has in the political questions of baronial justice and family dignity; although, like Worcester, he can feel the injured pride of the Percies' 'house', his pride is of a more intensely *personal* kind:

Send danger from the east unto the west,
So honour cross it from the north to south,
And let them grapple . . .
By heaven, methinks it were an easy leap
To pluck bright honour from the pale-faced moon,
Or dive into the bottom of the deep,
Where fathom-line could never touch the ground,
And pluck up drowned honour by the locks,
So he that doth redeem her thence might wear
Without corrival all her dignities . . .
(*1HIV*, I, iii, 193–5; 199–205)

Percy's real motivation then is not political: the 'great exploit' of rebellion appeals to him as a knightly adventure simply *because* it contains danger, risk, the opportunity to prove his strength and valour in chivalric action. The action is self-justifying, hardly needing either cause or consequence. The practical considerations of his power-hungry relatives Northumberland and Worcester seem to fall away from Hotspur's consciousness, and the acquisition of honour becomes an object in itself: the means justify the end. The excitement and physical appetite for action Hotspur feels push his language into a vivid poetry (something he later spurns): 'To pluck bright honour from the pale-faced moon'. The honour he seeks is necessarily *personal* – he wants to wear its dignities 'without corrival'. The values of chivalry have become in Hotspur a vividly imaginative and exciting, though aggressive and self-sufficient, individualism.

The king returns to that comparison between Hal and Hotspur at a central point of the play, III, ii. Again he invokes Hotspur as his

ideal, and harshly condemns Hal's way of life. He is, the play makes
clear, mistaken in several ways, and not just about Hal. The
contradictions in his own views emerge clearly here:

> For all the world
> As thou art to this hour was Richard then
> When I from France set foot at Ravenspurgh,
> And even as I was then is Percy now . . .
> He doth fill fields with harness in the realm,
> Turns head against the lion's armed jaws,
> And being no more in debt to years than thou
> Leads ancient lords and reverend bishops on
> To bloody battles, and to bruising arms.
> What never-dying honour hath he got
> Against renowned Douglas! whose high deeds,
> Whose hot incursions and great name in arms,
> Holds from all soldiers chief majority
> And military title capital
> Through all the kingdoms that acknowledge Christ.
>   (*1HIV*, iii, ii, 93–111)

The reference back to the return of Bolingbroke from banishment
clearly reveals the incongruities of the king's position. He is praising
Percy's 'military title capital', his never-dying honour, his high
deeds, his ability to fill fields with harness; he is 'Mars in swathling
clothes', an 'infant warrior'. And yet Hotspur is prosecuting all this
activity *against the authority and sovereignty of the king*: in an act of
rebellion which the king later describes as 'pellmell havoc and confusion', the 'churlish knot of all-abhorred war', 'broached mischief to
the unborn times'. How can the king bestow praise and approval on
those very values which oppose and threaten his own power and the
stability of the state? The answer rests in his comparison of Hal to
Richard II; of Hotspur to his own younger self when he returned from
banishment to seek restitution of his expropriated inheritance. Then
he was a rebel; *he* lived by those very values of chivalry which eventually deposed the legitimate king. And now his consciousness contains those antithetical values in conflict and contradiction: he is not
sure whether he is a king, or still a knight living by the code of honour.

The conception of kingship which emerges from Henry's speeches
here is very odd when closely inspected. It mingles the metaphysical
conception of divine kingship, the haughty and exclusive pride of

the aristocrat, and a clear-sighted sense of political expediency. He
rebukes Harry for being an 'alien' to the 'courts and princes' of the
royal blood; also for being allied to his 'riotous companions'. The
king claims that as Bolingbroke he kept himself aloof from the
people, practising an aristocratic exclusiveness; and that the brightness of 'sun-like majesty' can be much more effective if rarely seen:

> Had I so lavish of my presence been,
> So common-hackneyed in the eyes of men,
> So stale and cheap to vulgar company,
> Opinion, that did help me to the crown,
> Had still kept loyal to possession,
> And left me in reputeless banishment,
> A fellow of no mark nor likelihood.
> (*1HIV*, III, ii, 39–41)

The prince has, by contrast, mingled too freely with his subjects,
and lost the quality of 'majesty' which a king needs. It is clear from
this speech that the king does not actually believe that 'majesty' is a
divinely-sanctioned property; though he refers to 'sun-like majesty',
echoing the cosmic imagery of his predecessor, he is encouraging his
son to *cultivate* it, as he did. Once again he connects his son with
Richard II:

> The skipping King, he ambled up and down,
> With shallow jesters, and rash bavin wits,
> Soon kindled and soon burnt, carded his state,
> Mingled his royalty with cap'ring fools . . .
> Grew a companion to the common streets,
> Enfeoff'd himself to popularity,
> That, being daily swallowed by men's eyes,
> They surfeited with honey . . .
> . . . seen, but with such eyes
> As, sick and blunted with community,
> Afford no extraordinary gaze,
> Such as is bent on sun-like majesty
> When it shines seldom in admiring eyes . . .
> . . . And in that very line, Harry, standest thou,
> For thou hast lost thy princely privilege
> With vile participation.
> (*1HIV*, III, ii, 60–87, passim)

The king is supremely contemptuous of people, things and values
which inevitably constitute an element of his state: he expresses
an aristocratic scorn for 'vulgar company', 'the common streets',
'popularity', 'community', 'participation'. It is ironical to reflect how
these very words have become the common currency of political
language in democratic societies. Conventional accounts of the
plays assume that the prince is developing a more subtle conception
of 'kingship', studying popular life with a view to incorporating it
into the 'majesty' of the realm, uniting the 'common streets' with
the 'courts and princes' of the royal blood. In fact the prince replies
to his father's rebukes by promising only to be 'hereafter more
myself', without specifying what that self actually is. Is it a self with
a more complex grasp of political realities, determined to enrich
and strengthen royal power by seeking a relationship with the common people? Or a self committed to the values of chivalry, like his
father's younger self or Hotspur, who will seek to vanquish chivalry
by military action calculated to perpetuate it? Exclusive and exploitative contempt for the people is a value shared by absolutist
monarch and by feudal rebel. He agrees here that he will be prepared to adopt, or affect, the values of chivalry, in order to destroy
Percy and recover some of his lost dignity:

> I will redeem all this on Percy's head,
> And in the closing of some glorious day
> Be bold to tell you that I am your son . . .
> . . . For the time will come
> That I shall make this northern youth exchange
> His glorious deeds for my indignities.
> (1HIV, iii, ii, 132–46)

And of course he achieves this, becoming a model of chivalry to
outshine Hotspur. Vernon describes the Prince's martial manner in
a poetic language of exceptional brilliance and vividness (iv, i, 98–
110); Hal issues a challenge to Hotspur which is taken by Vernon as
a model of chivalric manners; and he kills Percy, who yields to him
all his 'proud titles', the loss of which he regrets more than the loss
of life. The Prince demonstrates that he *can* achieve success in this
sphere of activity, he *can* become the honourable chivalric hero: but
does he ever escape that ideology to become a new kind of national
sovereign? The link between the Prince and Hotspur is not simply

one of opposition for in a deeper sense they are counterparts: the only triumph of Henry's kingship is that victory on the field of Agincourt which brings him, in action and in language, strangely and ironically close to his old rival.

Insofar as *Henry IV* is a chronicle-history play, it extends the historical vision of *Richard II* into a new regime. Henry IV has inherited a society full of contradictions, which the available ideologies seem to be capable only of concealing or suppressing, not of reconciling. These contradictions *appear* to arise from the broken dynastic succession: in fact they pre-date that event, since they centre on the fundamental contradiction between monarchical and aristocratic power which Shakespeare saw as the characteristic structure of this epoch. The *Henry IV* plays show a *continuation* of that struggle, complicated but certainly not resolved by the change of dynasty, rather than a providential pattern of divine retribution for Henry's crime against nature. The feudal victory of Bolingbroke centralizes and deepens the unstable and contradictory forces of the society he hopes to rule.

The king himself is unable to resolve these problems, since his consciousness is itself divided and contradictory, split between monarchical and feudal ideologies. He comes to see history as an alien process of 'necessity' which human beings can contemplate but not control:

> O God, that one might read the book of fate,
> And see the revolution of the times
> Make mountains level, and the continent,
> Weary of solid firmness, melt itself
> Into the sea, and other times to see
> The beachy girdle of the ocean
> Too wide for Neptune's hips; how chance's mocks
> And changes fill the cup of alteration
> With divers liquors! O, if this were seen,
> The happiest youth, viewing his progress through,
> What perils past, what crosses to ensue,
> Would shut the book and sit him down to die.
> (*2HIV*, III, i, 45–56)

Henry defines history as 'necessity': the only way the process can be negotiated is by meeting it on its own terms – 'Are these things then necessities? Then let us meet them like necessities!' Though the king himself articulates the emotions of failure, he has genuine hopes that his son may be capable (subject to a reformation of character) of resolving the contradictions of the kingdom by political strategy. To control such a society the monarch must perforce accept the contradictory character required by history: he must display the resolute authority of a strong monarch, the conciliatory diplomacy of a feudal king, the Machiavellian subtlety of a successful prince, and the martial heroism of a noble warrior. The product of this unlikely recipe, and the consummation of rigid historical determinism, is Henry V.

A critical and historical analysis of *Richard II* and *Henry IV Part One* reveals them to be conscious acts of historiography: reconstructions of a feudal society analyzed in the process of dissolution, where its characteristic contradictions are most clearly visible. The plays are not thinly disguised studies of Tudor England in the 1590s; their historical quality was not introduced merely to hoodwink the censor. Nor do they obediently mime the official ideology of the state, reshaping the past into Tudor apology. They do not resurrect the medieval world as a lost golden age of organic social harmony; nor do they reduce Renaissance politics to a futile game symptomatic of a hopelessly tragic human condition. They revive the past as vanished, replayable fact, presented to a world in which the pastness of the past is clearly visible; they affirm the reality of historical transformation, and imagine the infinite possibilities of change.

The plays do not speak *directly* of the late sixteenth century though indirectly and implicitly they reflect certain constitutive characteristics of Elizabethan culture and society. Discussion of that reflective function belongs to a later stage of the argument. Meanwhile one serious potential objection remains to be dealt with: the existence of a body of concrete evidence from Shakespeare's own time, suggesting that these plays and other historical works were customarily understood as contemporary political statements disguised in the relative safety of past historical events. Such evidence has been held to suggest a widespread acceptance of the humanist identification of past and present, and to confirm the emphasis of the Tillyard school (initiated particularly by Lily B. Campbell) that the plays should be understood exclusively in the political context of the late sixteenth century. *Richard II*, for example, was censored in print by the excision of the deposition (lines 154–318 were omitted from IV, i in the Quarto editions of 1597 and 1598); apparently the act of showing or publishing the dethroning of a fourteenth-century monarch was considered of contemporary relevance by the censors. The play was used (almost certainly) as the opening volley in a rebellion of the nobility against Elizabeth's power in 1601: there is sufficient evidence to confirm the view that it was Shakespeare's *Richard II* which the Lord Chamberlain's Men staged at the Globe on 7 February 1601, at the request of the Earl of Essex's supporters. The play (or some other version of Richard's deposition) was apparently seen by Elizabeth herself as seditious: several months after the 1601 rising, Elizabeth passed some bitter remarks on Essex to the antiquary William Lambarde, including the apparently decisive self-identification, 'I am Richard II. Know ye not that?' and the angry, 'He that will forget God, will forget his benefactor: this tragedie was played forty times in open streets and houses'. When Sir John Hayward published in 1599 a book dealing with the last years of Richard II's reign (*The First Part of the Life and Reigne of King Henrie IIII*), dedicating it to the Earl of Essex, the Privy Council had no doubt as to the relevance of history to the present: Hayward was imprisoned and remained there apparently until after Elizabeth's death.[1]

In my view the significance of this evidence has been exaggerated. Without in any way wishing to underestimate the cautious and vigilant watchfulness of the Tudor state's security organs, I would want to emphasize that the evidence cited dates from a period of political instability culminating in a rebellion against the crown, and centres on the protagonist of that rebellion (in fact some of the information has been preserved only because Essex was tried for treason). The practice of identifying past and present was naturally intensified in a period of political tension, when the security services were particularly sensitive and the monarch herself particularly paranoid, both anxious to pursue and suppress subversive and incendiary ideas and personalities. If a similarly hypersensitive defensiveness about internal security had pertained throughout the 1590s, and if written versions of the past had automatically been judged as indirect contemporary comment, it is doubtful that the *genre* of the historical play would ever have emerged. Earlier plays like *Edward II* and *Henry VI* showed the deposition and murder of kings – one a Tudor ancestor – without, apparently, attracting censorship or legal interference. *Richard II* may well have been performed complete with deposition, licensed by the Revels Office as entirely innocent before the Essex faction began to point up the historical analogy. Sir John Hayward, under interrogation by Sir Edward Coke, defended himself by claiming the privilege of objective historiography; he 'wrote a history of 300 years past', which had no intended relevance to the time of writing.[2]

This problem can be conveniently confronted, paradoxically, by discussion of the play *Henry V* which is held by almost universal agreement to be a work of contemporary rather than historiographical relevance, and which actually contains a reference to the Earl of Essex – the only direct reference to a contemporary event in the whole of Shakespeare's work.

> [Henry V] . . . is the new national king, the herald of the Tudor monarchy, which is no longer a monarchy of the old type but different and necessary.[3]

On this issue Zdenek Stribrny's marxist analysis meets with complete agreement from J. H. Walter, a Tillyardian traditionalist, who sees Henry as a model king in terms of the humanistic political and moral thought of the Renaissance.[4] In fact the very opposite is the truth: Henry V is portrayed not as a Renaissance king, sovereign of a new nation-state, but as a feudal overlord; the play's historical vision of the kingdom he rules is an image of the declining feudal society of the fifteenth century, riven by the centrifugal appetites and energies of the landholding military caste. This society is forged by the king into a kind of unity impossible to identify with the unity of the sixteenth-century nation-state, since it is constituted only by the activity of war. 'England' in *Henry V* is not a united kingdom, only a victorious army; the king's achievement is not a peaceful and harmonious commonwealth, but a barren military triumph which conquers a land soon to be liberated from English rule, and exacerbates rather than arrests the inherent tendencies of feudal society towards dissolution.

The patriotic myth of Henry V as the ideal king, perfect leader and saviour of the nation was strong in Shakespeare's time, and has been revived by reconstitution of the play in certain critical moments of the nation's history: some of the consequences are examined in Chapter Seven. There is also an extensive history of negative or ironical criticism: but to its demystifying influence should be added the emphasis that Renaissance historiography was sufficiently varied and complex to entertain considerable flexibility and diversity of historical judgment. In Holinshed, for example, the justice of Henry's claim to the French crown is not exactly questioned, but it is certainly *doubted*; and against his context of a dubious ambition, the realities of fifteenth-century warfare are harshly sketched.[5] There is little in Holinshed's account of any providential theory of history, in which Henry's reign is blessed with a gracious respite from the action of divine vengeance; there is much more awareness of the real history of this late-feudal society. There is a full, complex account of a historical situation possible only in this late-feudal Europe, and relatively unthinkable in the sixteenth century. Henry VIII and Elizabeth were no warrior kings; they could hardly (at least after Henry VIII's youthful adventures in France) have undertaken the kind of knight-errantry which Henry V accomplished, leaving their country to look after itself while the monarch directed military campaigns in Europe. Henry V's style of kingship is more like that of Richard I than that of any Tudor monarch: it is still characterized by the crusading campaigns and military conquests which were the natural activities of the feudal nobility and their warrior kings, from William the Conquerer to Edward III. This is not of course to deny the very real political opportunities created by war, which are in evidence throughout history, from Elizabeth I's wars with Spain to Margaret Thatcher's war with Argentina: but rather to emphasize a historical distance which provided Shakespeare with the space necessary for interrogating the ideology of national unity achievable through foreign conquest.

   Henry V has certainly developed the notion of kingship from that held by his father in significant ways, but it remains bound within the essentially *feudal* ideology of the Lancastrian dynasty. Henry IV had dreamed of a crusade, a Christian military adventure, to unify his fractured kingdom: his son achieves exactly that, in the attenuated form of the conquest of France. In order to establish and secure the Lancastrian succession, Henry V will have to unite his kingdom; but in such a way that attention will be surely deflected from the internal causes of civil discontent and conflict. The enterprise is insolubly contradictory: to achieve internal unity by external force, 'action hence born out'; to establish a firm-rooted successive dynasty by obliterating the past; to foster the arts of peace by cultivating the arts of war. The play explores these paradoxes, showing how Henry's achievement is always framed, shadowed and ultimately destroyed by these same tense historical contradictions.

On the field of Agincourt, Henry expresses in famous lines a social idea which appears to be a kind of democratic nationalism:

> We few, we happy few, we band of brothers;
> For he today that sheds his blood with me
> Shall be my brother; be he ne'er so vile
> This day shall gentle his condition; . . .
>
> (IV, iii, 60–4)

But we should not confuse this subtle reconstruction of feudal ideology with a genuine nationalism. The only ground for this unity of the different social classes is the battle ground: and Henry's vision of a united nation is still firmly tied to the language of his ancestors. His egalitarianism co-exists in this very speech with a chivalric language evidently borrowed from his old rival Hotspur:

> But if it be a sin to covet honour,
> I am the most offending soul alive.
> . . . I would not lose so great an honour
> As one man more, methinks, would share me from,
> For the best hope I have.
>
> (IV, iii, 28–9; 31–3)

We cannot avoid recalling Hotspur:

> By heaven, methinks it were an easy leap
> To pluck bright honour from the pale-faced moon,
> . . . so he that doth redeem her thence might wear
> Without corrival all her dignities . . .
>
> (*1HIV*, I, iii, 199–205)

'I know not why' wrote Samuel Johnson, 'Shakespeare now gives the king nearly such a character as he formerly ridiculed in *Percy*'. The answer of course, is that the character of Henry, in its adherence to feudal ideology, remains very close to that of Percy. Certainly the differences are large and radical: for Henry, honour is not an individual property to be won by personal self-aggrandizement: it is a property to be won and possessed by the *nation* (England); and when it has been won, it is to be worn with modesty and humility: Henry expressly forbids 'boasting' after Agincourt; insists that the victory is God's victory; and refuses a Caesarian triumphal return to England, clearly conscious of how violent and divisive such progresses could be. But these shifts of emphasis cannot alter the fact that Henry sees social unity and national achievement entirely in terms of military honour: a nationalized feudal ideology.

The device of the Chorus is important in ensuring that the specific kind of interest and excitement generated by a play like *Henry V* cannot be identified with contemporary social situations or values in the way most critics assume. As Hazlitt argued, the kinds of heroism, kingship and conquest displayed in this play can be enjoyed collectively by a modern audience only when they are to some extent dissociated from their actual historical context.[6] The relationship between the 'heroic' and 'ironical' dimensions of the play is not in any balance or synthesis of incongruous truths; but in the play's definition of the heroic dimension as a purely *theatrical* reality, an ideology which can be impressive and exciting only in the theatre; and which can be (as it is by Henry) pulled off in the course of actual history, transferred to the realm of practice, only by uniting these values with their necessary corollaries – heroism linked to the waste and futility of war; kingship to Machiavellian adventurism; heroic conquest to the ruthless subjugation of an innocent people.[7] The play accomplishes the difficult feat of 'placing' both the heroic and the ironical theories of history: that is the nature (and the limit) of its contradictory 'unity'.

The most influential view of the Chorus in *Henry V* is that it is there to give the drama an *epic* character: to enlarge and elevate dramatic spectacle from the conflicts of person to the conflict of nations, from the limited space of the stage to the territory of international war. The Chorus urges the audience to supply, by a sustained imaginative participation, the kind of scale and realistic narrative detail possible in epic poem and novel, but not in drama. Cued by the Chorus's poetry, the audience can fill in the sense of space and of enormous, farspread human activity (particularly of a military kind) proper to the epic; and thereby provide the necessary context of great achievement, heroic struggle, enormous human effort and significant space, in which the epic hero's destiny can be unfolded and admired. In addition the Choruses provide the play with a neo-classical unity of action:

and the didactic purpose of holding up heroic action for admiration and imitation.[8]

But the Choruses have a double function. They *are* there to create an epic space for the drama in the imagination of the audience. But they are there also to draw attention to the *theatrical* nature of this event; a performance, in which history is reshaped and transformed by actors, before an audience, on a stage. The Choruses are there to foreground the *artificiality* of the dramatic event, placing a barrier between action and audience. The audience's imaginations are invited inside that barrier to enjoy direct participation in the drama; at the same time, the play is limiting the freedom of reference from the events on the stage back to ordinary everyday reality.

> A kingdom for a stage, princes to act
> And monarchs to behold the swelling scene.
>   (*HV*, Prologue, 3–4)

This does not simply demand an acceptance of certain dramatic conventions, so that kingdoms and princes can easily be substituted in the minds of the audience for the stage and actors. It also declares the artificiality of the dramatic medium, by calling attention to the stage, to the actors, and to an audience which knows full well that it is *not* composed entirely of 'monarchs'. The following lines create a vivid imaginative sense (typical of the play's imagery) of a terrifying, barely-suppressed brutality; the violence controlled by the militaristic, warlord-king:

> Then should the warlike Harry, like himself,
> Assume the port of Mars; and at his heels,
> Leash'd in like hounds, should famine, sword and fire
> Crouch for employment.
>   (Prologue, 5–8)

But the roused fear (drawing in the image of fire, famine and slaughter on one of the most brutal passages of Holinshed)[9] is immediately drained off, as the Chorus points to the innocuous mundanity of the stage itself – 'this unworthy scaffold', and of the theatre – 'this wooden O', this 'cockpit'. The phrases contain the violence of the action, and inscribe an imaginary barrier between theatrical and historical reality. The Chorus to act IV uses this technique to deflect the violence of Agincourt:

And so our scene must to the battle fly;
Where, O for pity! we shall much disgrace
With four or five most vile and ragged foils,
Right ill-disposed in brawl ridiculous
The name of Agincourt. Yet sit and see;
Minding true things by what their mock'ries be.
                                        (IV, Chorus, 48–53)

The way to convince an audience of the truth of dramatic illusion is not, clearly, to continually insist on the illusory nature of the representation. By defining the nature of this dramatic 'mock'ry', the play diminishes rather than enlarges the audience's readiness to receive it as 'true'.

The Choruses are concerned, then, not so much with bestowing epic qualities on the dramatic event, as with exposing the nature of theatrical illusion. The Chorus has its own kind of heroic language, but it is up to the audience to create an epic experience:

For 'tis your thoughts that now must deck our kings . . .
                                        (Prologue, 28)

In a play, history is created by a peculiar conjuncture of the dramatist's words, the actor's speech and gesture, and the audience's response. If epic is produced, it is produced only in and by these specific theatrical conditions. There is no heroic view of life to be carried away from the theatre – one that would be confirmed and reflected back by the public morality of society, as for the audience of Homer or of the *Beowulf*-poet. *Henry V* insists too strongly, through its Choruses, on the divergence between theatre and real events for any such simple relationship to hold.

Given these factors, it is no surprise to find that in *Henry V* epic qualities and heroic language are bestowed on unpromising material – on events and characters which cannot, in themselves, evoke anything like a wholehearted epic admiration. Patriotism, heroism, chivalry, the romance of war, can induce admiration and delight only when detached from their actual historical context and safely recreated in the security of the theatre purely as ideological entities. Once the real historical foundations of these ideologies are recognized, they lose their power to charm the imagination. The play is concerned both to isolate these ideologies and to extract from them

the maximum aesthetic and theatrical effect; while at the same
time demonstrating the historical actualities from which they are in
practice (though not in the theatre) inseparable.

The Chorus's final epilogue both claims and denies the reality,
the validity of Henry's achievement; once again foregrounding the
theatrical situation, it lavishes praise on Henry in conventional
terms:

> Thus far, with rough and all unable pen,
> Our bending author hath pursu'd the story;
> In little room confining mighty men,
> Mangling by starts the full course of their glory.
> Small time, but in that small most greatly liv'd
> This star of England: Fortune made his sword,
> By which the world's best garden he achieved,
> And of it left his son imperial lord.
> Harry the Sixth, in infant bands crown'd King
> Of France and England, did this king succeed;
> Whose state so many had the managing,
> That they lost France and made his England bleed:
> Which oft our stage hath shown; and, for their sake,
> In your fair minds let this acceptance take.
>
> (v, Chorus, 1–14)

Ironically, Shakespeare had written of the events succeeding Henry's
reign earlier, in *Henry VI*, 'which oft our stage hath shown': a comparison which neatly distances drama from history. The temporal
sequence of events is reversed, and the achievements of *Henry V*
viewed in the light of the disasters of his son's reign. Henry VI spoke
harshly indeed about his father's famous victories:

> But Clifford, tell me, didst thou never hear
> That things ill got had ever bad success?
> And happy always was it for that son
> Whose father for his hoarding went to hell?
> I'll leave my son my virtuous deeds behind;
> And would my father had left me no more!
>
> (*3HVI*, ii, ii, 45–50)

The stage can show Henry's brief triumph as convincingly as it can show his son's tragedy. But while the ironical and pessimistic perspective on history offered by the latter would be confirmed by everyday experience – even the everyday experience of play-going – the heroic achievement can be created only in the theatre, only by the 'fair minds' of the audience. What has been created here is the reverse of epic, where the epic hero enacts, for the admiration of the audience, some real problem of public morality; what has been created in this play is a self-mocking dramatic illusion, which inscribes a clear boundary between public morality and the ideological nature of its own 'celebration'.

Shakespeare's dramaturgy in *Henry V* is like that of Brecht: it promotes admiration, yet places obstacles in the path of spontaneous identification; it induces empathy *and* objectivity, but not in a mutually cancelling relationship, since the objectivity is a way of self-consciously perceiving the empathy. The spectator thinks feelingly, and feels with thought. Walter Benjamin's account of the effects of Brechtian theatre applies equally well to Shakespeare's achievement in *Henry V*:

> The naturalistic stage is in no sense a public platform; it is entirely illusionistic. Its own awareness that it is theatre cannot fertilize it; like every theatre of unfolding action, it must repress this awareness so as to pursue undistracted its aim of portraying the real. Epic theatre, by contrast, incessantly derives a lively and productive consciousness from the fact that it is theatre. This consciousness enables it to treat elements of reality as though it were setting up an experiment, with the 'conditions' at the end of the experiment, not at the beginning. Thus they are not brought closer to the spectator but distanced from him. When he recognizes them as real conditions it is not, as in naturalistic theatre, with complacency, but with astonishment. This astonishment is the means whereby epic theatre, in a hard, pure way, perceives a Socratic praxis.[10]

It is in the light of this reading of *Henry V* as demystifying historiography and as drama of alienation that we should approach the crucial reference to Essex in the opening Chorus to act v. This seems to be the most striking confirmation of the orthodox view that Henry is a type of prototype of the Tudor monarch, and the play's historical focus Shakespeare's contemporary England. In drawing an analogy with Essex's ill-starred Irish campaign of 1599, the Chorus makes 'the only *direct* allusion to contemporary events in Shakespeare's plays', an allusion therefore regarded as 'uniquely significant':[11]

> But now behold,
> In the quick forge and working-house of thought,
> How London doth pour out her citizens.
> The mayor and all his brethren in best sort,
> Like to the senators of antique Rome,
> With the plebians swarming at their heels,
> Go forth and fetch their conquering Caesar in:
> As, by a lower but by loving likelihood,
> Were now the general of our gracious empress,
> As in good time he may, from Ireland coming,
> Bringing rebellion broached on his sword,
> How many would the peaceful city quit
> To welcome him!
>
> (v, Chorus, 22–34)

The unique contemporary allusion appears to effect a direct articulation of the epic heroism of the past with the potentiality for such action in the present: in much the same way as the reconstruction of *Henry V* in the Second World War period attempted to reconstitute the old heroic emotions in a contemporary crisis. Essex's Irish expedition, undertaken to quell the nationalist rebellion and destroy its leader the Earl of Tyrone, began in triumph in March 1599, with the government and Queen expecting total victory over the rebel forces; and ended in (what Elizabeth and her council decided was) ignominious defeat in September of the same year, when Essex returned alone, his forces depleted by sustained guerilla attrition, with a list of defeats and a humiliating truce. The play is usually dated from this reference, with presuppositions about its epic and heroic mode permitted to determine the dating: according to the Arden edition, this self-evidently heroic play must have been written and performed closer to March than September 1599, since Essex's fortunes declined rapidly after the capture of Cahir Castle in May – Essex's only significant military achievement of the expedition, described by the implacable Elizabeth as taking 'an Irish hold from a rabble of rogues'. Both the ambivalence of the play, the ambiguity of the Chorus's speech, and the complexity of that historical moment, should make us sceptical about such a procedure. It is possible that the play testifies to a brief but significant moment of unity shortly after Essex's departure, with the empress and her general reconciled in expectation of victory: but to see the play as reflecting or supporting that moment would require far greater confidence in the play as traditional epic than can be derived from the text. The comparison of Essex to 'conquering Caesar' cannot possibly be taken at face value, since we know (with unusual certainty) that Shakespeare's dramatic treatment of Julius Caesar himself was written, at the very most, a matter of a few months after *Henry V*, and was being performed in the autumn of 1599 at the newly constructed Globe playhouse. That play begins with a military triumph designed to vindicate Caesar's victory over Pompey and his rule over Rome: from the very beginning of the drama we witness the violent and divisive effects of such a display of martial authority in a context of civil conflict, from the refractory tribunes to the divided conscience of Brutus, from the defaced images of the emperor to the 'bleeding piece of earth' left by assassins at the base of Caesar's monument. The arts of war are inimical to the arts of peace, in ancient Rome, Plantagenet England or Elizabethan London: in the Chorus's speech the people would have to 'quit' the peaceful city in order to experience the vicarious violence of a military triumph. There was more than one view of Essex and his Irish campaign: a different interpretation of the reference might point to a different date. It is possible that the Chorus wcomplimenting either Essex or Elizabeth, but unlikely that it could be both. Essex went to Ireland under the cloud of Elizabeth's displeasure: she was extremely sceptical about his chances of success, and made no secret of the fact; she was opposed to Essex's strategy, her dispatches insisting with growing hysteria that he should march north into Ulster to engage with Tyrone, which Essex persistently refused to do. After making his peace with the Irish leader, Essex returned (breaking the Queen's specific injunction) to endure interrogation by the Privy Council and house arrest lasting for a year. Within six months of his release his head was on the block. If the play was acted at Court, and the compliment intended towards Elizabeth, it was probably ironical, with the emphasis on Essex's ambitions and on the sarcastic implications of the phrase 'in good

time'. It is equally possible that the play was aimed at a more popular audience more prepared to regard Essex as a potential hero; an
audience containing also perhaps some of the nobles who later
commissioned a performance of *Richard II* to inaugurate the Essex
rebellion. Who could lay a better claim to those heroic ancestors,
the tetchy old woman on the throne or the popular young hero of
the hour?[12]

Without a definite date it is impossible to argue conclusively
for any of those possibilities: and to argue backwards towards a
date from presuppositions about the text is simply to confirm preconceived opinions. All that can be done is to infer from the
text and from its contingent history the most probable meaning
attributable to the allusion: and I will argue from the play's confrontation of heroic and anti-heroic modes, its structured ambivalence, that Essex's version of heroism is demystified and interrogated as thoroughly as Henry's. The allusion does not bring the
spirit of Agincourt up to date, but rather diagnoses Essex as a
curious throwback to the imagined historical world of the play: a
noble who became a warrior not from any personal aptitude or
military talent, but because of his birth; a man who could live in
the accepted noble style only by dependence on court favour, and
could neither abandon that life nor sustain a reciprocal relationship
with the court; a soldier who confused military responsibility with
political power, and turned his sword from the external enemy
towards his sovereign.

There is no simple, positive identification of the heroism of the
past with the heroism of the present. Shakespeare seized on a
particularly contradictory character in a particularly complex historical situation, and found there the appropriate analogy for the
contradictory revelations of his historiography.

Chapter Five

Drama and the Nation

WELL before the inauguration of the Tillyard School, the figure of 'Shakespeare', the Renaissance drama in general, the whole structure of Elizabethan society, had all been brought to represent the cultural expression of a peculiarly unified period of British national history. Half a century before the great historical break of the Civil War which, according to influential theoreticians like T. S. Eliot and F. R. Leavis, established decisive realignments in British society which would prevent the re-establishing of the old medieval harmony, English culture produced an art-form which was essentially a *common* property; supported and shared by all classes of society, from commissioned court performances and exclusive private playhouses to the big public theatres patronized by everybody from apprentice to earl. The Elizabethan drama represents, according to this theory, a unique commingling of the popular and the sophisticated, drawing on the vigorous popular traditions of folk-drama and religious ritual to produce a highly developed form of theatre palatable to labourers, artisans, merchants, gentry, aristocracy; the people in their inn-yards, the nobility in their great houses, the creamed-off social elite of the Court. Despite the differentiation of social classes in these separate cultural spaces, and even within the public theatre itself, the same repertory was common to all members of society. This 'common culture' has been widely regarded as evidence of an extraordinary degree of cohesion and unanimity in Elizabethan society: the evident diversity and contradictory coherence of the cultural achievement is read back into the society to discover a lost golden age of peace, prosperity and social harmony:

> What makes the age outstanding in literary history, however, is
> its range of interests and vitality of language; and here other

factors contributed besides the humanism of the Universities and
the Court. One of these was the persistence of popular customs
of speech and thought and entertainment rooted in the communal life of medieval towns and villages. To some extent the old
traditions obstructed the new. But they also combined, inasmuch
as the Tudors established a firm and broadly based national
community; and by combining they invigorated the whole idiom
of literature. The Elizabethan literary language, especially that
of professional writers like Shakespeare, is addressed to a mixed
public, more trained in listening than in reading, and more
accustomed to group life than to privacy. . . . These factors
together largely explain why the drama was the chief form of
Elizabethan art . . . drama was a communal art.[1]

Contemplating this lost paradise of pre-lapsarian historical innocence ended by the Civil War appears to be a mere exercise in
historical nostalgia: a cultural atavism, reactionary in sentiment,
impotent to negotiate the complexities of the present. Such a formulation is however far from the truth: the following pages will reveal
some of the extraordinary energy and resourcefulness applied to
reconstructing and making relevant that ahistorical Elizabethan
community. The lost social harmony of Tudor England, though
impossible of restoration, is nevertheless produced in all these
interventions as accessible to modern thought and feeling by the
various activities of reading, criticism and theatrical performance.
This version of 'Shakespeare' is not mournfully regretted but vig-
orously activated within the apparatus of culture and education
to provide the ground for a common, shared social discourse,
a mechanism of ideological reconciliation. The image of a unified
Tudor culture, accessible in the plays of Shakespeare, is thus
effectively inserted into and naturalized within contemporary culture, thereby assuming a definite material function in modern
society.

What is the historical basis of this modern 'Shakespeare' myth, of
this cultural unanimity supposed to have produced in its drama, and
pre-eminently in Shakespeare, such a potent aesthetic force for
national unification and social harmony? It should be possible, by
venturing some generalizations about the growth of the drama in
Shakespeare's time, to show that these plays do not express a pre-
existent national unity, and are not therefore as readily available for

conservative or reactionary reproduction as critics of all political persuasions have frequently assumed.

The drama of Shakespeare's theatre was metropolitan, and the historical conditions determining that cultural location were of very recent origin. A metropolis is not a nation, nor can a capital city properly be held to represent a nation; the identification being especially inappropriate when considering a society like Tudor England, recently but sharply differentiated from a dissolving post-feudal society by its New Monarchy, reformed Church, state bureaucracy and emergent capitalist economy. A 'nation', after all, is not a fixed community but a relative and historically specific social formation.

Before the period of Shakespeare's theatre the drama was 'national' in a much more universal sense. The various pre-Reformation dramatic traditions, cultural expressions of medieval society, were all more thoroughly incorporated into the universal social life of the nation: the nation defined not as the Court or the capital but as the complex structural totality of social life in town and country, village and hall, metropolis and province. The oldest tradition was the popular folk-drama, about which very little is known even from its surviving remnants: conjecturally it can be supposed a universal because popular form of dramatic activity, possibly linked with magic, ritual and the superstitions of primitive religion; it was rooted in the material conditions and everyday experience of rural life in small village communities or agricultural small towns.[2] Feudal drama and entertainment were based on the demesne or estate, and related back to traditions of private entertainment in which resident performers or travelling entertainers would play to a nobleman's or gentleman's household. The morality plays of the early Tudor period exemplify this type of drama, which was evidently performed in the hall, a centre of social life in a feudal community and a meeting-place of all social classes. In this common dining-room, which was also the focus of social and administrative life on the estate, entertainment took place in the midst of ordinary social activity; communal entertainment, commissioned by the lord, in which an undifferentiated community participated without any commercial transaction, save the exercise of the lord's bounty.[3] Finally there was the religious drama, as universal as the Church: controlled by the ecclesiastical power, taking place within the Church itself as dramatized ritual, or sustained by local craft guilds as the street-theatre of the mystery play cycles.

The Tudor period marks the end of this truly *national* drama and the establishment of a specialized metropolitan drama playing to a much smaller constituency. This was Shakespeare's theatre, which bore a relation to the totality of national life similar to that of our so-called Royal 'National' Theatre today. The conditions for the establishment of that theatre were systematically created by various legislative actions of the Tudor state, combining with certain economic developments equally inseparable from the history of that state:

> The movement of England during the sixteenth century from participation as a segment of Catholic Europe to religious and political independence in a continent of critically balanced antagonisms was parralleled by a change in the nation's dramatic life from a vital, largely amateur activity which threaded every level of society to a mainly metropolitan professional business, favoured by the court, patronised by the nobility, and arousing anger and disapproval in a powerful segment of the middle class.[4]

When Henry VIII substituted his authority for that of the Pope as Head of the Church, the king automatically assumed complete control of the drama: and the history of drama under the Tudor state is partly a history of increasing state interference and tightening bureaucratic control, centralizing the cultural power of the state enormously. The state had to extirpate the religious drama altogether, since it was the seasonal ritual drama of the Roman Church,[5] in the process cultural power was stripped not only from the church but from those municipal authorities and amateur local interests responsible for supporting the religious drama. A religious dramatic event became a potentially seditious public assembly overnight: and the Crown exercised control over such activities through local ecclesiastical and secular authorities. An Ecclesiastical Commission appointed by the Crown had censored and suppressed the provincial mystery cycles out of existence by 1569. Tudor attempts to construct a Protestant drama were narrowly academic, divorced from popular culture, and short-lived: so in practice the Reformation produced the conditions for a secular drama, licensed, regulated and controlled by the state authorities.[6]

How did this transition from a universal national drama to a drama based on the Tudor state's own conception of the 'nation' happen, and happen so rapidly? The 1572 'Act for the Punishment of Vagabonds', though in another sense belonging to a long history of the state's attempt to regulate the activities of marginal social groups like the unemployed, beggars, itinerant traders and travelling entertainers, has rightly been recognized as a legalistic prelude to the establishing of the new Tudor 'national' theatre.[7] The Act appears at first glance to be a confirmation of surviving feudal relationships, since it required that an acting company must have the protection or patronage of a great noble in order to freely exercise its craft.

> All and every person and persons being whole and mighty in Body and able to labour, having not Land or Master, nor using any lawful Merchandise, Craft or Mystery whereby he or she might get his or her living, and can give no reckoning how he or she doth lawfully get his or her living; and all Fencers, Bear-Wards, Common Players in Interludes and Minstrels, not belonging to any Baron of this Realm or towards any other honourable Personage of greater Degree; all Jugglers, Pedlars, Tinkers and Petty Chapmen; which said Fencers, Bear-Wards, Common Players in Interludes, Minstrels, Jugglers, Pedlars, Tinkers and Petty Chapmen, shall wander abroad and have not Licence of two Justices of the Peace at the least . . . shall be taken adjudged and deemed Rogues, Vagabonds and Sturdy Beggars.[8]

The Act was not, however, constituting or ratifying dramatic companies as household retainers of the nobility: the companies were already independent commercial organizations run entirely on profit-making lines, and they received from the powerful magnates protection rather than patronage, a badge of respectability rather than a living: as James Burbage's letter to the Earl of Leicester testifies:

> May it please your honour to understand that forasmuch as there is a certain Proclamation out for the reviving of a Statute as touching retainers, as your Lordship knoweth better than we can inform you thereof: We therefore, your humble Servants and daily Orators your players, for avoiding all inconveniences that may grow by reason of the said Statute, are bold to trouble your Lordship with this our Suit, humbly desiring your honour that (as

you have been always our good Lord and Master) you will now vouchsafe to retain us at this present as your household servants and daily waiters, not that we mean to crave any further stipend or benefit at your Lordship's hands but our liveries as we have had, and also your honour's license to certify that we are your household servants . . .[9]

Royal as well as noble protection was available to a preferred company: 'Leicester's Men' received in 1574 a patent licensing them to play where they pleased from Elizabeth herself:

Elizabeth by the grace of God Queen of England, etc., to all Justices, Mayors, Sheriffs, Bailiffs, Head Constables, Under Constables, and all other our officers and ministers, greeting. Know ye that we of our especial grace, certain knowledge and mere motion have licensed and authorised, and by these presents do licence and authorise, our loving subjects, James Burbage, John Perkin, John Lanham, William Johnson, and Robert Wilson, servants to our Trusty and well-beloved Cousin and Counsellor the Earl of Leicester, to use, exercise and occupy the art and faculty of playing Comedies, Tragedies, Interludes, Stage plays . . .[10]

It was evidently with the protection of this patent that Burbage built the first purpose-built playhouse, the Theatre, in 1576.[11]

The Elizabethan acting company therefore was constituted by a *rapprochement* of old and new social relationships. Their protection came from the ruling class itself, and ostensibly they were entertainers by appointment to the court and nobility: Leicester's, Sussex's, Warwick's, Essex's and Oxford's Men held the field until in 1583 the government creamed off those adjudged to be the best players and formed one privileged company, the Queen's Majestie's Servants. The number of companies permitted to perform in London simultaneously was strictly limited at different times to two, three or four: so the theatrical world (as far the public theatres were concerned) was dominated by an elite of professionals closely linked with the ruling class. And yet the companies were fully independent commercial organisations, dependent for their profits on the audiences of the public theatres. The decisive break with feudal relations came with the construction of these purpose-built playhouses, run entirely on profitable lines; an economic pattern which discloses with absolute clarity the fact that the players were selling a commodity for cash. Despite their close relationships with the traditional ruling class, the Elizabethan acting company represented a kind of cultural bourgeoisie, producing and selling a commodity to those prepared to pay:

> Under the protective shield of their lord's badge, invoking a declining, obsolescent form of service, which was in their case sometimes little better than a legal fiction, the players established themselves as purveyors of a commodity for which the general public was prepared regularly to put down its cash.[12]

Shakespeare himself was an actor and resident writer in the Lord Chamberlain's company: but his fortune was made not by either of these activities but by his 'share' in the company and his investment in the Globe playhouse.

The 'nation' outside London became less attractive as a commercial prospect than the capital itself: the companies travelled to the provinces only when plague or competition forced them to do so, and a company would frequently split as a consequence:

> . . . the commercialism of the players . . . directed them to London. The Shakespearean drama was written for companies that used their playbooks solely to make their living, and by far the best living was to be found in London. Except for the occasional university student like Japser Mayne, no poet wrote with anything but the London companies in mind. All the major playhouses were built in London. . . . In London there were regular venues, regular audiences, regular incomes. Every player's ambition was to belong to a company resident in London. And equally the only place where a play could be marketed was in London.[13]

The Elizabethan stage marks the end of the truly *national* drama, and the beginning of the almost exclusively metropolitan drama for which Shakespeare wrote. His drama was 'national' in a sense that has to be located in the specific kind of nation-state that developed out of medieval Europe, a process signalled in England by the Reformation. When the Tudor administration began to suppress by legal violence the traditional religious drama as part of its campaign against Catholicism and political dissent, it initiated a process of theatrical 'nationalization' which produced the drama of Shakespeare's stage – a centralized and professionalized theatre, adopted by the ruling class but actually a bourgeois industry, flourishing in the intensive cultural life of the metropolis and kept firmly under government control. Before Shakespeare, drama was amateur, universal, unlocalized, and represented a rich cultural vitality active throughout the national community. In Shakespeare's time London was a forcing-house of talent which privileged excellence and virtuosity, the self-evident value of saleable commodities, consumed by a small metropolitan constituency. The Tudor state thus produced a drama very much in the image of its own dominant tendencies towards centralization and appropriation of political and cultural power, wielded by a centralized bureaucratic government. The origins of Shakespearean drama are thus inseparable from the emergence of the secular national state, parent of that bourgeois state which is still with us today, and which even now preserves intact some of the cultural patterns established in the sixteenth century (such as the 'Royal National Theatre').

The Tudor state deliberately and systematically provided a limited space for the production of a national culture which would express, confirm and naturalize its own power. To this extent the Elizabethan drama can be seen, not as the reflection or expression of a pre-existent national culture, but as a systematically constructed ideology of national unity designed to confirm the state's authority. Cultural power was gradually and intentionally drawn, along with political power, towards the centre, thus constituting a national ideology which mirrored the national sovereignty of the state.

An *ideology* of national unity is the product of a divided and contradictory society seeking resolution of its internal discords by a cultural *concordat*. When subjected to a marxist analysis, that ideology discloses the contradictions it is designed to suppress. In the literary discourses that form a constituent element of this ideology a materialist criticism will discover, not an astonishing cultural variety victoriously controlled into a serene harmony, but the stresses and tensions, the discords and contradictions running along the fault-lines of a society: the fractured integrity of an ideological coherence. The criticism therefore which seeks to resurrect for us the global cohesion of a lost social totality by reproducing its

ideology, is involved in an act of willing complicity with the mystifi-
cations of that ideology: it is committed to a revival of the ideology
as a whole, with all its suppressions and absences, its repudiation of
historical contradictions, its denial of the dialectics of historical
change. To evaluate Shakespearean drama as in any sense a simple
expression of Tudor ideology, whether the operation is conducted by
the archaeological scholarship of orthodox criticism or the sceptical
disclosures of New Historicism, is to ratify the seamless unity of that
ideology rather than analyzing its innate incoherences.

Shakespeare's historical dramas were not an expression or symptom of a harmonious nation, but an ideology of national unity
developed in the limited cultural space prescribed by the state for
that purpose. An effective ideology must provide the necessary
arena for a strictly limited play of contradictions; and we have seen
how in manipulating different theories of historiography, the drama
brought into play a broad range of possibilities reflecting the diverse
cultural tendencies of the society. But there is a wider play of contradictions beyond authorial consciousness, rooted in the tensions
and divisions of history, mystified in the seductive self-evidence of
ideology, and visible to a materialist understanding of the historical
functioning of cultural discourses.

Some account has been given of those historical conditions which
rendered the English histories apparently available for conservative
and reactionary reproduction. The following chapters will analyse in
detail the operation of that process, moving towards a position where
both reactionary and progressive reproduction can be evaluated in
political and aesthetic terms. The social conditions of the Elizabethan drama must now be re-examined to discover the historical
grounds for a progressive reproduction of 'Shakespeare'.

We have considered the peculiar character of Shakespeare's
'plays' in the originating moment of their production: 'productions'
is what they were, and though sold on a market as a commodity,
they had nothing of the fetishism we think of as inseparable from the
commodity in bourgeois society. They became commodities in the
bourgeois sense when printed: fixed in the determinacy of the written word, imprisoned within the constraining binder of a volume,
labelled with the distinguishing mark of the commodity, price. But
as dramatic performances they were, in a historically specific sense,
free.

In a particular fundamental sense Shakespeare's 'text' eludes the abstract formulation, the changeless fixity of the immanent text, because its original form is that of *drama*: a cultural practice in which the text is necessarily external to, therefore ancillary to, the enacted performance. The alliance between literary criticism and the theatre, often a relationship of great cultural and ideological conflict, has been developed in the present century to an intimate rapport, particularly on the ground of Shakespeare's drama, a *rapprochement* of literary and theoretical practices which suppresses and elides the contradictions between them. Historically, however, the plays were *drama* before they were *literature*: and it is clearly of the utmost significance to this argument that at the originating moment of their production those plays had no recognizable existence as literary texts.

The 'text' of a Shakespeare play widely taken for granted by contemporary criticism and education is the modern edition, the result of centuries of scholarly enquiry, bibliographical analysis and critical discussion, in which the 'play' appears supplemented with scholarly and critical introductions, explanatory notes, appendices giving extracts from sources, etc. The 'play' itself has been constituted as a literary object, held firmly in place by the constricting frame of scholarship and criticism which mediates the play to the modern reader. This form of the 'text' originated in the scholarly editions of the eighteenth century, and the text is recognizably similar in each case. Stripped of all critical apparatus, the text of a play in a modern edition resembles with sufficient exactness the play as it appeared in the first compilation of Shakespeare's works, the First Folio of 1623, or one of the so-called 'good Quarto' editions. Naturally these variant forms bear the traces of their institutional uses: the modern text clearly a text for 'critical study', assimilated to the needs of the educational system; the heavyweight eighteenth-century version a text for antiquarian exploration; the First Folio a text for reading. The earliest printed editions display much more inconsistency in their transmission of the play, because of their proximity to the specific economic and cultural practices of those individuals and groups responsible for writing, owning, performing and printing the plays.

A typical Elizabethan play designed for performance in a public playhouse was written for, perhaps commissioned by, an acting company, and became the company's property. There was no copyright in the modern sense:[14] to speak of performance, copying or printing 'rights' is in any case anachronistic, since no such rights existed in law, and the companies had to protect their property and endeavour to secure their monopoly as best they could in a fiercely competitive economic climate. To the entrepreneur who ran a theatre and backed a company, or to the collective of sharers who both owned and worked the company, the play was commercially viable only as a performance: to have it published would be neither lucrative nor prudent, since there was no law to prevent a rival company from acting it elsewhere. A company would be determined to restrict the copying of the play-text until its appeal in the theatre had been temporarily exhausted, when a few pounds could be salvaged by selling the play to a printer: determined, in short, to prevent the play from becoming literature. Apart from the author's manuscript, only one complete copy of the play, for use as a prompt-book, would be needed; even the actors could not see the whole play written or printed, but would receive copies of their own parts, located into the action by cues. The great Elizabethan acting companies can be compared with the major film companies of today, which seek to prevent the copying, performance and distribution of their productions on video-tape. 'Piracy' was prevalent in Elizabethan London too: a play-text could be assembled from a performance, either by means of shorthand transcription or an actor's recollection, and printed without the company's permission. The appearance of such pirated editions would often precipitate a premature printing of the company's original version. Even the various pirated and 'Quarto' texts, which interestingly bear the marks of their origins in performance, are very much a secondary stage of production subsequent to the original appearance of the work as drama:

> Except for a few of the poets, nobody gave a thought to posterity. The companies that bought the plays were actively hostile to the idea of printing them. The players were there to give entertainment and to take money. There was no reason to make the product durable or to record it for future generations. So the plays lived in a medium as ephemeral as the sounds through which they came to life.[15]

The 'text' in this situation is a text-for-performance: a basic structure on which the theatrical presentation could be mounted, a musical score for the actors' improvisation. There was no authentic text outside the acting company to correct and control the dramatic event. Since the actor-sharers were the directors of their own company, the play-text their property, and the writer himself possibly an active company member (Shakespeare was actor, sharer and resident writer in the Lord Chamberlain's Men), a dramatic production must have been more a matter of collaborative interpretation and active improvizing, than of the faithful and scrupulous representation of a pre-existent text. The decisive theoretical break occurs between the play-as-literature and the play-as-drama: only the first is reproducible as a fetishized object.[16] If in performance the play was not directed by a fixed textual structure, then the performance was in an absolute sense the making of the play: a process influenced by many contingent factors, including the play-text, the presence or absence of the writer as an active participant, the character of the players themselves, the physical conditions of the playhouse, the tangible presence of a vociferously participating audience. As *drama* the play holds an enormously greater potentiality for 'iterability', for the production of plurality of meaning, than the written or printed text. This undeniable plurality, however, is no hypothesis of speculative idealism, but a historically determined quality inscribed into the play by the specific material conditions of its production. Just as the historiographical character of the plays should be understood in terms of the process of historical genesis, so their dramatic qualities should not be separated from their formative origin in the public playhouses of Elizabethan London.

In a largely pre-literate society without a printing industry, a dramatic *performance* is the essential identity, the material reality of the cultural form. The Elizabethan theatre, though it was the first fully developed cultural 'industry', had its roots in that popular oral tradition. Before the appearance of purpose-built playhouses the natural locations of popular drama were the street and inn-yard: drama grew up in close kinship and in competition with other forms of popular entertainment. The Globe Theatre stood symbolically beside the Bear Gardens on London's Bankside. Such physical conditions produce a theatre in which there is always very close proximity and very direct *rapprochement* between actors and audience; in which the traditions of popular entertainment are very much alive and to the fore; in which the clarity of daylight makes it impossible for an audience to lose itself in self-forgetful rapture; and in which acting conventions have to be highly conventionalized (an actor playing naturalistically in an inn-yard is likely to be mistaken for a waiter).

In the Elizabethan public playhouse these conditions still held. The actors played on a thrust stage completely surrounded by a tightly-packed audience, standing in the yard and seated in the galleries. Daylight performance made the audience as visible as the actors: the audience was not, as in a modern theatre, isolated in the darkness of an auditorium and concentrating single-mindedly on the brightly-lit rectangle of the stage. Acting was stylized rather than naturalistic; and non-illusionistic – the actors could not deny the presence of an audience.

The companies were organized as an *ensemble*, the players themselves being the self-employed commercial directors of the enterprise: the 'sharers' took the main parts and assigned other parts to hired hands. Although the players in the purpose-built public playhouses could obviously have used illusionistic scenery and elaborate props, they did not: in the style of the popular drama from which the Elizabethan theatre evolved, they were content with rudimentary props and made no attempt at scenic illusion. A company would in any case be prepared to take a play from the public playhouse to an indoor private theatre, a nobleman's house or the Court, a flexibility which would place strict limits on the use of theatrical resources.[17] To an extent the Elizabethan theatre maintained some of the unlocalized qualities of the popular drama – a practice to which Sir Philip Sidney indignantly objected, in the belief that such dramatic liberty violated the fundamental laws of drama:

> For where the stage should always represent but one place, and the uttermost time presupposed in it should be, both by Aristotle's precept and common reason, but one day, there is both many days, and many places, inartificially imagined . . . you shall have Asia of the one side, and Africa of the other, and so many other under-kingdoms, that the player, when he cometh in, must ever begin with telling where he is, or else the tale will not be conceived.[18]

The non-illusionist conventions natural to an unlocalized drama seemed unreasonable to the neo-classical conception of dramatic truth.

The drama which developed within the strictly circumscribed cultural space provided for it by the Tudor state, was, for a brief space, as a consequence of its roots in popular culture, a remarkably free form of discourse. Though not by any means free from state regulation and control, the pressures of patronage and surviving feudal relationships, censorship and legal interference; yet it was free from the authoritarian dominance of the literary text, free from the authoritarian control of the director, and free from the tyranny of illusionistic theatrical conventions. Each performance was provisional, exploratory and unfinished; unique, unrepeatable and experimental; as living as the relationship between actors and audience, as ephemeral as the sounds of their voices.

Such a theatre was, to a degree, naturally saturnalian; it was linked to that tradition of popular cultural resistance discussed earlier. Its lively and pluralistic generation of meaning would not be contained within the rigid ideological frame of Tudor propaganda; within the political science of the old Christian or the new secular humanism; or within the emerging priorities of bourgeois historiography:

> . . . in Shakespeare's day . . . a close, almost exclusive attention to the actors sustained enjoyment and discovery. The originality did not spring from some new mode of staging or some new dominant theme, but was the result of an exploration of Shakespeare's plays by actors who lived with his roles and modified their performances from night to night, and acted with giant imagination and resource for a free audience . . . a free, actor-centred theatre would provide an encounter with Shakespeare's plays at which everything was at risk, and from their prepared positions the actors, with the audience, could probe, penetrate and ride high upon the plays in their moment-by-moment life.[19]

It is my argument that this pluralistic quality of the plays is historically specific, inscribed into them by the historical conditions of their production. The following chapters focus on particular case-studies in the ideological reproduction of Shakespeare's historical drama: on the critical history of Falstaff, on cultural productions of *Henry V*, and on theatrical productions of the history cycles. These comparisons distinguish clearly and sharply between reactionary and progressive reproduction; and between productions designed to preserve intact the Tudor ideology of national unity, and productions which revive the historical conditions of Shakespeare's theatre to make staging history a radical cultural intervention.

Chapter Six

Carnival and History:
Henry IV

It is a commonplace that the figure of Falstaff, or the 'world' that figure inhabits or creates, constitutes some kind of internal *opposition* to the ethical conventions, political priorities and structures of authority and power embodied in the sovereign hegemony of king, prince and court: the state. Falstaff is at the centre of a popular comic history, located within the deterministic framework of the chronicle–history play, which challenges and subverts the imperatives of necessitarian historiography. The chronicle–history frame is qualified and criticized by a confrontation of different dramatic discourses within the drama, a confrontation which brings into play genuinely historical tensions and contradictions, drawn both from Shakespeare's own time and from the reconstructed time of the historical past.

The kind of 'opposition' represented by Falstaff is often compared with the other oppositional tendencies which challenge the state in these plays: Falstaff's moral rebelliousness and illegality are seen as analogous to those forces of political subversion – the rebellion of the Percies and the Archbishop of York's conspiracy – which shake the stability of the Lancastrian dynasty. But though moral riotousness and political opposition are often arbitrarily connected by hostile propaganda, a state which ruthlessly suppresses the latter often finds space for the former – regarded perhaps as the legitimate exercise of freedom guaranteed to a despotic ruling class by the 'stability' of its government (e.g. the court of the Stuarts). It has been recognized that the revelry and satire of Falstaff constitute kinds of social practice which were afforded a legitimate space in medieval culture. Medieval European hierarchies, secular and ecclesiastical, sought to preserve the rigidity of their social relations, to control and incorporate internal tensions and oppositions, by allowing, at fixed times, temporary suspensions of rule, order

and precedence: festive holidays in which moral freedom and opposition to political authority, the flouting of moral conventions and
the inversion of ordinary social structures, were allowed to flourish.
These periods of temporary suspension were closely analogous to,
possibly related back to, religious practices of antiquity:

> Many peoples have been used to observe an annual period of
> licence, when the customary restraints of law and morality are
> thrown aside, when the whole population give themselves up to
> extravagant mirth and jollity, and when the darker passions find
> a vent which would never be allowed them in the more staid and
> sober course of ordinary life. Such outbursts of the pent-up
> forces of human nature, too often degenerating into wild orgies
> of lust and crime, occur most commonly at the end of the year,
> and are frequently associated . . . with one or other of the
> agricultural seasons, especially with the time of sowing or of
> harvest.[1]

Dance, song, feasting, moral freedom, were a natural element of
most pre-Christian European religions, and were sternly condemned
as unchristian, immoral licence by zealous and reforming Christian
clerics, from the early Church fathers (who attacked the Roman
Saturnalia) to the sixteenth-century Puritans. More generally they
were modified, and incorporated into Christian observance (in the
same way as the more prudent and discerning Christian missionaries
tried to *adapt* rather than supplant the beliefs of those they wished
to convert), so that the pagan fertility myths of the Mummers' Play
became a Christmas or Springtime celebration.[2] Such social practices were far from being simply a period of release, with bouts of
drinking and lust and frenzied dancing: they were often characterized by a specific ritual shape, involving the suspension of ordinary
structures of authority. The Roman Saturnalia reveals a clear ritual
structure within the general surrender to appetite and passion: within
it social relationships were not merely suspended but *inverted*:

> Now of all these periods of license the one which is best known
> and which in modern languages has given its name to the rest, is
> the Saturnalia . . . no feature of the festival is more remarkable,
> nothing in it seems to have struck the ancients themselves more
> than the licence granted to slaves at this time. The distinction

between the free and servile classes was temporarily abolished. The slave might rail at his master, intoxicate himself like his betters, sit down at table with them, and not even a word of reproof would be administered to him for conduct which at any other season might have been punished with stripes, imprisonment, or death. Nay, more, masters actually changed places with their slaves and waited on them at table; and not till the serf had done eating and drinking was the board cleared and dinner set for his master.[3]

The custom was called saturnalian because it purported to be a temporary imitation of the 'Golden Age' society of peace, fertility, freedom and common wealth, without private property or slavery, presided over by the God Saturn: 'The Saturnalia passed for nothing more or less than a temporary revival or restoration of the reign of that merry monarch'.[4] The nostalgic sentimentalism of Roman patricians and the utopian longings of their slaves met on the common ground of saturnalian revelry and ritual: a clear acknowledgment that such a society must have been preferable to the present order, co-existed with a more pragmatic sense of the essentially limited nature of human ideals and aspirations, a sad recognition that 'order' (i.e. the contemporary state) can be suspended, but never, in practice, abolished or transformed. So the Saturnalia, and the associated rituals of medieval Europe, were:

> . . . an interregnum during which the customary restraints of law and morality are suspended and the ordinary rulers abdicate their authority in favour of a temporary regent, a sort of puppet king, who bears a more or less indefinite, capricious and precarious sway over a community given up for a time to riot, turbulence and disorder.[5]

Similar customs are visible in later English folk-ceremonies by which the rural people celebrated spring or summer: festivities in praise of fertility would involve the election of a mock ruler – a 'May King', a 'Summer Lord', a 'Mock Mayor' – or a King and Queen whose mock marriage would seem to symbolize some ancient myth of fertility. Such festivities, it is suspected, would probably include the exercise of practical fertility among the celebrants: 'It may be taken for granted that the summer festivals knew from the beginning that element of sexual licence which fourteen centuries of Christianity have not wholly been able to banish'.[6]

Those ancient cults and practices can be linked to Shakespeare's time by a famous passage from the Puritan Phillip Stubbes' *Anatomy of Abuses* (1583):

> Against May, Whitsunday, or other time, all the young men and maids, old men and wives, run gadding overnight to the woods, groves, hills and mountains, where they spend all night in pleasant pastimes; and in the morning they return, bringing with them birch and branches of trees, to deck their assemblies withall. And no marvel, for there is a great Lord present amongst them, as Superintendent and Lord over their pastimes and sports, namely, Sathan, prince of hell. But the chiefest jewel they bring from thence is their May-pole, which they bring home with great veneration . . . And then they fall to dance about it, like as the heathen people did at the dedication of the Idols, whereof this is a perfect pattern, or rather the thing itself.[7]

Stubbes also inveighs against the custom of electing a 'Lord of Misrule' to preside over ritual celebrations. Those May celebrations persisted in folk-culture and continued to be the target of Puritan attack: various legislative attempts to control or suppress them seemed to have little success before 1644. On the basis of this folk culture saturnalian customs developed throughout medieval society: in cathedral and collegiate schools the Church permitted festivities such as the Feast of Fools, a revelry presided over by a member of the lower clergy reigning as temporary sovereign; and where such customs were suppressed by reforming clerics, the local bourgeoisie would often revive them as civic festivities. In Universities, Inns of Court and in the Royal Court itself, such revels flourished under a 'Lord of Misrule' or king of fools: Henry VIII often participated personally in such celebrations.

The relation to these popular traditions of the Elizabethan drama has been well enough understood and documented – E. K. Chambers's pioneering work built upon the findings of Frazer and the early anthropologists to produce a new perspective on the relation between drama and social custom; and the field still remains dominated by the fine studies of C. L. Barber and Robert Weimann.[8] There is still room, however, for further theoretical work on this relation, especially on the specific *social* significance of saturnalian custom and its passage into drama: and this work is made infinitely more feasible by the fairly recent 'discovery' of Mikhail Bakhtin's theories on 'carnivalization' in medieval and Renaissance literature, developed in his study of Rabelais (1940).[9]

In the Middle Ages, Bakhtin writes: 'a boundless world of humorous forms and manifestations opposed the official and serious tone of medieval ecclesiastical and feudal culture . . . the culture of folk carnival humour'. These forms were, according to Bakhtin's most illuminating emphasis, basically *popular* expressions of folk culture: though they were built into the formal structure of medieval culture, they contained and signified (like the Roman Saturnalia) a completely different conception of human society:

> All those forms of protocol and ritual based on laughter and consecrated by tradition existed in all the countries of medieval Europe; they were sharply distinct from the serious, official, ecclesiastical, feudal and political cult forms and ceremonials. They offered a completely different, non-official, extra-ecclesiastical and extra-political aspect of the world, of man, and of human relations; they built a second world in which all medieval people participated more or less, in which they lived during a given time of the year.[10]

Clearly the 'carnival' (Bakhtin's generic title for all saturnalian customs and practices) was a contradictory social institution: its whole *raison d'être* was that of opposition to established authority; it rejected all official norms and conventions; inverted established hierarchies; flouted, satirized and parodied the rituals, institutions and personalities of power. And yet it was countenanced, permitted, even fostered by those very authorities.

> The medieval feast had, as it were, the two faces of Janus. Its official, ecclesiastical face was turned to the past and sanctioned the existing order, but the face of the people of the market place looked into the future and laughed, attending the funeral of the past and present.[11]

Only a very rigid, hierarchical and static society needs such organized release and limited, temporary liberation; only a very stable, confident society can afford to permit them. By the late sixteenth century matters were different; the continuities of pagan ritual and belief were being harshly attacked by the Puritans; the precarious religious settlement made any mockery of religious authority (even, later in Elizabeth's reign, of Catholicism)[12] impossible; and the various attempts to stabilize a rapidly changing social and class structure, continued under the Stuarts, made the image of the world turned upside down particularly distasteful to established authority. The potency of these ideas can be measured by the fact that later, in the Civil War period, such comic inversions became the basis of serious, revolutionary social criticism. From the medieval rituals in which the text 'He hath put down the mighty from their seats, and exalted them of low degree' inaugurated a temporary inversion of social hierarchy, to the radical social theories of Winstanley and the Fifth Monarchy men, there is a definite though complex and contradictory historical continuity.[13]

Bakhtin argues that such carnival customs expressed and embodied an oppositional ideology: and that in such events the people themselves could temporarily live out an ideology of alternative values: 'The carnival and similar marketplace festivals . . . were the second life of the people, who for a time entered into the utopian realm of community, freedom, equality and abundance'.[14] In carnival all were equal: all everyday order and hierarchy dissolved, leaving people reborn to new and more truly human relations. These relations required a new philosophy, a new language, which Bakhtin calls 'dynamic expression': a new kind of logic in which the real world is criticized by living out a fantasy of its dissolution – the world turned upside down, the logic of parody and travesty, comic humiliation of power and greatness, comic uncrowning of authority and the crowning of the low.

It should then be possible to analyze any example of carnival festivity or saturnalian custom, and any literary production flowing from these social forms, in terms of this contradiction: from the point of view of the people, carnival is an expression of the independent values, the humanism of popular culture, a fantasy of equality, freedom and abundance which challenges the social order; from the point of view of authority, carnival is a means of incorporating and controlling the energies and anti-authoritarian emotions aroused by carnival licence. This cultural contradiction, this confrontation of popular and authoritarian discourses, will prove a sound basis for defining the function of Falstaff. It will first

be necessary to provide a detailed account of Bakhtin's theory of
carnival.

Bakhtin finds that the central *image* of the carnival attitude is that
of the *body*: the 'material bodily principle' which is always regarded
as 'deeply positive'. It is a symbol for (or rather a direct imaginative
expression of) 'the people, constantly growing and renewed'. As a
conception of human nature this image of the people as a giant
(gargantuan) collective body pre-dates the formation of a strictly-
defined and differentiated atomized individual which, in Bakhtin's
terms, is a development of the Renaissance (in Rabelais, for
example, the individual body has not yet been completely severed
from the general body of the people):

> In grotesque realism the bodily element is deeply positive . . .
> something universal, representing all the people . . . The com-
> plex nature of Renaissance realism has not as yet been sufficiently
> disclosed. Two types of imagery reflecting the conception of the
> world have met at crossroads; one of them ascends to the folk cul-
> ture of humour, while the other is the bourgeois conception of the
> complete atomised being. The conflict of these two contradictory
> trends is typical of Renaissance realism. The ever-growing, in-
> exhaustible, ever-laughing principle which uncrowns and renews
> is combined with its opposite: the petty, inert, 'material principle'
> of class society.[14]

The dominant *style* of carnival discourse is the *grotesque*: '. . . all
that is bodily becomes grandiose, exaggerated, immeasurable'.[15]
The carnivalizing imagination creates gargantuan images of huge
bodies, enormous appetites, surrealistic fantasies of absurdly inflated physical properties.

Carnival is humorous and satirical, and its laughter always *mat-
erializes*: concretizes the spiritual in the physical, the ideal in the
material, the 'upper' strata of life and society into the 'lower'.
Ideals, pretensions, elevated conceptions of human nature cannot
survive the enormous assertions of human sensuality: the pride of
physical life mocks and degrades everything which seeks to transcend or escape it. Hence this grotesque humour of the body
provides a firm basis for satire (a word often historically confused
with the half-human, half-bestial figure of the satyr).

While the 'bourgeois ego' limits human life to the birth and death

of a differentiated individual, the grotesque bodily image of carnival is that of a perpetually unfinished process of change and
renewal: 'The grotesque image reflects a phenomenon in transformation, an as yet unfinished metamorphosis, of death and birth,
growth and becoming.'[16] The grotesque body is therefore deeply
ambivalent, since it contains both processes of creation and destruction, vitality and dissolution – a simultaneity of the antitheses of life
glimpsed in one dimension: 'In this image we find both poles of
transformation, the old and the new, the dying and the procreating,
the beginning and the end of the metamorphosis.'[17]

The grotesque image is not sealed off from the outer world: it
merges into its environment as if symbolizing some unity of man
and nature. Hence in carnival and carnivalesque literature there
is a recurrent emphasis on the physical points of entry and exit
(mouth, nose, genitals, anus) and on processes of reproduction and
defecation – processes which guarantee the perpetuity of 'the ever
unfinished, ever creating body'. Where classicism in art later represented the body as complete, self-sufficient, enclosed and perfect,
with its relation to the outer world sealed off, the grotesque insisted
on that relation by displaying and caricaturing the body in its
external relations.

Subsequent to the Middle Ages the grotesque became generally
subject to a moralistic perspective which severely limited its power
and significance:

> During the domination of the classical man in all the areas of art
> and literature of the seventeenth and early eighteenth centuries,
> the grotesque related to the culture of folk humour was excluded
> from great literature; it descended to the low comic level or was
> subject to the epithet 'gross naturalism'. . . . During this period
> (actually starting in the seventeenth century) we observe a pro-
> cess of gradual narrowing down of the ritual, spectacle and
> carnival forms of folk culture . . .
> Having lost its living tie with folk culture and having become a
> literary genre, the grotesque underwent certain changes. There
> was a formalisation of carnival-grotesque images, which permit-
> ted them to be used in many different ways and for various
> purposes. This formalisation was not only exterior; the contents
> of the carnival-grotesque element, its artistic, heuristic, and
> unifying forces were preserved in all essential manifestations

during the seventeenth and eighteenth centuries: in the *commedia dell'arte* (which kept a close link with its carnival origin) in Moliere's comedies . . . in the comic novel and travesty of the seventeenth century, in the tales of Voltaire and Diderot, in the work of Swift . . . in all these writings, despite their differences in character and tendency, the carnival-grotesque form exercises the same function: to consecrate inventive freedom, to permit the combination of a variety of different elements and their rapprochement, to liberate from the prevailing point of view of the world, from conventions and established truths, from cliches, from all that is humdrum and universally accepted. This carnival spirit offers the chance to have a new outlook on the world, to realise the relative nature of all that exists, and to enter a completely new order of things.[18]

Falstaff clearly performs the function, in *Henry IV Parts One* and *Two*, of carnival. He constitutes a constant focus of opposition to the official and serious tone of authority and power: his discourse confronts and challenges those of king and state. His attitude to authority is always parodic and satirical: he mocks authority, flouts power, responds to the pressures of social duty and civic obligation by retreating into Bacchanalian revelry. His world is a world of ease, moral licence, appetite and desire; of humour and ridicule, theatricals and satire, of community, freedom and abundance; a world created by inverting the abstract society, the oppression and the hierarchy of the official world. In the tavern the fool reigns as sovereign; on the high road the thief is an honest man; while in the royal court the cares and duties of state frown on the frivolity and absurdity of saturnalian revelry. To this extent Falstaff can be located in that *popular* tradition of carnival and utopian comedy defined by Bakhtin.

Bakhtin's most innovatory and useful emphasis lies on the *oppositional* character of popular traditions. Falstaff's relation to 'folk culture' may seem remote, though he bears vestigial (or perhaps simply parallel) traces of ancient fertility gods, mythical figures like the Silenus, refers to popular culture and the figures of popular ritual dance and drama (ballads, morality-plays, the May-game and morris-dance figure, Maid Marian), and undergoes at the end of *Henry IV Part One* a comic resurrection probably imitated from the popular drama. But he certainly bears a strong relation to popular traditions of the sixteenth century, some elements of which were isolated by Dover Wilson[19] (the morality-play relation for example); and his various languages all derive from popular culture – the cant of criminals, the accents of anti-Puritan parody and satire, the language of tavern and high-road. His flexible command of different popular discourses goes with another factor, to be discussed at length below: variety of dramatic roles, which bear no coherent relation to what we call 'character', but operate only as part of a specific relation between actor and audience.

Falstaff *is* Bakhtin's 'material bodily principle' writ large: his enormous size and uncontrolled appetite characterize him as a collective rather than an individual being. His self-descriptions employ a grotesque style of caricature and exaggeration to create the monstrous image of a figure larger than life, bigger than any conceivable individual:

> Have you any levers to lift me up again, being down?
>
> (*1HIV*, ii, ii, 34)

> I do here walk before thee like a sow that hath overwhelmed all her litter but one.
>
> (*2HIV*, i, ii, 10–11

– and he frequently discourses in his own brand of grotesque fantasy, which works by inflating the small into the enormous: his subsequent narrative of the robbery (*1HIV*, ii, iv. 160–212) or his disquisition on Bardolph's nose (*1HIV*, iii, 23–49). The collective being is created by foregrounding this concrete image of the material body, but also by means linguistic and dramatic: Falstaff is not a coherent individual subject but a polyphonic clamour of discourses, a fluid counterfeiter of dramatic impersonations.

Falstaff's satirical humour 'degrades' – that is, translates the abstract into the concrete, the spiritual into the physical: 'A plague of sighing and grief! It blows a man up like a bladder!' (*1HIV*, ii, iv, 327–8). The conventional physical effects of grief are inverted, producing fatness rather than emaciation: the breath exhaled in sighs becomes the gaseous inflation of an unsettled stomach. The Prince observes that Falstaff's enormous sensual concreteness contains no space for non-material entities: 'There's no room for faith, truth nor honesty in this bosom of thine: it is all filled up with guts and midriff' (*1HIV*, iii, iii, 152–3).

For Bakhtin the grotesque bodily image 'reflects a phenomenon in transformation', contains the processes of both creation and dissolution. This deep ambivalence is utterly characteristic of Falstaff, who seems to constitute a medium in which these antithetical processes generate simultaneously. Physical sloth and inertia co-exist with vivid vitality of imagination; age and youth are interchangeable. During the Gad's Hill robbery Falstaff poses, under cover of darkness, as a lithe young gallant mugging the elderly and obese bourgeoisie:

> Ah, whoreson caterpillars, bacon-fed knaves, they hate us youth!
> . . . No, ye fat chuffs, I would your store were here! On, bacons, on! What, ye knaves! young men must live!
>
> (*1HIV*, ii, ii, 81–2; 84–6)

and later to the Lord Chief Justice:

> You that are old consider not the capacities of us that are young; you do measure the heat of our livers with the bitterness of your galls; and we that are in the vaward of our youth, I must confess, are wags too!
>
> (*2HIV*, i, ii, 172–6)

To moralize these passages would give us a pitiable image of age masquerading as youth. In fact, they present the audacious paradoxes of carnival, in which death and life, age and youth co-exist in the same figure, held together in impossible simultaneity by the force, zest and gaiety of carnival humour, balanced but unillusioned, poised but explosively liberating. The Prince again acknowledges this as Falstaff's essential nature in seasonal metaphors: 'Farewell, the latter spring! Farewell, All-Hallown summer!'; which anticipates Bakhtin's: 'in this image we find both poles of transformation, the old and the new, the dying and the procreating, the beginning and the end of the metamorphosis.[20]

Bakhtin's account of the demise of the carnival and the grotesque in literature as neo-classicism advanced, coincides precisely with the fate of Falstaff in criticism. The modern critical traditions derive from John Dover Wilson's *The Fortunes of Falstaff* (1943), a monument of ideological consolidation dating from that amazingly fertile period of Shakespeare reproduction (discussed below), the

Second World War. Dover Wilson argues that the later eighteenth century inaugurated a diversionary tendency of Falstaff criticism: where Dr Johnson had been able to hold, with neo-classical centrality, a 'balanced' view (which Dover Wilson attempts to reconstitute), romanticism, *via* the sentimentalism of Maurice Morgann and the republicanism of Hazlitt, introduced an 'imbalance' into the poised edifice of criticism, establishing as norms certain radical attitudes: disloyalty and distaste towards the prince, unqualified admiration for Falstaff, a preference for comic opposition over conservative royalism, for instinct and desire over reason and self-control, for moral and political subversion over the preservation of 'order' in the state.[21] Dr Johnson, apparently, 'still lived in Shakespeare's world, a world which was held together, and could only be held together by authority based on and working through a carefully preserved gradation of rank. He was never tired of proclaiming the virtues of the Principle of Subordination . . .'[22] According to Dover Wilson, Johnson 'shared Shakespeare's political assumptions', which are embodied in Ulysses' speech on 'degree' in *Troilus and Cressida*; and was therefore able to understand Shakespeare where the romantics could not. Dover Wilson does not, however, claim to derive his critical authority from the same ground of sympathetic – because partisan – comprehension. In fact his position is identical to that of Tillyard, whose *Shakespeare's History Plays* (already referred to, and discussed at length below) belongs to the same historical moment, the same cultural intervention, as Dover Wilson's book on Falstaff: both share the apparently scholarly (but implicitly polemical) privileging of 'order', defined as a hierarchical state ruled by the 'Principle of Subordination'. Dover Wilson's cultural/ideological strategy is clear: to re-establish a pristine but disrupted 'order' in the criticism of *Henry IV*, in Shakespeare studies, and thence in the problematical society of war-time Britain. The political intention is obvious, but naturally unacknowledged; it is articulated instead as a *moral* reconstituting of the proper context for appreciating Falstaff:

> Shakespeare's audience enjoyed the fascination of Prince Hal's 'white-bearded Satan' for two whole plays, as perhaps no character on the world's stage had ever been enjoyed before. But they knew, from the beginning, that the reign of this marvellous Lord of Misrule must have an end, that Falstaff must be rejected by the

Prodigal Prince, when the time for reformation came. And they no more thought of questioning or disapproving of that finale, than their ancestors would have thought of protesting against the vice being carried off to Hell at the end of the interlude.[23]

'Shakespeare's audience' here is a fictional construction invented merely to confirm the critic's own views. Yet Dover Wilson can confidently ascribe to that phantom a definitive moral perspective in which Falstaff plays a strictly temporary and limited role: an isolated space of pleasure circumscribed by the unshakeable certainties of moral truth. With even greater confidence Dover Wilson asserts his definition of the moral judgment Shakespeare's audience would have passed on Prince Hal's riotous youth:

Vanity . . . was a cardinal iniquity in a young prince or nobleman of the sixteenth and seventeenth century; . . . this is the view that his father and his own conscience take of his misreadings; and as the spectator would take it as well, we must regard it as the thesis to which Shakespeare addressed himself.[24]

In short, the play is being located within a moralistic framework developed by critics like Tillyard and Dover Wilson during the Second World War, a moralistic perspective entirely out of sympathy with the popular traditions of carnival comedy from which Falstaff developed. Once this structure was erected and consolidated and the threat posed by Falstaff to bourgeois criticism deflected, it became possible to affirm a nostalgic and sentimental pleasure in what Falstaff had to offer. This balancing act, a strategic counterpointing of constraint and canonization, is skilfully engineered in Dover Wilson's conclusion:

Falstaff, for all his descent from a medieval devil, has become a kind of god in the mythology of modern man, a god who does for our imaginations very much what Bacchus or Silenus did for those of the ancients; and this because we find it extraordinarily exhilarating to contemplate a being free of all the conventions, codes and moral ties that control us as members of a human society, . . .

Yet the English spirit has ever needed two wings for its flight, Order as well as Liberty . . . this balance which the play keeps between the bliss of freedom and the claims of the common weal has been disturbed by modern critics . . . I have endeavoured to do something to readjust the balance. In effect, it has meant trying to put Falstaff in his place . . . I offer no apologies for constraining the old boar to feed in the old frank . . .[25]

Dover Wilson, scholar, critic and public servant, has evidently inherited the world and the ideology of Prince Henry: there is an unbroken continuity of the 'English spirit' between himself and

. . . English Harry, in whose person Shakespeare crowns *noblesse oblige*, generosity and magnanimity, respect for law, and the selfless devotion to duty which comprise the traditional ideals of our public service.[26]

Falstaff can be afforded only a severely limited space in this scheme of things, which is evidently Dover Wilson's bizarre conception of an actual world, his view of the point where the play's ideology merges into a reality outside itself: but once his influence within it has been securely controlled by 'balanced' criticism, he can be safely distanced into myth, given the freedom of an unreal realm of 'imagination', and canonized as a quaint, lovable but innocuous minor divinity.

A measure of the powerfully influential character of this view on subsequent criticsm of the *Henry IV* plays, is the extent to which C. L. Barber's study of saturnalian comedy depends upon it. Barber adopts the same image of the Prince as Tillyard and Dover Wilson:

. . . the play is centered on Prince Hal, developing in such a way as to exhibit in the prince an inclusive, sovereign nature fitted for kingship.[27]

Barber, like Tillyard and Dover Wilson, considers the play's central issue to be that of the Prince's position relative to 'misrule': will he prove noble or degenerate? will he learn to exercise strict control over saturnalian licence, or will his 'holiday' become his 'everyday'?

The interregnum of a Lord of Misrule, delightful in its moment, might develop into the anarchic reign of a favorite dominating a dissolute King. Hal's secret, which he confides early to the audience, is that for him Falstaff is merely a pastime, to be dismissed in due course . . .[28]

Even within Barber's extremely subtle and perceptive account can be discerned a gravitation towards the 'official', permissive view of saturnalian comedy rather than its popular, subversive view: misrule operates only in relation to rule, disorder cannot exist without order, a mock king derives his meaning from the real king and can have no independent status or validity – 'the dynamic relation of comedy to serious action is saturnalian rather than satiric . . . the misrule works, through the whole dramatic rhythm, to consolidate rule'.[29] Barber acknowledges, in a very interesting passage[30] that Falstaff represented some force potentially subversive: not the 'dependent holiday scepticism' which could be comfortably accommodated within a monolithic medieval society, but, in the much more diverse and rapidly changing society of Elizabethan England, a 'dangerously self-sufficient everyday scepticism' threatening to fracture the imposed perimeters, expand the allotted space of licensed saturnalian revelry. He argues further that the rejection of Falstaff can only be accomplished by the employment of primitive magic in the hands of a king whose 'inclusive, sovereign nature' has been drastically reduced and narrowed. Yet Barber will not admit that Falstaff represents a power which the play can barely contain because the historical contradiction it brings into play by confronting popular and establishment discourses are so sharp and insoluble: to do so would break down the sustained effort to achieve and maintain 'balance'. Instead Barber sees the rejection as the inevitable, the only possible outcome of the play's interrogation or 'trial' of Falstaff: 'The result of the trial is to make us see perfectly the necessity for the rejection of Falstaff as a man, as a favorite of the king, as the leader of an interest at court.'[31]

The editor of the Arden Shakespeare texts of *Henry IV* is able to quote approvingly from both Dover Wilson and Barber, and to support the idea of the plays as a 'unified vision' with the names of New Critics Cleanth Brooks and Robert B. Heilman.[32] He writes, in the Tillyard tradition, of 'the great idea of England', quotes (with qualification but with overall approval) Dover Wilson's '*Henry IV* is Shakespeare's vision of the "happy breed of men" that was his England', and endorses C. L. Barber's view that in saturnalian comedy misrule operates to consolidate rule.[33] There is a gestural recognition of Falstaff's comic opposition, but a correspondingly firm insistence that Shakespeare was not 'amoral' or 'infinitely tolerant':

> There is history here, as well as comedy – history which requires responsible action . . . [Shakespeare] upholds good government, in the macrocosm of the state, and the microcosm of man . . . his vision is of men living, however conflictingly, in a nation, a political-moral family.[34]

The rejection of Falstaff is 'necessary, well-prepared, and executed without undue severity'; 'Shakespeare *has* here achieved a balanced complexity of wisdom'.[35]

It would be possible then to locate Falstaff within that popular tradition of carnival and utopian fantasy defined by Bakhtin, and to argue that the moralistic defamation of Falstaff is analogous to the demise of carnival humour as it lost its living tie with folk culture and became subject to the moral and aesthetic dominance of neo-classicism. Yet there is clearly much in Falstaff's dramatic contribution to contradict the categorization here employed: much to support the reductive strictures of the moralists. By the end of *Henry IV Part Two*, Falstaff has become something much more akin to Bakhtin's concept of the 'isolated bourgeois ego': 'I have a whole school of tongues in this belly of mine, and not a tongue of them all speaks any other word but my name.' The inflated egoism displayed here is not carnival: the clamorous popular voices of the collective being have been reduced to monotone: the 'isolated bourgeois ego' has secured complete totalitarian rule over the complex multifarious variety of carnivalized humanity. This dramatic tendency evidently has such power that it induces criticism emanating from various positions on the left to collaborate with conventional criticism in isolating egoistic individualism as Falstaff's sole or primary dramatic role. The passages on the *Henry IV* plays in John F. Danby's *Shakespeare's Doctrine of Nature* (1961) recognize no fundamental contradiction between dominant and subordinate worlds in the plays: though mutually exclusive, the separate spheres share a general condition of moral and political malaise, '. . . with no common term except the disease of each'. In 'an England pervaded throughout court tavern and country retreat by pitiless fraud', Falstaff, far from constituting any serious opposition, 'is himself the most pitiless creature in the play'. The related energies of 'Appetite' and 'Power' are the universal motivations driving this corrupt and diseased political body.[36] More recently, Elliot Krieger's marxist analysis of Shakespearean comedy reaffirms Danby's emphasis, defining Falstaff as a predatory, competitive self, dedicated entirely to appetite and exploitative consumption:

> Falstaff opposes only the forces of authority that place limits on his own autonomy, whereas he works to maintain and uphold *his* authority – the autonomy of the ego.[37]

Evidently then we are confronted here either with a process of degeneration or a site of contradictions: or possibly with a combination of the two. Does Falstaff begin as the 'ever-growing, inexhaustible, ever-laughing principle' and end as 'the isolated bourgeois ego'? Is the 'character' actually a site of perpetual conflict between these antithetical principles: a literary figure offering to an audience *alternative* positions of intelligibility? Do those opposing forces, if present from the outset, shift their positions of relative power? Conventional criticism, when it does not seek to invalidate Falstaff *ab ovo*, opts for the first of these possibilities: *Henry IV Part Two* is usually regarded as the history of Falstaff's degeneration towards deserved dismissal. I will argue that Falstaff is in fact a site of contradictions: that the relation between the contradictory forces is unstable and changing; that under the pressure of external determinations built into the play's historical vision, its fundamental aesthetic form, and its location in the originating moment of its production, the balance of forces develops in tension until it reaches an ultimate breakdown at the end of *Henry IV Part Two*.

Fal.   Now, Hal, what time of day is it, lad?

Prince Thou art so fat-witted with drinking of old sack, and unbuttoning thee after supper, and sleeping upon benches after noon, that thou hast forgotten to demand that truly which thou wouldst truly know. What a devil has thou to do with the time of the day? Unless hours were cups of sack, and minutes capons, and clocks the tongues of bawds, and dials the signs of leaping-houses, and the blessed sun himself a fair hot wench in flame-coloured

taffeta, I see no reason why thou shouldst be so super-
fluous to demand the time of the day.

                                    (*1HIV*, i, ii, 1–12)

The specific context of the Prince's fantasy is provided by the
material principle of the physical body, which is here seen in a
characteristically relaxed condition ('unbuttoning', 'sleeping'). The
emphases are on physical appetites, of eating, drinking and sex
('old sack', 'capons', 'a fair hot wench'); on the carnival device of
degrading the intellectual or spiritual into the physical ('fat-
witted'); and on the kind of *inversion* of the established world-order
(signified here by the language and imagery of time) which is the
constitutive activity of the carnivalistic imagination. Falstaff's existence, alleges the Prince, rejects the discipline of the hour: and this
apparent privileging of time as the structure of social order could be
(and has been) taken as a moralistic condemnation of Falstaff's
essential *raison d'être*. But this is to ignore the mode of the Prince's
speech, which is precisely that discourse of fantasy in which the
inversion of the existing world-order produces an exhilarating sense
of liberation: those ideologies implied by the concept of time (moral
seriousness, civic duty, work) are interrogated by this practice of
inversion. The signs of time – hours, minutes, clocks, dials, the
blessed sun – are all liberated from the fixity of their common social
meanings, wrenched from their legitimate place in the hierarchy of
language, and degraded to the dimension of physical pleasure. The
Prince may seem to be castigating Falstaff's freedom from accepted
limitation, routine, system and convention: but his playful manipu-
lation of those signs which act as guarantees of social order shows
him equally excited by the liberty of carnival discourse. Fantasy,
Rosemary Jackson has argued, is based on 'an obdurate refusal of
prevailing definitions of the "real" or "possible"',[38] it subverts rules
and conventions taken to be normative. It is the inverse side of
reason's orthodoxy; and therefore can reveal 'reason' and 'reality'
to be arbitrary, shifting constructs rather than the solid foundations
of human existence and social order. In terms of this definition the
Prince's imagination is characteristically fantastic: he participates in
a discourse which calls into question the very rules and conventions
on which he is to base his ultimate power as king.

    Falstaff's response is to reaffirm and develop this freedom of
language: he also turns the world upside down in fantasy:

Indeed, you come near me now, Hal, for we that take purses by the moon and the seven stars, and not 'by Phoebus, he, that wand'ring knight so fair' . . . when thou art king let not us that are squires of the night's body be called thieves of the day's beauty: let us be Diana's foresters, gentlemen of the shade, minions of the moon; and let men say we be men of good government, being governed as the sea is, by our noble and chaste mistress the moon, under whose countenance we steal.

(*1HIV*, i, ii, 13–15; 23–29)

Falstaff identifies himself and the Prince with a culture of inversion: in which the reality of the world is to be sought in darkness rather than in light, ruled by the moon rather than the sun; and in which 'good government' is reversed from its normal moral and political associations (firm political rule of the state, strenuous personal discipline of the self) to signify a universal surrender to natural appetite ('being governed as the sea is . . .') in a kingdom of thieves. This discourse of criminality affords a context in which moral criticism can be positively rejected from the alternative ground of a counter-culture: the law calls them thieves, morality condemns them for wasting time and besmirching the day's brightness; but they can confidently invoke their own values, the professional ethics of their own occupation; they have their own 'brightness' in the shadowy glamour of romance ('knights', 'squires', 'minions'); they serve another god. The world is turned upside down in both these fantasies: the Prince's vision of a world in which those objects regarded as securities of reality are carnivalized, transformed into images of appetite and vice, is no different from Falstaff's imaginative ability to invert the world of positive reality in his fantasy of criminal romance.

The stock critical problem concerning the Prince's 'real attitude' to Falstaff, invariably discussed with reference to the soliloquy which ends the scene ('I know you all, and will awhile uphold The unyok'd humour of your idleness') is then misplaced. The real question is not: how does the Prince really regard Falstaff? But rather: what kind of dramatic relationship is constituted by this sharing of a fantastic discourse? Carnival does not merely 'rub off' onto the Prince when he is in Falstaff's company: he can command its language in his own right:

. . . What a disgrace is it to me to remember thy name! or to know thy face tomorrow! or to take note how many pairs of silk stockings thou hast – viz. these, and those that were thy peach-coloured ones! or to bear the inventory of thy shirts – as, one for superfluity, and another for use! But that the tennis-court keeper knows better than I, for it is a low ebb of linen with thee when thou keepest not racket there; as thou has not done a great while, because the rest of thy low countries have made a shift to eat up thy holland. And God knows whether those that bawl out the ruins of thy linen shall inherit his kingdom: but the midwives say the children are not in the fault; whereupon the world increases, and kindreds are mightily strengthened.

(*2HIV*, ii, ii, 12–26)

The Prince's diatribe against Poins is usually understood as an expression of his increasing disgust with his low companions, customarily regarded as a symptom of his growing remorse and imminent reformation. In fact, the speech is an exercise in exactly the mode of satirical fantasy the Prince shares with Falstaff. In the course of apparently criticizing Poins, the Prince's wit constructs a fantasy world in which games, vices, topical allusions, religious parody, all interact in an inverted image of received reality: where the lower regions of the body devour the higher; where a race of illegitimate children are envisaged as the inheritors of a 'kingdom'; and where the Prince's own problematic relation with the royal family ('kindreds') is projected as a fantasy of family strength confirmed, not dissipated, by the prodigality of vice, the abundant proliferation of bastards. The Prince's subsequent attempt (58–60) to dissociate himself from Falstaff appears, in the light of his speech, to be the denial of a constitutive element of himself or of his dramatic role: when he later rejects Falstaff as a figure of his own 'dream', he also renounces, from himself and from his theatrical potentialities, the liberating power of fantasy.

It is true, as conventional wisdom would be swift to point out, that the Prince signals this intention as early as the soliloquy which closes *Henry IV Part One*, i, ii:

I know you all, and will awhile uphold
The unyoked humour of your idleness.
Yet herein will I imitate the sun,

Who doth permit the base contagious clouds
To smother up his beauty from the world,
That, when he please again to be himself,
Being wanted, he may be more wondered at
By breaking through the foul and ugly mists
Of vapours that did seem to strangle him.
If all the year were playing holidays,
To sport would be as tedious as to work . . .
                              (*1HIV*, I, ii, 190–200)

The relation between 'work' and 'holiday' articulated here is very
much a dominant/subordinate antithesis: 'holiday' is a temporary
release from the permanent responsibilities of 'work', a transient
suspension of quotidian duties and obligations. The Prince expresses
the 'official' attitude towards saturnalian licence: its strictly limited
function is that of confirming, by a liberation as temporary as it is
violent, as impermanent as it is affirmative, statutory authority and
constituted order. The image of the sun is rehabilitating: what
Falstaff has inverted, the Prince sets upright again; light and the
sun are re-established in their dominant relation to darkness and
clouds. Authority places a limit on carnival freedom, re-establishes
what carnival overturns.

The mode of soliloquy should also be recognized as determining
the dramatic effect of the Prince's confession. By soliloquizing, a
character expresses a clearly defined individuality, an isolated single-
ness expressing a formidable self-consciousness. Falstaff is often
associated with the individualism of soliloquy, since some of his
most memorable utterances belong to the mode. It is worth pointing
out that in *Henry IV Part One* he hardly uses it at all. In this
particular scene, for the first sixty lines he does not even use the
pronoun 'I': but speaks of 'we' and 'us', invoking his identity as
member of a collective. The Prince consistently employs the first
person singular, and with the departure of Falstaff and Poins he is
able to turn aside from the action and address the audience directly,
displaying his capacity for detachment and egoistic self-assertion.
The device also allows for the possibility of an 'alienation-effect',
since soliloquy was actually (in Shakespeare's theatre) colloquy, an
exchange between actor and audience, which partly suspends the
dramatic illusion, making the audience aware of the character as an
individual separable from the action in which he is participating, his

identity not wholly absorbed into the dramatic interaction with other characters. The Prince is briefly prised away from the illusionistic narrative, offering himself for inspection to the audience's curiosity. The device can have many different effects: here it shows the Prince uniquely capable of individuation, a singling-out from the collective enterprise of the drama into solitary self-assertion and self-justification. This differs strikingly from Falstaff's habit of overt self-dramatizing, since unlike Falstaff, the Prince lays claim to an authentic individual identity independent of his dramatic roles: whatever role he plays, he assures the audience, he will implicitly remain, and at some future point will become in reality, 'himself'.[39] Falstaff never lays claim to such an authentic self: he exists only as a series of dramatic roles, a succession of self-conscious *rapprochements* between actor and audience. His discourse is certainly self-reflexive, but never invokes a distinct personality; rather it alludes to the self as a gargantuan collective creature of myth, a grotesque and hugely inflated caricature. Whether Falstaff is addressing the audience, as in his reaction to the Page's cheek:

> The brain of this foolish-compounded clay, man, is not able to invent anything that intends to laughter more than I invent, or is invented on me . . .
>
> *(2HIV*, i, ii, 5–8)

– or for another character, as in his parodic boasting to the Lord Chief Justice:

> I would to God my name were not so terrible to the enemy as it is . . .
>
> *(2HIV*, i, ii, 217–19)

– he never claims the possession of a distinct centre of self: in the first instance he is openly revealing himself to the audience as a theatrical figure, a dramatic conceit; in the second he manipulates the audience's awareness that this 'name' is an empty title, cheated from the Prince by a comic act of deceit and expropriation. Falstaff's much discussed and much maligned egoism can scarcely be equated with moral categories: there is no self to centre on.[40]

The Prince's life, unlike Falstaff's, is obviously a part of history: its significant episodes are constrained within the fixed, predetermined process of historical event viewed retrospectively as a *fait accompli*. However long he tarries in Eastcheap, Shrewsbury and Agincourt are his fixed destinations. With Falstaff he can experience a relative autonomy which is strictly limited and temporary: he can play roles other than that determined for him by the course of historical necessity, the freer roles established for him by popular romance-history as distinct from Protestant chronicle. But at some point his identity will inevitably be subsumed into the intransigent fixity of fact, the 'known' of history. The Prince anticipates this point as the recovery or realization of 'himself': an undertaking offered in the form of a promise to his father in the scene already discussed:

> I shall hereafter, my thrice gracious lord,
> Be more myself.
> > (*1HIV*, iii, ii, 93–4)

The 'self' he offers to become sounds suspiciously like the chivalric public image required by the king:

> I will redeem all this on Percy's head . . .
> And that shall be the day, whene'er it lights,
> That this same child of honour and renown,
> This gallant Hotspur, this all-praised knight,
> And your unthought-of Harry chance to meet.
> For every honour sitting on his helm,
> Would they were multitudes . . . !
> > (*1HIV*, iii, ii, 132; 139–43)

When the moment of self-realization arrives, it becomes evident that in the process the Prince loses all independent individual being and submits to the tyranny of historical determinism: the famous passage describing his battle array dissolves the person into the derealization of chivalric romance, beautiful but banal, eloquent but empty:

> I saw young Harry with his beaver on,
> His cushes on his thighs, gallantly armed,
> Rise from the ground like feather'd Mercury,
> And vaulted with such ease into his seat
> And if an angel dropp'd down from the clouds

To turn and wind a fiery Pegasus,
And witch the world with noble horsemanship.
(*1HIV*, iv, i, 104–10)

The glamour of this poetry has proved universally captivating. In fact its abstract romanticism represents a final absorption of the free individual into history. The Prince appears transformed into a figure of heroic myth; an illustration from Froissart, the mythical protagonist of an Elizabethan romance epic or a Stuart court masque, our Sidney and our perfect man. This, it could be argued, is role-playing with a vengeance, and that is true, but the role is a pre-determined one, fitted to the individual by historical destiny: the 'self' is a mere dissolution into the current of a deterministic process. Falstaff is not a part of history in the same sense, although he had a historical genesis. His origins are by contrast obscure and contradictory, bestowing on him a much greater potentiality for change. He continues to do the opposite of what is required of him: here he plays the coward, in *Henry IV Part Two* the mock-hero. The Prince has ultimately only one role, one destiny: a splendid figure of chivalric myth, the apotheosis of an antiquated culture already rendered archaic and ridiculous by Hotspur's suicidal violence and Falstaff's destructive satire.

It has of course been recognised, notably by Dover Wilson, that in relation to literary and dramatic tradition, Falstaff is a composite figure, a coalescence of various stock-figures – the morality vice, the bragging soldier, the parody-Puritan. But, for Dover Wilson and others, this heterogenous background points nonetheless to a consistent dramatic design and to a unified character with a coherent symbolic role in the play's ideological structure. At the heart of Dover Wilson's criticism is a contradiction: he attempts on the one hand to isolate from the composite 'character' the various identities that character assumes, thus liberating the 'actor' from his roles; yet he argues on the other hand that it is proper for Falstaff to be defined and judged, within the play and criticism, strictly in terms of those roles. There is an acknowledgment of the fluidity of this corporate, collective being who can play a highwayman, a Puritan, a morality vice, a bragging soldier all in the course of a few scenes; yet an intransigent insistence that the actor be severely punished for the evil implicit in some of his roles. Evidently there are difficulties of definition here: but if we think of Falstaff as a kind of professional player (like another of his ancestors, the licensed fool) it should be possible to differentiate the actor from his impersonations, while acknowledging that he exists as an actor only in the playing of these roles.

Dover Wilson's difficulty can be detected in his efforts to deal with the curious element of Puritanism in Falstaff's dramatic repertory, his tendency to deploy Puritan idiom, language and theological concepts. In seeking to incorporate this feature into a conception of coherent character, Dover Wilson (never shy of casuistical argument) has his ingenuity sorely stretched. The Puritan pose Falstaff adopts is, he claims, that of mock-repentance which should belong, in its genuine form, to the Prince, hero of the Prodigal Son myth alleged to be the play's true moral structure. But to show the Prince repenting would be to admit that he has done something of which to repent. 'Since Henry V is the ideal king of English history, Shakespeare must take great care, even in the days of his "wildness", to guard him from the breath of scandal'.[41] In order to protect the Prince's tender reputation, the role of repentant is transferred ('illogically', Dover Wilson admits) to Falstaff. Here lies the contradiction between moralistic and theatrical interpretation: if Falstaff is arbitrarily handed the role of Puritan – which exists therefore only as a specific and transient relation between actor and audience at a particular moment of the drama – then similarly *all* Falstaff's role could be regarded as separable from his character. Is Falstaff, perhaps, not so much a character who acts in certain ways, according to type, but rather one who has the character of an actor? That is not of course a punishable moral offence – unless Falstaff were to be consigned not to the Lord Chief Justice, but to the evangelical zeal of the theatre's enemies, Phillip Stubbes and William Prynne.

Falstaff's essential theatricality is recognized in an interesting passage by A. R. Humphreys in his Arden edition of *Henry IV Part One*:

> Who, in fact is 'he'? 'He', really, is the comic personality given a chance by the dramatist to revel in a comic role. . . . To schematise Falstaff's shotsilk variety into stable colour is absurd: his dramatic sphere of popular comedy allows a rapid shifting of attitudes. . . . The attempt to fix Falstaff into a formula of psychological realism must finally fail. Brilliant at timely evasions, he escapes this strait-jacket as he escapes any other.[42]

Yet these recognitions do not deter the writer from fitting Falstaff into a formula of *moral* realism: '. . . the king stands for rule, Falstaff for misrule, and Falstaff, like the rebel lords, is to be suppressed'.[43]

In the dramatic development itself, Falstaff's shift into Puritan discourse is abrupt, unprecedented and inexplicable. At one moment he is playing the mercurial highwayman, the gallant and eloquent outlaw possessed with the glamour of his occupation; within twenty lines he has adopted the sanctimonious accents of the stage-Puritan:

> I prithee sweet wag, shall there be gallows standing in England when thou art King? and resolution thus fubbed as it is with the rusty curb of old father Antic the law? Do not thou when thou art king hang a thief.
>
> (*1HIV*, i, ii, 56–60)

> . . . But Hal, I prithee trouble me no more with vanity . . . now am I, if a man should speak truly, little better than one of the wicked. I must give over this life, and I will give it over . . . if men were to be saved by merit, what hole in hell were hot enough for him?
>
> (*1HIV*, i, ii, 79–105)

The Prince satirizes this theological idiom as hypocrisy; his reply to Falstaff's nostalgia for repentance is to recall him to his original role, which is evidently more stimulating to the royal taste:

> *Prince.* Where shall we take a purse tomorrow Jack?
> *Fal.* 'Zounds, where thou wilt, lad . . .
> *Prince.* I see a good amendment of life in thee, from praying to purse-taking.
>
> (*1HIV*, i, ii, 96–100)

Poins, entering at the tail-end of this dialogue, shows himself familiar with the pose: 'What says Monsieur Remorse?' By *Henry IV Part Two*, Falstaff has shifted position again: still employing the same familiarity with scriptural idiom, he is now a satirist of Puritan merchants and tradesmen – the 'smooth-pates' (roundheads) of the City:

Let him be damned like the glutton! Pray God his tongue be
hotter! . . . The whoreson smooth-pates do now wear nothing
but high shoes and bunches of keys at their girdles . . .

(*2HIV*, I, ii, 34–9)

If these allusions to Puritanism are constituents of Falstaff's 'character', it would be necessary to produce a plausible psychological
explanation for his transition from convinced (though straying)
Calvinist to satirist of his former faith. There is plainly no profit
in this approach. In order to explore some more fruitful possibilities, it will be necessary to trace the historical origins of Falstaff's
puritanical streak.

I propose to regard the element of Puritanism in the light of two
perspectives, the theatrical and the historical; to demonstrate its
separate function in each context; and to clarify the nature of their
articulation.

Falstaff originated in a historical character very unlike Shakespeare's creation: Sir John Oldcastle, High Sheriff of Herefordshire,
'a valiant soldier and a hardy gentleman', who was associated with
the Lollard rebellion of Henry V's reign, and ultimately tried and
burnt as a Wycliffite heretic. Subsequent historical tradition first
condemned him as a heretic and fomenter of dissent, whose com-
panionship with Henry dated from the Prince's riotous youth; at
some point the 'heresy' of Oldcastle merged with the 'riotousness'
of Henry's legendary past, though factually the two are of course
quite antithetical. This fifteenth-century legend regarded Oldcastle
as a rebel justly punished by a prudent king. In the sixteenth century
his reputation was rehabilitated: after the Reformation the new
orthodoxy of writers like Bale, Halle and Foxe canonized him as a
martyr of the early Protestant faith. In terms of this perspective, his
rejection by the (Catholic) monarch was not for wildness, but for
the zeal and integrity of his belief. In the earliest acted versions of
Henry IV Part One, Falstaff was called Oldcastle (the name survives
as a speech-prefix '*Old*' at I, ii, 19 of the Quarto text); and the
Epilogue to *Henry IV Part Two* explicitly, if perhaps mischievously,
distinguishes Falstaff from Oldcastle. The alteration of names was
evidently a response to complaints against various plays (including
The Famous Victories of Henry V) dealing with the king's youth,
and including Oldcastle as one of his riotous companions, from
the Brooke family (Lords Cobham, descendants of Oldcastle, and

powerful nobles of Elizabeth's court). A dramatic riposte appeared in the form of a play (probably commissioned by the Brookes) written by four dramatists,[44] *The True and Honourable History of the Life of Sir John Oldcastle* (printed 1600), which reconstituted Oldcastle's memory as a Protestant martyr. Here Oldcastle–Falstaff becomes a model feudal lord (like Woodstock in the anonymous play) with a strong, though far from militant, Protestant faith. The king counsels him to 'forsake [his] gross opinion'; but Oldcastle insists that the only quality distinguishing his belief is his refusal to give allegiance to the Pope. Henry is not hostile to this view; he is 'loath to press' his subjects' consciences, and is satisfied with Oldcastle's loyalty, provided that he does not organise religious dissent (see *Oldcastle* II, iii). The play dissociates Oldcastle from the armed insurrection of Lollards; and equally from a plot of nobles (the Earl of Cambridge's conspiracy), to expect him to join them. Oldcastle is in complete agreement with the king on the subject of religion: the subject's conscience is in his own keeping, provided that it remains loyal to the sovereign; institutional reform of religious practices is a matter for the king. A captured Lollard rebel pleads that their motive was to seek 'Reformation of Religion'; to which Henry replies:

> Reforme religion! What it that ye sought?
> I pray who gave you that authority?
> Belike then, we do hold the sceptre up
> And sit within the throne but for a cipher.
>   (*Oldcastle*, IV, ii)

The play retrospectively resolves the historical conflicts of religion in the light of Henry VIII's Reformation: the king holds absolute power over state and church, and no subject has the 'authority' to question the king's judgment on practices of worship.

The serious and positive treatment of Puritanism in this play offers a sharp contrast with Shakespeare, and might lead us to suspect that in theatrical terms the Puritan elements in Falstaff's dramatic character was merely vestigial: the echoes of a character and a controversy long before forgotten, existing only in a clownish character in some popular comic histories, which ignored or remained oblivious of the bitter religious struggles of the early Protestant church, and revived into memory only by the intervention of some influential nobles, piqued at the blotting of their ancestor's escutcheon. Falstaff's Puritan parody and his anti- Puritan satire would have exactly the same function: that of inviting the audience to enjoy a burlesque on the popular butts of Elizabethan and Jacobean stage satire (cf. Ben Jonson's *The Alchemist* and *Bartholomew Fair*), with perhaps a concealed jibe at Puritan interference with the theatre. Falstaff's sorties into this are not, like Jonson's, sustained exercises in social and religious satire: they show a character simply 'dropping into' a style of comic performance familiar to the audience (a style which would amuse both the apprentices who served the City Puritans and the gentry who despised them), *for the sake of the performance alone.* The style is constructed as a temporary *rapprochement* between actor and audience, in which the audience relishes the actor's role-playing for its own sake; the question of integrating the role into a psychologically coherent 'character' would simply never arise.

The explanation provided by the theatrical context would, however, deprive the Puritan trace of *any* historical significance, while in fact the relevant historical context, though remote and difficult to link with the drama, exercises a visible determining pressure on it. If we consider Falstaff/Oldcastle not as an autonomous figure quite independent of historical determination, but as a mediation of real historical forces, we find that Shakespeare's play stands in an interesting relation to *The True and Honourable History.* Both plays are concerned with the personal relationship between the prince/king and a favourite, explored in a context of rebellion against the state – baronial conspiracy in both, in one a popular religious rising. The Percies' rebellion in *Henry IV Part One*, the Archbishop of York's conspiracy in *Henry IV Part Two*, and the Earl of Cambridge's plot in *The True and Honourable History* (as in *Henry V*) all represent the familiar pattern of aristocratic dissaffection with the power and policy of the crown. *The True and Honourable History* centres on a rebellion of a different kind. The Lollard rising (which certainly regarded Oldcastle as its leader, though his whereabouts on 9 January 1414 remains a mystery) was a popular insurrection of a general kind, led by members of the gentry articulating very widespread religious grievances and having as its motive the intention of capturing the king, destroying the clergy and re-establishing the Church on its original foundations of pure primitive Christianity. The practical power of the movement, thought not its broad strength of feeling, was exaggerated by contemporaries, who saw it as a revolutionary movement aimed at the wholesale demolition of the social fabric. It was certainly a serious threat (recognized as such by modern historians) and the only serious internal domestic disturbance Henry had to deal with throughout his reign. Its distinction is that like the Peasants' Revolt of the fourteenth century, it involved sections of the people and not just the great temporal lords and their private armies – many of those arrested and executed were craftsmen. *The True and Honourable History* is very concerned to attain a clear contemporary perspective on the event: to endorse its religious views and condemn its militant methods. The Lollard rebellion is an absence in *Henry IV*; an omission which, despite the importance attached to it by the chronicles, would not be strikingly surprising or significant (matters of religion were not lightly dealt with on Shakespeare's stage, except in orthodox and protected plays like *The True and Honourable History*) if it were not for the presence of Falstaff. Oldcastle is completely dissociated from any kind of subversive intention or activity, for the play, which purports to be an accurate historical account designed to set the record straight, is actually a blatant rewriting of history: it rehabilitates Oldcastle as a loyal, respectable middle-of-the-road Anglican ever willing to comply with his sovereign's policy on matters of religion, and denies him any revolutionary or subversive character. In *The True and Honourable History*, the leader of the Lollard rebellion ceases to be a heretic or a rebel; in *Henry IV* (although 'Oldcastle is not the man') he appears as both.

We are presented here with a remarkable historical pattern. In 1596–7, a mere forty years before Puritanism went to war against the king as a revolutionary force, Shakespeare was dramatizing the history of a period in which Protestantism, in a brief but striking presage of the future, appeared as the revolutionary force it was to become. Shakespeare did not treat the Lollard rebellion directly (though he knew of it from the chronicles, and had already displayed an interest in popular insurrection in *Henry VI Part Two*); and yet the sense in *Henry IV* of a second oppositional force, challenging the crown on a popular front separate from the familiar baronial struggle, is so strong as to have been universally recognized. Within the composite character of Falstaff appear details which echo those past and future struggles, implicitly invoking a hidden history, signifying by concealment a genuinely

radical historical force. What had been (and would become again) a
serious threat to royal sovereignty appears, not as itself, but *transformed into comedy*: the political saturnalia of *Henry VI Part Two*
becomes the moral saturnalia of *Henry IV Part One*. Both envisage
and ardently desire the over-turning of the world: one in fantasy,
the other in deadly earnest.

One possible explanation for this transformation of popular resistance into comic opposition is that of censorship and ideological
constraint: real historical pressures calculated to deflect oppositional
energies into fantasy. But this is only partially satisfactory: even without censorship Shakespeare could hardly be imagined writing a
partisan account of a Puritan or popular rebellion. The rising dramatized in *Henry VI Part Two* is clearly a mirror-image of the
destructiveness of the feudal nobility, and Cade's utopian fantasies
are imaginatively attractive: but the play deflects any sympathetic
or supportive responses; there is no viable solution here to the
historical problems of feudalism. Utopian fantasy as it appears
in Falstaff, in its anarchistic resistance to available political alter-
natives, constitutes a political discourse uncompromising in its ex-
tremity of demand for freedom, peace, justice and plenty. Falstaff's
utopian cry, 'Shall there be gallows standing in England when thou
art king?' seems universally accepted as a piece of egoistic criminal
ambition; even in a society which has rejected the barbarity of
capital punishment, it rarely strikes anyone that this image of a
society without punishment is a vigorous and beautiful dream of
human aspiration. Utopian anarchism demands freedom without
limit: though never wholly practicable, its validity consists in its
restless and insatiable interrogation of practical politics. Such a
spirit would demand of a Lollard rebellion or a Puritan revolution –
as indeed the utopianism of radical sects was to demand in the
seventeenth century – liberty for whom, and on what terms?

The metaphor of drama itself, self-reflexively contained within a
dramatic action, and through it the various meanings and associations of 'play', is the most natural symbol – both signifier and
embodiment – of the festive, carnival principle. Attendance at a
play in Shakespeare's London was, literally, for those who laboured
for their living, a holiday: as performances took place in daylight
they inevitably overlapped with the disciplines of work (one of the
great objections of the City to the theatre was that it 'seduced
idle persons from their labours'). The theatre was (as it still is) a

privileged space of special licence and liberty, in which there can take place a suspension of the ordinary rules and conventions of social order: a place in which 'play' temporarily becomes a norm. The stubborn realities of existence become malleable in the solvent of theatrical fantasy: rigid hierarchical relations can be inverted, kings can become clowns and vice versa; the stage presents the compelling image of a humanity able to transform itself by acts of will, able to liberate itself from the intransigence of historical fact. In one sense, Elizabethan theatre was actually a modern, secularized form of those ancient religious rituals discussed earlier: an attenuated form, since the participant in a religious ritual has become the fee-paying spectator who only watches the enactment of a symbolic rite. Like the popular drama which influenced it, the Elizabethan drama performed some of the functions of saturnalian ritual. Certainly the very close association, characteristic of this period, between the drama and various forms of popular entertainment (bear and bull-baiting, fencing, juggling, clowning, dance, song and feasting) suggests a general connection with carnival. A visit to a theatre must have been a festive, holiday occasion and experience. In an important scene of *Henry IV Part One*, drama is explicitly foregrounded as an emblem of the licence, liberty and festive ritual associated with Falstaff: drama becomes the appropriate metaphor for the play's internally oppositional carnival culture.

The 'play extempore', performed in *Henry IV Part One*, II, iv by Falstaff and the Prince, is located in one of the originating venues of metropolitan dramatic art – a tavern. Inn-yards, in which the troupes of travelling players would perform their shows, were the normal focus of playing before the construction of purpose-built theatres which began in 1576, and various London taverns (the Red Bull, the Bell, the Bel Savage, the Cross Keys) continued to compete with the public playhouses until 1594, when the Privy Council banned inns still used as inns from staging plays. The Boar's Head in Whitechapel simply changed its function, as did the Red Bull, from inn to playhouse: retaining its taproom, together with four parlours and eleven bedrooms.[45] The scene invokes an image of drama as spontaneous improvisation and as popular entertainment, taking place in a locale dedicated to pleasure and holiday licence. As always when Shakespeare employs the device of play-within-a-play, the foregrounding of dramatic conventions is effective in inducing a consciousness of the medium itself, an attitude of critical curiosity towards the artifice of the play; in this case as the actors (already fitted with their characters) play out roles of considerable significance to their 'real' (i.e. dramatic) lives, the device operates to disclose the contradiction between the infinite flexibility and changebleness of popular mimetic forms – improvisation, burlesque, parody, inversion, topsy-turveydom – and the intransigent rigidity of social fact, of historical necessity or of theatrical chronicle.

The prince has already earlier in the scene performed an impromptu imitation of Hotspur, and proposed that Falstaff should assist him in acting out Percy's relations with his wife. The genuine peril represented by Hotspur is absented but implied by the Prince's fantastic caricature: we are made aware that this revelry is taking place in a space of temporary freedom circumscribed by the urgent calls of historical destiny. A messenger from the court bearing news of the rebellion is 'sent packing' by Falstaff at Hal's request: an atmosphere of holiday is established in explicit contradiction to the summonses of duty and public responsibility. The dissolution of the kingdom into civil war calls forth from the assembled company only enthusiastic fantasies of pleasure in destruction, of utopian longings fulfilled by the breakdown of political authority:

> *Fal.*   Worcester is stolen away tonight; thy father's beard is
> turned white with the news; you may buy land now as
> cheap as stinking mackerel.
> *Prince.* Why then, it is like if there come a hot June, and this civil
> buffeting hold, we shall buy maidenheads as they buy
> hob-nails, by the hundreds.
> *Fal.*   By the mass, lad, thou sayest true, it is like we shall have
> good trading that way.
>
> (*1HIV*, ii, iv, 354–61)

The Arden editor interprets this as an anticipation of moral inhibitions slackening in the heat of civil conflict: but such an explanation fails to take into account the implications of 'buying' and 'trading': or the proximity of this sexist fantasy to Hotspur's macho antics of the previous scene, which display the chivalric hero renouncing the romantic elements of his culture and privileging male violence as an absolute value:

> . . . This is no world
> To play with mammets, and to tilt with lips . . .
>
> (*1HIV*, ii, iii)

This quality of 'honour' which has become so aggressively contemptuous towards women, is demystified in Hal's and Falstaff's talk
of buying and selling maidenheads: the likely result of Hotspur's
archaic violence is the world of the unscrupulous commercial
entrepreneur, exploiting a free-market economy in which the most
precious human attributes are reduced to commodities. Hal and
Falstaff provide a comic-carnivalizing critique of the chivalric hero's
feudal fantasies (already opened to interrogation by the comedy of
Hotspur himself): the real world is criticised by living out a fantasy
of its dissolution.

The shift into improvised drama immediately makes possible
the central action of carnival misrule: the crowning of the fool
as king:

> *Prince.* Do thou stand for my father and examine me upon the
> particulars of my life.
> *Fal.* Shall I? Content! This chair shall be my state, this dagger
> my sceptre, and this cushion my crown.
> *Prince.* Thy state is taken for a joint-stool, thy golden sceptre
> for a leaden dagger, and they precious rich crown for a
> pitiful bald crown.
>
> (*1HIV*, ii, iv, 371–7)

The art being practised here is that of parody and travesty; the style
burlesque; the perspective satirical. The burlesque style consists in
calling attention to those dramatic properties which would normally
function as meaningful signs within the conventions of a specific
dramatic discourse: when prised away from that discourse and
examined as material objects, they appear trivial and absurd by
comparison with what they would otherwise 'naturally' signify.
(The Chorus in *Henry V* similarly calls attention to the 'vile and
ragged foils' which an audience would otherwise cheerfully accept
as emblematic of the broadswords of Agincourt.) This passage from
Henry IV Part One compares interestingly with a similar passage
from Thomas Heywood's *Edward the Fourth Part Two*, describing
an analogous tavern improvisation:

> Then comes a slave, one of these drunken sots,
> In with a tavern-reckoning for a supplication,
> Disguised with a cushion on his head,
> A drawers apron for a heralds coat,
> And tells the Court, the King of England craves
> One of his worthy honours dog-kennels,
> To be his lodgings for a day or two,
> With some such other tavern-foolery.[46]

Here the burlesque style is more in the reportage than in the original act of improvisation: intoxicated with the power of his own foolery, this 'slave' seems far less aware than the narrator of the absurdity of his performance. The satirical edge is directed towards the ludicrous pretensions involved in the act of counterfeiting royal majesty with common domestic materials. The paired opposites – 'tavern-reckoning' / 'supplication', 'cushion' / 'crown', 'drawers apron' / 'heralds coat', 'dog-kennel' / 'lodging' – operate ironically to confirm the distance separating royalty from the low-life of the tavern, majesty from everyday living. In Shakespeare the burlesque is already present in the playing, explicitly inserted as a constituent of the performance by an acknowledged master of parody and satire. The mockery is not simply directed *against* Falstaff as a pretender to undeserved status and royal celebrity: it is directed against the pomp and ceremony of royalty itself and against certain dramatic discourses which in their inflated rhetoric and linguistic esotericism render the high style of monarchic culture vulnerable to satirical demystification.[47]

Falstaff's reference to his stage-properties is technically an act of dramatic construction: it signals the inception of a temporary theatrical illusion, dependent upon a tacit agreement with the audience. The Prince promptly deconstructs what Falstaff has constructed; he alienates the audience from any possibility of further dramatic illusion by explicitly drawing attention to the mundanity of the materials on which such illusion (in this kind of theatre) is always based. The Prince's use of 'alienation-effect' does not however destroy the dramatic potentiality of the improvisation: between them the two actors construct something analogous to the Chorus in *Henry V* which simultaneously calls upon the audience to accept dramatic conventions and to be consciously aware of their arbitrary and artificial nature. We believe that the actor really is

Falstaff, we are not going to believe that he becomes the king: yet we are willing to accept a theatrical simulation, which the Prince's demystifying satire does not disperse, since it is already self-consciously and self-reflexively theatrical. Falstaff himself enacts his role with a plentiful use of such burlesque devices, irony flourishing in the space between language and object:

> Give me a cup of sack, to make my eyes look red . . .
>
> Stand aside, nobility . . .
>
> [*To the Hostess*] Weep not, sweet Queen, for trickling tears are vain.

The Hostess herself extends this technique to an overt recognition of the actor behind the role:

> O Jesu, he doth it as like one of these harlotry players as ever I see!

Falstaff's parody of royalty and of academic drama comes to an end when the Prince insists on their exchanging roles so that he can play the king:

> Does thou speak like a king? Do thou stand for me, and I'll play my father.

This gesture is effectively a re-inversion of carnival, a deposing of the crowned fool and his replacement by the true heir apparent. Falstaff continues to enjoy the freedom of dramatic impersonation, while the Prince takes on a role suspiciously like that allotted to him by his historical destiny. The open space of dramatic liberty is clearly narrowing: though at this point it is not entirely foreclosed, and the show goes on. In response to the Prince's mock-catechism Falstaff recalls the roaring boy of *The Famous Victories*, and deploys the linguistic freedom of popular drama:

> *Prince.* The complaints I hear of thee are grevious.
>
> *Fal.*   'Sblood, my lord, they are false: nay, I'll tickle ye for a young prince, i'faith.

It is surely misleading to understand the Prince's diatribe which follows simply as a homily of moral exhortation. Critics and editors have noted the references to morality-plays ('grace . . . devil . . . vice . . . iniquity . . . vanity'), the denunciatory images of gluttony and disease, the moral antitheses which seem to lock Falstaff firmly into the framework of an implied ethical orthodoxy: 'reverend . . . grey . . . father . . . good . . . cunning . . . worthy' here systematically contrasted with 'vice . . . iniquity . . . vanity . . . villainy . . . craft'. But the prince's verbal assault is composed entirely in that discourse of grotesque fantasy we have noted as a common language linking him with Falstaff: the inflated images of enormous bodies, insatiable appetites, food and drink ('huge bombard of sack, . . . stuffed cloak-bag of guts . . . roasted Manningtree ox with the pudding in his belly') and the interestingly varied associations of the town of Manningtree in Essex, documented by the Arden edition (feasting, fairs, popular drama and civil disturbance) elicit not moralistic disgust but excitement at the caricaturing absurdity of carnival fantasy. In the final, authentic renunciation of Falstaff the Prince is very careful to avoid such language, well aware that indulgence in it links him firmly to Falstaff's oppositional discourse:

> Leave gormandizing; know the grave doth gape
> For thee thrice wider than for other men.
> Reply not to me with a fool-born jest, . . .
>   (*2HIV*, v, iv, 54–6)

From a moralistic perspective the Prince's speech of II, iv is a diatribe of disgust: from the point of view of popular, carnival culture a hymn to the grotesque bodily image. Even the series of moral antitheses can be regarded as old age affecting youthful vice: or as the power of the grotesque to fuse age and youth in a single moment. The morality-play Vice is clearly the most interesting theatrical 'character' in such drama; and similarly the image of the incurably vicious ruffian is more attractive than that of the grey reverend father to which it is opposed. But the energy, vitality, dramatic richness and satirical gusto of the scene are provided by the *style* which holds the opposites together in creative dialectic. Carnival and popular theatre are here identified: those popular forms which signify freedom and changeableness, variety and contradiction, the *rapprochement* of different discourses, jointly oppose the rigidity of official culture. Carnival liberty is opposed to historical necessity.

The effect of this speech on Falstaff is sufficient to indicate that it partially conceals an authoritarian motive: the celebration of holiday is constrained within a rigid adherence to the order of 'everyday'. Falstaff's immediate reaction to the Prince's speech is a masterly stroke of theatre which easily upstages the phoney king – systematic comic misunderstanding:

> I would your grace would take me with you: whom means your Grace?

But this gives way to a speech of defence and justification which involves a curious reduction of that gargantuan, mythical 'tun of man' to a mere name, reiterated with obsessive repetitiousness, as if under the pressure of an implicit moral rejection the popular collective being shrinks closer to the defensive security of the 'isolated bourgeois ego':

> . . . sweet Jack Falstaff, kind Jack Falstaff, true Jack Falstaff, valiant Jack Falstaff . . .

Falstaff already seems to have a whole school of tongues in that belly of his, which pronounce no other word but his name. This shrinkage of identity, this sharp concentration of the ego, has occurred as the aspirations and liberties of carnival have been subordinated to the calculating anxiety of an uneasy state:

> *Fal.*   . . . banish plump Jack, and banish all the world.
>
> *Prince.* I do, I will.
>
> (*1HIV*, ii, iv, 474–5)

Shakespeare made the Battle of Shrewsbury both a historical and a theatrical climax to the first part of *Henry IV*. In terms of historical pattern, the battle appears to be a decisive defeat for the rebel forces (although the play acknowledges by a number of details that the rebellion is far from over), a reclamation of the Prince to moral obligation and public responsibility, a unification of the hitherto divided royal family. Dramatically, the battle was the kind of theatrical action and spectacle that popular audiences delighted in: the title given to the play in the Stationers' Register for 1597 (1598), and the title pages of all the Quarto editions promote the 'Battel', together with 'the conceipted mirthe of Sir John Fastolf' as major attractions. For a popular audience the duel of the two heroes must have functioned much like a Hollywood western show-down: and the continuity of that ancient heroic pattern (older than the *Iliad*, as new as the latest spaghetti western) tends to universalize it, to separate the heroic combat from the specific historical context which produced it. The significance of the duel between prince and heroic rebel was not necessarily confined to the 'theme of England': the destiny of the nation, the fate of the Lancastrian dynasty recede as the decisive issue becomes reduced to the primitive ritual pattern of single combat, man to man; a pattern which could offer an audience voluntary participation in an ideology of war seemingly detached from the complex historical determinants of the general conflict.

To put it another way: is the Battle of Shrewsbury a crucial struggle for national defence, or a testing of particular individuals in a trial of chivalry? We have already seen that there can be no straightforward identification of the two. Both issues are present in the play, but there is a rigid division of significance between the different characters. For the king, Shrewsbury is a defence of the public order and the legitimate government against an unjustified insurrection. The king addresses Worcester:

> You have deceiv'd our trust . . .
> . . . Will you again unknit
> This churlish knot of all-abhorred war,
> And move in that obedient orb again
> Where you did give a fair and natural light,
> And be no more an exhal'd meteor,
> A prodigy of fear, and a portent
> Of broached mischief to the unborn times?
>   (*1HIV*, v, i, 11, 15–21)

In seeking to overthrow the established regime the rebels have committed a betrayal of 'trust': where the Lancastrian monarchy guarantees stability, the rebels seek to introduce change: 'hurly-burly innovation', 'pellmell havoc and confusion'. The political language is elaborated by the metaphors of planetary movement into a discourse which sanctions the Lancastrian power as a 'natural' structure – the nobleman should be a satellite to the kingly sun, his motion disciplined to an orbit of obedience, not displaying the erratic independence of the meteor, out of place and pattern. For the king, the issue is political and metaphysical: the state must be defended, not merely because it represents order and stability, but because its order is a function of the natural order of the universe.

When the Prince intervenes, the language of political and universal order gives way to the discourse of chivalry:

> Tell your nephew,
> The Prince of Wales doth join with all the world
> In praise of Henry Percy: by my hopes,
> This present enterprise set off his head,
> I do not think a braver gentleman,
> More active-valiant or more valiant-young,
> More daring or more bold, is now alive
> To grace this latter age with noble deeds.
> (*1HIV*, v, i, 83–92)

To the Prince, Shrewsbury is not a struggle to establish peace and justice, but an ordeal of chivalry with his rival Hotspur, an opportunity to display chivalric prowess, to 'try fortune with him in a single fight'. The language is elaborately courteous ('I do not think a braver gentleman'), heroic ('valiant . . . daring . . . bold') and consciously archaic – 'To grace this latter age with noble deeds' actually admits that the proffered challenge echoes a heroic age of the distant past. Though the king admires his son's new-found chivalric manner, he brushes aside the idea of a trial by combat with as little ceremony as Octavius can be imagined using when dismissing Mark Antony's challenge: 'Albeit, considerations infinite/ Do make against it' (v, i, 102–3). By adopting the language of chivalry the Prince detaches himself from the tangled complexity of 'considerations infinite' and writes the competition between himself and Hotspur into a vivid poem of feudal romance and chivalric adventure, where justice is guaranteed by the victory of the sword.

The Prince's foregrounding of heroic values, his marginalizing of political issues by the apparent universality of chivalric romance, determine the specific character of Falstaff's intervention into Shrewsbury. In his 'misuse of the king's press', his unscrupulous exploitation of his recruits, he is clearly subverting the values of the state as embodied in the king, setting individual appropriation higher than the good of the commonwealth, rejecting not only the discipline of war, but all the public responsibilities of a subject. He appears to espouse an individualist and exploitative ideology. Yet the energies of carnival, the grotesque imagination and the physical appetites of the material body are still there to interrogate the values of war: metaphors of food and drink culminate in a final couplet which explicitly evaluates fighting in terms of feasting:

> Fill me a bottle of sack . . . soused gurnet . . . toasts and butter . . . cream . . . butter . . .
> To the latter end of a fray, and the beginning of a feast
> Fits a dull fighter and a keen guest.
>
> *(1HIV*, IV, ii, *passim)*

To emphasize only the accumulative and exploitative quality of this, as Elliot Krieger does, is to oversimplify. Falstaff is not an individualist speculator articulating his exploitative ideology in metaphors of consumption: his discourse is still linked to the carnivalizing imagination, which proposes a healthy appetite for physical pleasure, a professional sensuality, as superior to the strenuous discipline and heroic sacrifices of war. There is an implicit appeal to positive values rooted in common emotion and popular sentiment, despite the fact that those values are contradictorily harnessed to an individualist ideology. Just as in the 'play extempore' we saw the collective being of Falstaff forced into the defensiveness of an isolated ego by the pressures of moral exhortation and political anxiety, so here the harsh exigencies of battle, which enforce strict uniformity by the most rigid code of discipline, leave the dissenter insufficient space to cultivate a coherent opposition, and press him towards the escapist device of individual evasion. The position of the deserter is always contradictory: according to military codes desertion is the grossest act of cowardice and betrayal, the sin that cannot be forgiven; yet from outside that code we view the deserter sympathetically, as representative of a fundamental right of dissent, the final option for challenging the values of war by individual abstention. Falstaff's language and behaviour articulate an opposition of values: feasting against fighting, carnival against chivalry; the common sense of the good soldier Schweik against the suicidal violence of the military hero.

The quality of Falstaff's opposition is the more potent because the Lancastrian ideology of war is, at this stage, so incurably feudal and chivalric: hence Falstaff's major contribution to the interrogation of war is not his comic travesty of recruitment but his 'catechism' of the dominant chivalric value, 'honour'. He expresses, not a comprehensive indictment of war, but a challenge to the kind of thirst for individual honour which motivates Hotspur and (apparently) the Prince. Falstaff criticizes the fragile insubstantiality of this noble virtue, its irrelevance to the real business of living for the common people, to whom honour is indeed 'a mere scutcheon', a dusty heralidic ensign decorating the tomb of a dead aristocrat. In this context, Falstaff's irrepressible demand: 'Give me life!', is more potent and persuasive than a plea for personal excusal. Insofar as war is defined in terms of military honour, chivalric adventure, feudal romance, the popular voice can identify it as an alien occupation; insofar as the 'order' of the state is bound up with those values (as we have seen it to be in the contradictory consciousness of the king and the heroic role-playing of the prince) it renders itself equally vulnerable to question. When the Prince meets Falstaff on the battle-field, and urges him strenuously to take the fighting seriously, it is in the name of 'honour' that he appeals:

> What, stands thou idle here? Lend me my sword:
> Many a nobleman lies stark and stiff
> Under the hoofs of vaunting enemies,
> Whose deaths are yet unrevenged.
>   (*HIV*, v, iii, 40–4)

Falstaff again opposes war with carnival: his pistol-case contains a bottle of sack. The prince's question 'is it a time to jest and dally now?' seems to brook no qualification: yet for a popular audience unimplicated in the revenge code of the feudal nobility, in the 'holiday' of a theatre, the answer cannot be guaranteed. A distinct note of popular sentiment is introduced into the scene by Falstaff's reference to 'Turk Gregory':

> Turk Gregory never did such deeds in arms as I have done this day . . .

The parody of heroic language focuses (apparently) on Gregory

XIII, a warlike Pope, demonized by Protestant writers, who, according to Dover Wilson, 'was in 1579 fighting with Nero and the Grand Turk as one of "the three tyrants of the world" in coloured prints sold on the streets of London'.[48] Falstaff uses these figures of popular culture to turn the Battle of Shrewsbury into a mummers' play. Popular and establishment discourses are juxtaposed to produce a confrontation of values: and the audience which delighted in the show-down between Hotspur and the Prince was also given the opportunity to register its preference for holiday over battle, for Falstaff's comic travesty over the Prince's stern chivalric resolution.

We are not simply presented with an antithesis of individual perspectives in Falstaff and the Prince: the interaction between the chronicle and comic dramatic modes permits a flexible interaction of the various characters, king, prince and clown. This can be illustrated by exploring the link between the feigned death of Falstaff and the 'counterfeiting' employed by the king. As I have shown disguise functions differently in comic and in chronicle history plays. *Henry IV Part One* employs a mixed method, in which the king's disguise is a comic device used successfully to evade a tragic situation. The king does not disguise himself, but disguises others as himself: he thus becomes one with his subjects, but sheds his vulnerability to them, and they die as sacrifices to preserve the monarch's safety. When Falstaff feigns death his 'counterfeiting' parallels the king's: both use disguise to extricate themselves from danger; just as Falstaff can be killed and rise again, so the king can apparently die and be resurrected. Comic history, with its magical power to transform rigid historical fact into fantasy, is consciously manipulated by Henry for his own ends; temporarily and by proxy he participates in what is Falstaff's natural mode of existence.

The chronicle-history climaxes with the death of Hotspur: the high-point of the set-piece battle is the heroic duel, ornamented with formal speeches of defiance from each hero, *in extremis* confession from the vanquished, courteous tribute to the slain enemy by the victor.

The Prince's epitaph on Percy and his corresponding tribute to Falstaff appear to constitute an appropriate point of closure: the twin speeches achieve a balance of styles, a unity of action, the sense of a pattern approaching completion. The Prince displays equal generosity to both his dramatic rivals, balanced between the heroic peroration for Hotspur and the comic tribute to Falstaff. Heroic death absolves Hotspur from the 'ignominy' of rebellion, which should be effaced from his epitaph; what remains of him is the corpse of a 'gentleman' purged of all 'ill-weaved ambition', passively unresistant to the Prince's elaborate display of courtesy. Falstaff's 'scutcheon' signifies no honour, but is a *plaudite* for the success of his dramatic role – 'Death hath not struck so fat a deer today' (v, iv, 106) – an applause tempered with a definitive moral qualification:

> O, I should have a heavy miss of thee
> If I were much in love with vanity.
> (v, iv, 104–5)

What Falstaff, and through him the popular dramatic tradition that he represents, can contribute to the formal aesthetic and moral closure of the chronicle-history form is the element of predictable but surprising change: predictable because we are not *really* surprised when Falstaff rises from death, since we recognize it as characteristic, but surprising because we experience the liberation of a fantasy resurrection violating the aesthetic unity imposed by the Prince's exit. The comedian returns, and the jaws of death prove to be a set of false teeth. The irresistible energy of popular drama insists on variety and changeableness in continuity, subverts the neat balancing and synthesis of formal chronicle drama, and throws the action again into the openness of infinite possibility.

> Embowell'd? If thou embowel me today, I'll give you leave to powder me and eat me too tomorrow.
> (v, iv, 110–11)

The disparate associations here of 'embowel' form a pun which enacts the confrontation of history and holiday: the insatiable physical appetites of the material body deny the harsh necessitarianism of death, in a play of possibilities only the theatre can enact.

The difference between the king's counterfeiting and Falstaff's is that while the king's is opportunist, Falstaff's belongs properly to popular drama: it is clowning and parodic, it inverts and fractures the permitted framework of chronicle history to re-create the delight of a world re-made in the image of fantasy. Though the

Prince was himself the agent of attempted closure, he pays hearty tribute to Falstaff's capacity to resist and deny it. In doing so he not only embraces and extends toleration to the carnival spirit; he also admits that his own attitude to 'honour' remains not unlike Falstaff's. Hotspur died regretting the loss of honour more than that of life; Falstaff siezes honour he has no right or claim to; the Prince gives up honour as soon as he acquires it, as though the death of Percy was more significant politically than in terms of heroic victory or chivalric achievement.

The ultimate collision and sundering of the Prince and Falstaff, the famous 'rejection-scene' at the end of *Henry IV Part Two* is enacted by a final confrontation of patrician and plebian dramatic discourses, of ruling-class and popular cultures. The occasion is a national ritual of church and state, the coronation of the Prince as King Henry V. The King has already, in v, ii, articulated the ideology of national unity and social harmony which the coronation pageant is designed to celebrate: he has made peace with his brothers and the nobility, and assured the Lord Chief Justice that 'the great body of our state' (defined here, in the standard Elizabethan usage, as the joint power of king and nobility, 'prince and peer', not as the whole body of society) is safely and harmoniously reintegrated. The royal progress to Westminster Abbey, a formal ritual expressing political and ecclesiastical dignity and power, is, however, accompanied or pursued by a procession of a different kind: a grotesque antimasque which falls into a parodic and oppositional relation to the majesty and solemnity of the royal pageant:

> *Trumpets sound, the King and his train pass over the stage: after them enter Falstaff, Shallow, Pistol, Bardolph, and the Page.*

Falstaff's company attempts to transform the coronation into a carnival, in which the clown can speak with familiarity of the king as an equal – 'God save thee, my sweet boy!' – and in which the subversive energies of saturnalism licence challenge the formality of patrician ritual with a comic flurry of intense dramatic activity:

> *Fal.* [*to Shallow*] O, if I had had time to have made new liveries,
>   I would have bestowed the thousand pound I borrowed of

you. But 'tis no matter, this poor show doth better, infer the zeal I had to see him.

Shal. It doth so.

Fal. It shows my earnestness of affection –

Shal. It doth so.

Fal. My devotion –

Shal. It doth, it doth, it doth.

Fal. As it were, to ride day and night, and not to deliberate, not to remember, not to have patience to shift me –

Shal. It is best, certain.

Fal. But to stand, stained with travel, and sweating with desire to see him, thinking of nothing else, putting all affairs else in oblivion, as if there were nothing else to be done but to see him . . .

Pist. My knight, I will inflame thy noble liver,
And make thee rage.
Thy Doll, and Helen of thy noble thoughts,
Is in base durance and contagious prison,
Hal'd thither
By most mechanical and dirty hand.
Rouse up Revenge from ebon den with fell Alecto's snake,
For Doll is in.

                                        (*2HIV*, v, v, 11–38)

Falstaff dramatizes himself in yet another role, that of the parasite or flattering courtier: his speeches are not, as the sentimentalists held, earnest protestations of personal affection, but self-conscious, impersonal role-plays in which he constructs himself a character by self-reflexive caricature. He is supported on the one hand by Shallow's opportunistic encouragement, and on the other by Pistol's rhetorical indignation. This parodic antimasque confronts the official ritual with the dynamic energies of comic drama; with the flexibility and dramatic freedom of the comic-history mode, in which characters can act free of historical determination; with a *rapprochement* of different styles – the naturalistic situation, for example, in which Falstaff mingles with a crowd at a public event, is incongruously juxtaposed with Pistol's incurable penchant for literary parody. Dover Wilson's reaction to this conjuncture will give a fair indication of its true quality: he imposes a rhetorical insistence on preserving intact the solemnity of the coronation ritual, freeing its inviolable sacredness from the threat of parody or subversion:

> . . . at this moment, with the crown of England newly placed upon his head, the chrism still glistening upon his forehead, and his spirit uplifted by one of the most solemn acts of dedication and consecration which the Christian Church has to offer, all his thoughts will be concentrated upon the great task to which he has been called, its duties and responsibilities.[50]

Meanwhile the Falstaff-action is condemned in a revealing phrase: v, iv, in which Doll is hauled to prison by most mechanical and dirty hand, is described as 'gruesome-grotesque', displaying 'the ugliest side of Eastcheap life'. Bakhtin defined the 'grotesque' as the characteristic style of carnival discourse: here the word has lost all positive meaning and is used as a term of moral opprobrium. There can be no room in this orthodox, rehabilitating criticism for a sympathetic view of the grotesque, of carnival, of comic opposition: those styles which exist to 'consecrate inventive freedom', to encourage the *rapprochement* of different discourses, to liberate from the prevailing point of view of the world, must have their functions severely limited, subordinated to the hegemony of moral order, political hierarchy and the oppressive uniformity of an official culture.

The Prince's speech of rejection (v, v, 47) imposes on the situation silence, stillness and formality; and establishes a definite rupture between official and popular cultures. His accents are those of the City attacking the popular drama:

> How ill white hairs become a fool and jester!

Confronted by the miraculous and comic resurrection of Falstaff on the field of Shrewsbury (reminiscent of popular dramas such as the mummers' plays) at the end of *Henry IV Part One*, the Prince acknowledges the power invoked by that dramatic *tour de force*:

> . . . is it fantasy that plays upon our eyesight?
> (*1HIV*, v, iv, 134)

On becoming king he renounces both the playful freedom of theatrical illusion and the generous humour of saturnalian liberty:

> . . . being awak'd, I do despise my dream.
> *(2HIV*, v, v, 52)

Prior to Shakespeare's drama there existed a tradition of popular culture, a sub-culture, incorporated into yet intrinsically in tension with the official culture of the Tudor nation-state. This culture was democratic and utopian rather than hierarchical and pragmatic, imaginative and fantastic rather than realistic and historicist. It voiced some of the aspirations of sections of the common people – peasant, artisan, apprentice, lower bourgeoisie and clergy; and above all, it was, to some degree, *hostile* to the official culture which sanctioned it. In view of all this it is possible to detach the figure of Falstaff from the moralistic perspective into which the play fails to place him, and into which criticism since the early twentieth century has struggled to incorporate him, and to recognize as positive and liberating many aspects of the figure which seem, from the moralistic perspective, to be negative and oppressing. The important thing to recognise is that these dramas bring into play separate and incompatible visions of history; they identify the popular vision with the institution of drama itself; they celebrate the dialectical conflict of these contradictory cultural energies; and they articulate a profound regret at the final effect of closure which signals the impending victory of one dominant conception of 'history' over the complex plurality of Renaissance historiographical practices.

Chapter Seven

Reproductions: Henry V

THE year 1944 represents a remarkable focus of Shakespeare reproduction, and a decisive moment in the ideological reconstruction of the English history plays, especially *Henry V*. 1944 saw the appearance of three texts which represent three different ideological interventions into the culture of war-time Britain: all concerned generally with Shakespeare, particularly with the English history plays, and pre-eminently with *Henry V*. G. Wilson Knight published a patriotic essay, *The Olive and the Sword*, which had been printed as a pamphlet in 1940, and performed as a play.[1] Laurence Olivier's film of *Henry V*, in the making since 1943, was released. Finally there appeared the text which has already concerned us, and which has proved by far the most influential: E. M. Tillyard's *Shakespeare's History Plays*.

In the 1930s critics associated with the *Scrutiny* movement had consolidated 'Shakespeare' as an ideological force of cultural and national unity: in the dual form of a *historical* constituting of Shakespeare as the authentic voice of an organically homogeneous period of English culture; and a *literary-critical* emphasis on textual reading as the only surviving means available of participating in and reconstructing that lost totality. *Scrutiny* insisted on the social provenance and social relevance of literature: but nonetheless privileged *criticism* as the only effective means of gaining access to or recreating the lost harmony of English culture. The social effects of the Second World War placed this ideology under some pressure. The national war effort demanded total participation from every section of society: culture too should apply its powers to the necessary and immediate tasks in hand. *Scrutiny* went its own way, scarcely acknowledging the existence of war. But other kinds of cultural intervention took the call to arms seriously. As both the national poet and a symbol of organic unity in British society,

Shakespeare was clearly a candidate for enlistment. The spirit of his 'patriotism' was evoked very early: on 22 February 1939, Neville Chamberlain was quoting from *King John*:

Come the three corners of the world in arms,
And we shall shock them . . .[2]

Wilson Knight's essay represents an early attempt to force literary criticism into the public arena: to break away from *Scrutiny's* concentration on the text and on academic reconstruction, to place the ideological power of 'Shakespeare' at the service of the national war effort.

At this point 'Shakespeare', as the visible, concrete embodiment of a lost social harmony, was brought into direct complicity with that ideology of national unity which the leading sections of British society – government, press and broadcasting media, trade union leadership – were fighting to forge and perpetuate throughout the war. This powerful myth of national unity has been subjected recently to some interrogation by historians, who have demonstrated some of the mechanisms of its construction, and exposed some of the less heroic realities of war on the Home Front. Angus Calder's book on British society in the Second World War seriously questions the myth of the People's War:[3] his evidence and arguments emphasize the discontent as well as the heroism, the persistence of social divisions and conflicts from the 1930s as well as the development of new more open social relationships. His conclusion is that the war brought no fundamental change in British society:

> Those who made the 'People's War' a slogan argued that the war could promote a revolution in British society. After 1945, it was for a long time fashionable to talk as if something like a revolution had in fact occurred. But at this distance, we see clearly enough that the effect of the war was not to sweep society on to a new course, but to hasten its progress along the old grooves.[4]

And Henry Pelling's *Britain in the Second World War*[5] confirms this view that the war did not lead to profound social changes.

This historical problem can be seen as the context in which to describe and evaluate these cultural interventions into a national crisis. If the large scale social changes which actually *did* take place – the spread of democratic participation in social life, the breaking-down of class barriers, the employment of women, etc. – did not succeed in creating a new society, it must in some measure be due to the success of those political and cultural forces which succeeded in reconstructing British society on the old lines. An examination of the process by which some elements of that myth were constructed may throw some light on the nature of the myth itself.

G. Wilson Knight's essay is as much a piece of war-time propaganda as an essay in literary criticism – if anything, more propaganda than scholarship, since the starting-point of the argument is very explicitly not 'literature' but the contemporary situation. His language is not the mannered urbanity of scholarly discourse, but the fierce rhetoric proper to a national crisis: he begins with a direct appeal to the spirit of national unity ('our English heritage') which in his view was forged in 1940 by the imminent threat of invasion, and which he regards as the 'soul of the nation':

> Four years ago [1940] the sudden fusion of parties into a single united British Front gave confidence and purpose to a nation in peril. Only when all parties are felt as, in the depths, at one, can the soul of a nation be revealed: as in a human life, when different attributes, body, heart, and mind, pulse together, the soul is known . . . the soul of England has yet to find, or rather hear, its own voice.[6]

The soul of the nation is national unity: in 1940 England found its soul. But the soul has yet to discover its true 'voice'. The true voice of the authentic English soul is apparently to be heard in its literary tradition:

> We have for four years been fighting, alone or in partnership, the reptilian dragon-forces of unregenerate, and therefore unshaped and inhuman instinct, energies breathing fire and slaughter across Europe, because such is our destiny, asserted by our time-honoured national symbol, Saint George, the dragon slayer, whose name our present sovereign bears; and we shall first search out that destiny not in platitudes or half-belief nor any reasonings of our own fabrication, but where alone it rests authentic, in the great heritage we possess of English letters, the greatest accumulation of national prophecy; where the soul of England, which is her essential sovereignty, speaks clearly – in Shakespeare, Milton, Pope, Byron, Blake, Wordsworth, Tennyson, Hardy and many more.[7]

Clearly 'English literature' is regarded here as an object with its own independent mode of existence: it is the true voice of the nation. Yet the idea of the nation's soul 'finding' its voice implies something closer to a conscious and deliberate appropriation and reconstruction of a 'literature' for its usefulness in the contemporary crisis. Knight wishes to assert that literature has spoken of national unity all along – only its utterance has not been heeded. But the urgency of his concern with a pressing present reality suggests strongly that the voice is that of a ventriloquist, with Shakespeare his articulate dummy. The above passage engineers an important slide from the political concept of national unity to the *metaphysical* idea of 'sovereignty'; metaphysical because Knight does not use it as a political term to define the heart of power in a state (in his Britain, constitutionally Parliament) but to allude rather to a spirit of national emotion which manifests itself in the sovereign, but is possessed by the people as a whole. (It would be amusing to consider what some members of Knight's pantheon – Milton, Byron, Blake, Hardy – would have thought of his royalist 'sovereignty'.)

The greatest expression of this sovereignty, the most authentic expression of England's soul, is Shakespeare:

> If ever a new Messiah is to come, he will come, says the greatest of all American writers, Herman Melville, in the name of Shakespeare. We need expect no Messiah, but we might at this hour, turn to Shakespeare, a national prophet if ever there was one, concerned deeply with the royal soul of England. That royalty has direct Christian and chivalric affinities. Shakespeare's life-work might be characterised as expanding, through a series of great plays, the one central legend of St George and the Dragon. Let us face and accept our destiny in the name both of Shakespeare and Saint George, the patron saint of our literature and nation.[8]

This rhetoric of metaphysical terminology seeks to identify a number of key terms – the nation, the nation's soul, and its voice (literature), the sovereign, Christ, Shakespeare and St George. The logical absurdity of this argument can easily be exposed: but such exposure does not exhaust its significance, which consists in the directness with which Knight defined the ideological function of literature as he conceived and practised it:

I aim to show what reserves for the refuelling of national confidence exist in Shakespeare's poetry.[9]

Among the 'reserves' capable of 'refuelling' the national confidence
(strikingly mechanistic metaphors, these, for such an idealist metaphysic) are Shakespeare's history plays:

> Shakespeare wrote at a time when, after centuries of civil war,
> England first became nationally self-conscious . . . the voice of
> the new nation is Shakespeare.
>   His historical plays are mainly studies of internal disorder
> during the centuries leading to the England of Elizabeth. Shakes-
> peare's thinking functions continuously in terms of order. . . .
> The issues troubling Europe today are here in embryo; and the
> desire for world-order which fabricated the League of Nations is
> an expansion of a desire pulsing throughout Shakespeare.[10]

Shakespeare's historical dramas were, for Wilson Knight, parables
of 'order' and 'disorder': expressions of an unsentimental patriotism
which faces up to the prevalence and the perils of 'disorder', and
proudly affirms the potentiality and the imperative necessity of
'order'. Such political terms are used with an apparent innocence of
political meaning: what social system constitutes this apparently
unquestionable 'order'? In fact Knight's theory is metaphysical
rather than political: social order is defined as the English nation
united in the symbol of the Crown:

> The Crown symbolises the nation's soul-life, which is also the
> greater self of each subject.[11]

This formulation recalls Matthew Arnold's theory of class: we all
have a lesser self, which encourages us to consider our own personal
interests or the interests of family, faction, social group or class; and
a greater self, which urges us to identify with the corporate body of
the nation. The form of that identification is the Crown: '. . . our
sole final allegiance is to that whole of which all these are parts and
whose symbol is the Crown'.[12] The category of 'order' is thus a
substitute for the political definition of a social formation – in this
case a bourgeois-democratic state governed by Parliament with an
anachronistic figurehead in the form of a vestigial monarchy – and

Shakespeare's plays are used to support and confirm an appeal to 'order' which signifies, in effect, a qualified adherence to the *status quo*. The appeal to order is exactly, in fact, that emotion of national unity, which was fostered during the Second World War not just to defeat fascism but to secure the ideological unification of the bitterly divided Britain of the 1930s.

Henry V becomes the focal point of Shakespeare's vision of 'order'. Knight can see no irony, ambiguity, or contradiction at all in the play. Henry is 'a Christian warrior, leading, after long periods of civil war, a united nation to foreign conquest', 'a blend of righteousness with power', 'a blend of Christian faith and martial heroism', and the play is 'a new epic and heroic drama, blending Christian virtue with martial prowess'.[13] The over-working of the word 'blend' visible in these quotations is significant: it is one of many such metaphors – 'concord', 'harmony', etc. – displaying the critic's concern to identify the play's formal unity with the unity of England, and both with the desired unity of Britain in 1944. Knight's Henry never puts a foot wrong: even in his masquerade as a common soldier in act IV, he does not commit the error of 'the pernicious socialist doctrine' by levelling himself down to his subjects' status: by their heroism they level themselves up to his royalty.[14]

Wilson Knight's views may seem bizarre – but they underwent no substantial change over the next forty years. In June 1982 he said of the Falklands War:

> I have for long accepted the validity of our country's historical contribution, seeing the British Empire as a precursor, or proto-type, of world-order. I have relied always on the Shakespearean vision as set forth in my war-time production *This Sceptred Isle*. . . . Our key throughout is Cranmer's royal prophecy at the conclusion of Shakespeare's last play, *Henry VIII*, Shakespeare's final words to his countrymen. This I still hold to be our one authoritative statement, every word deeply significant, as forecast of the world-order at which we should aim. Though democratic, it involves not just democracy alone, but democracy in strict subservience to the crown as a symbol linking love to power and the social order to the divine . . . I tend to support our activities, now or in the future, in so far as they may be felt to be expanding British tradition and our national heritage to world proportions, in attunement with Shakespearean prophecy.[15]

The relation of Laurence Olivier's film of *Henry V* to the contemporary war-time situation of its production (1943–4) is as explicit as that of Wilson Knight's jingoistic essay. The film bears an epigraph:

> To the Commandos and Airborne Troops of Great Britain, the spirit of whose ancestors it has been humbly attempted to recapture in some ënsuing scenes, this film is dedicated.

Part of the film's intention was clearly identical with that of Wilson Knight – 'to show what reserves for the refuelling of national confidence exist in Shakespeare's poetry'. Olivier, who was in Hollywood when the war began, learned to fly there in order to join the Fleet Air Arm. In uniform he played the role of patriotic orator to the Home Front: too old for active service, he found opportunities for contributing to the war effort in the form of ideological and cultural service. According to Clayton C. Hutton he had to be persuaded by the Ministry of Information to abandon his duties in the Fleet Air Arm in order to make *Henry V*.[16] The film came out too late to coincide with D-Day (the date of which had of course been kept secret) but was still dedicated to the troops involved in the Normandy landings.

Those scenes of the film which seem to have made the maximum impact and to have lingered most strongly in the popular imagination (to judge by the number of ill-informed, published comments I have come across)[17] are those which belong to its patriotic application of the play to the current national crisis: Henry's Churchillian speeches before Harfleur and Agincourt; the dejection, courage and soul-searching of the long night before Agincourt (clearly recalling the mood of 1940); the inserted battle-scenes, filmed with all the resources of modern film technology – depicting what Shakespeare's Chorus despaired of depicting: the colourful panoply of chivalry, the glamour of historical pageant, the thrill of victory, the confident, militaristic emotions of 1944. Yet all these details belong to one part of the film: its dramatization of acts III and IV of Shakespeare's play; and by themselves do not by any means exhaust or even adequately describe the film's contribution to Shakespeare reproduction.

Shakespeare's Chorus speaks constantly of the difficulties involved in producing an 'epic' drama under Elizabethan stage conditions –

the impossibility of presenting with any authenticity or realism the
great national events and vivid historical spectacles which constitute
the play's ostensible subject:

> . . . But pardon, gentles all,
> The flat unraised spirits that hath dar'd
> On this unworthy scaffold to bring forth
> So great an object: can this cockpit hold
> The vasty fields of France? Or may we cram
> Within this wooden O the very casques
> That did affright the air at Agincourt?
>
> (*HV*, Prologue)

Olivier came to the play equipped with all the formidable technology for portraying reality developed by the modern cinema: all
the freedom of the camera to move from interior to exterior, studio
to location; all the financial and material resources of setting and
costume necessary to provide authentic historical colour; all the
technology necessary to film something like the French cavalry
charge at Agincourt. Why did Olivier not simply dispense with the
Choruses – a testimony to aesthetic limitations long since trans-
cended – and present the film 'realistically' within the conventions
of historical reconstruction that Shakespeare's Chorus seems to
yearn for? Why, with all these aesthetic resources at command,
does the film begin with a reconstruction of an Elizabethan theatre
– locking the play back into the constricting framework which its
own poetry struggles so hard to escape?

The decision to incorporate into the film devices and aesthetic
strategies derived from the dramatic technique of the Chorus provides the film with an ideological tendency which is quite different
from – potentially contrary to – its ideology of patriotism, national
unity and just war. The film's passage into a 'realistic' reconstruction
of Agincourt is mediated by a series of devices which in their different ways distance the art of film from reality, displaying the artificiality of the medium in such a way as to qualify (though not, ultimately,
to dispel) the passionate conviction of the patriotic emotion.

Various speculations have been attempted about Olivier's motives
for locating the drama back into the historical context of the Elizabethan theatre. It has been suggested that the intention was primarily

theatrical – to make a film of a stage production, rather than a screen adaptation of a play. Or perhaps the motive was more academic – the equivalent of a scholarly appendix on contemporary stage conditions. Or it was an exercise in cultural philanthropy – purveying the cream of high culture to a popular audience. It does not seem to have been realized that the film, in imitating Shakespeare's Chorus, also incorporates some of the aesthetic devices which work within Shakespeare's drama to undermine the play's traditionalist and official ideology.

The film begins with a shot of empty space – a scrap of paper is windblown through a vacant blue sky; whirled towards the camera, it resolves into a handbill advertising a performance of *Henry V* at the Globe Theatre. Insofar as this device demands literal interpretation, it represents exactly that: a handbill tossed by the wind through the sky of Elizabethan London. But that blue sky is also empty space and time: the handbill, before it becomes the title-page of a play, is a scrap of paper arbitrarily carried forward from the past, indecipherable until it unfolds before the camera, meaningless until it is *read*. The film seems to begin by suggesting that the play floats in a turbulent vacuum of history until a process of visual *reproduction* transforms it into history of a new kind. The faintly disorientating character of this device contrasts sharply with the more familiar evocation of a firm, objectively existent historical tradition which is there to be read off from Shakespeare's text, or the legend of Henry V, or the soul of the English nation.

The camera then displays a reconstructed model (very obviously a model, patently artificial) of Elizabethan London, and a slow crane-shot comes to rest on the Globe Theatre. The camera then penetrates to the interior of the theate, to show an audience collecting for a performance. A rich assemblage of visual detail seeks to portray a reconstruction of the theatre's atmosphere and tone in a very lively, noisy and sociable gathering, with much public self-display of the nobility, the sale of food and drink; all accompanied by William Walton's effective pseudo-Elizabethan music. The performance proper begins, not with a curtain raised to display a naturalistic *mise en scène*, but with a boy displaying a large printed card bearing the play's title – a convention of the Elizabethan theatre (and, incidentally, of Brecht's epic theatre) which disrupts any attempt at naturalistic illusion. There is no attempt at all to translate theatre into film: what is being filmed is a theatre in action.

Throughout Shakespeare's act I the theatrical conditions are visible: sections of the audience – those seated on the stage and those on the floor or in the galleries – the prompter, the tiring-room, and so on. Critics committed to the independence of film as an art, and hostile to any dependence of film on the literary media, have shown impatience with what they see as the inappropriate survival here of theatrical form.[18] But it is much more important to describe the specific aesthetic and ideological effects of this foregrounding of production devices. As long as the theatrical context remains visible (up to the end of Shakespeare's act II) the audience can retain the possibility of seeing Henry primarily as an *actor* rather than as a historical character; and this is much more than the ostentatious virtuosity of a famous screen actor displayed before the cameras. With this suggestion supplied, the audience can easily make an imaginative jump from theatre to history: this is a king who seems to rule more by the accomplished deployment of theatrical techniques than by statesmanship or good government. The radical and subversive element of Shakespeare's play consists mainly in this tendency of the drama to foreground the artificiality of its dramatic devices; and to create a perspective in which the king can display himself as an *actor* rather than a naturalistic character. Our first glimpse of Henry in the film is not on the stage as king, but in the tiring room as a nervous actor, numb with stagefright, anxiously clearing his throat: prior to making his entrance to immediate and rapturous applause from a noisy and very visible audience, Henry presents himself to the audience as an actor, with scant respect for the conventions of naturalist drama.

The scene with the clergymen is played as farce, with continual and voluble interventions by the audience; and the high point of Henry's self-dramatization occurs in the film (as it does in the play) in his reaction to the Dauphin's insulting gift of tennis-balls. In this scene the camera employs a device developed by Olivier to overcome some of the difficulties involved in translating drama into film:

> The film climax is a close-up; the Shakespearean climax is a fine gesture and a loud voice. I remember going to George Cukor's *Romeo and Juliet*. As a film director he did what seemed the right thing when he took the potion scene with Norma Shearer – he crept right up to a huge head, the ordinary film climax. But it was in fact a mistake. She, being a good technician in film-making,

cut the power of her acting down as the camera approached her for the climax of that speech leading up to taking the potion – 'Romeo, I come! This do I drink to thee.' At the moment of climax she was acting very smally, because the camera was near. That was not the way it should have been. So the very first test I made for *Henry V* I tried to see how it would work in reverse. It was in the scene with the French Ambassador, and as I raised up my voice the camera went back . . .[19]

Olivier was speaking here primarily of the function of this technique as it concerned the actor, but the device also makes an important contribution to the 'epic' quality of the film, especially in the realistic, exterior location scenes used to represent Agincourt. The movement from close-up to long-shot does not just allow scope for the actor to intensify his performance; it also, more fundamentally, increases the size and multiplies the content of the frame: it supplies more abundance of visual detail thereby bringing more objects, images and characters into significant relationship. Henry's 'Crispin Crispian' speech (iv, iii) before Agincourt begins as a close shot from below depicting Henry himself (whose face, in close-up and soliloquy, has been dominating the screen in the previous sequence). As his speech rises to a climax the camera pulls back and up, to reveal the assembled masses of fighting men around him, all excited by his militaristic rhetoric and infected with his martial enthusiasm. The frame expands from a focus on the leader's personality to an image of the leader as centre of his loyal army: from the psychological to the epic; from the monarch to the nation.

The same technique, used to film the earlier scene with the French Ambassador, has an entirely different effect. A close-up shot shows Henry's controlled passion of indignation at the Dauphin's insult. As his speech of reply (i, ii, 259–97) rises to a climax, the camera pulls back to reveal – not a naturalistic social setting, but a stage, other costumed actors, an audience, a theatre. The effect is heightened by a deliberate emphasis on Henry as an actor playing to the audience: one shot taken from the back of the stage displays him *acting* before his enthusiastic spectators. His exit line at the end of the scene is delivered as a flourish directly to the audience.

As in Shakespeare's play, then, the king is characterized as an *actor* rather than a monarch: the drama displays his capacity to masquerade and perform, his ability to generate acclamation and excitement in the *theatrical* context. The *playing* is very obviously *play*. To see this, as many have done, as a naturalistic method of presenting theatre on the screen, is to seriously underestimate the subtlety of the film's aesthetic devices; to see the film as concerned simply to offer a 'straight' patriotic version of *Henry V* is to interpret selected parts rather than the film's significant whole.

Consider for example the effect of interpolating the scene of Falstaff's death. This is played, and filmed, very 'straight': it is the point where the visible theatrical framework gives way to the painted backdrop scenery and realistic locations of the later sequences; and it is deprived of all Shakespeare's humour. The effect aimed at by invented action, text, visual image and music, is one of overwhelming pathos. Falstaff is shown on his death-bed: he rouses faintly to repeat his lines from *Henry IV Part Two*:

> God save thy Grace, King Hal, my royal Hal!
> . . . God save thee, my sweet boy!
> (*2HIV*, v, v, 41–3)

The grim tones of the new king's reply appear in voice-over: 'I know thee not, old man.' Falstaff falls back, flocculates and expires. The scene closes with a shot from outside the chamber window: a curtain is drawn across it. Meanwhile we hear Pistol and his companions departing for the war; Pistol quotes, in another interesting interpolation, lines from Marlowe's *Tamburlaine*:

> Is it not passing brave to be a king
> And ride in triumph through Persepolis?

The theatrical metaphors are very obvious here, and very much in the spirit of Shakespeare's play. The drawn curtain marks the end, not so much of Falstaff's life, as of his role. Has the king destroyed him because he cannot tolerate such theatrical competition, because he will not be upstaged by his former comrade? Pistol's main function in Shakespeare's play is to parody, by projecting a Marlovian megalomania, the king's tendency to dramatize himself as the old-fashioned epic hero. His interpolated *Tamburlaine* echo is taken up and confirmed by the next film-scene, which contains a brief précis of act II, scene ii at Southampton, with the Earl of Cambridge's conspiracy completely removed. Henry is shown dramatizing himself as a crusader, military leader, would-be conquering hero; and very much enjoying his role. The immediate juxtaposition of this colourful pageant with the melancholy chiaroscuro of Falstaff's death supplies an undertone of calculated cruelty to Henry's extravagant display of theatrical virtuosity. Evidently it *is* passing brave to be a king and ride in triumph through Persepolis, though it is passing unfair to be a rejected and betrayed companion and die in loneliness and poverty.

Once the film settles into realistic locations for the battle of Agincourt (locations which occupy a small part of the film, yet which have, significantly, attracted a disproportionate amount of attention) the theatrical framework disappears completely, and with it the film's radical and subversive potentialities. The viewer is immersed in a *real* world which becomes increasingly analogous to the world of contemporary history. Scenes such as that between Henry and the soldiers (IV, i) with all the fear and anxiety of a night before battle, and scenes of naturalistically presented military action showing the defensive preparations of the English and the showy chivalry of the French, were evidently too close to the contemporary experience of war for the film to free itself from or even to offer qualification of, what becomes its dominant ideology. *Action* replaces *acting*; the serious business of fighting suppresses the freedom of theatrical play; the world of the film becomes more like the Britain of 1940. The critical exigencies of the contemporary situation pull the film back, away from its aesthetic experiments, into complicity with the ideologies of patriotism, war enthusiasm and national unity. This suspension of the viewer's complex awareness of the theatrical event, this immersion of the viewer into a carefully constructed facsimile of a 'real' world, is so successful that it is with a shock that we see the theatre reappear at the end. The illusions of naturalism and of conventional theatre have succeeded in dominating the imagination: and through those illusions the film's ideological integrity is reasserted.

Forty years later, the theatre critic of the *Daily Mail* divided his day between Westminster Abbey and another production of *Henry V* at Stratford-upon-Avon:

> Offhand I can't remember a day when it seemed so marvellous or mad to be English. Suddenly the chronic inconvenience of London's transport strike and the continuing horrors of the mining dispute were put into the merciful perspective of history.

It began in Westminster Abbey where I sat close to the Queen Mother and watched her fight back tears and surrender to smiles with a packed congregation as the funniest hours of her reign were celebrated in the familiar words and music of Sir Noel Coward.

And it ended here at Stratford, with a young, brave and poetic Henry bridging the centuries between by reminding us of the unlikely spirit which won Agincourt. Nothing much seemed so very different . . .

What links the vision of young Mr Kenneth Branagh, making his Royal Shakespeare debut as a raw, stocky warrior, with Coward's latterday musings, is the patriotic poet which lurked beneath their different facades . . .

To hear Mr Branagh wonder incredulously at the valour of his rag-tag-and-bobtail troops was to hear echoes of Derek Jacobi reading the moving war diaries of Coward at the unveiling of his memorial stone.

And when Branagh squats among his men, blackened with the efforts of war, and urges them once more into the breach – well, – we had heard that sentiment back in the Abbey when Penelope Keith set the sea of hankerchiefs dabbing at moist eyes . . .

I won't press the coincidence. Suffice to say that neither the service at the Abbey nor Adrian Noble's spare, bare production at Stratford were mere tub-thumping exercises in mindless nationalism.

There was pain, irony, wit and humanity in both. As Ian McDairmid's conversational chorus informs us: Henry had a kingdom for a stage. Which of course was like Coward turning his stage into a kingdom. Both, in their way make a little thing like a transport shut-down seem irrelevant. All this from old masters and new blood! Between Harry's Harfleur spirit and Coward's London Pride, it did not, after all, seem improbable that there are still good reasons to be in England now that April's almost here.[20]

Jack Tinker makes an interesting distinction here between 'patriotism' (of the handkerchief-dabbing type) and 'nationalism' (of the tub-thumping variety). To have a forceful and vigorous ideology of nationalism, you have to have a forceful and vigorous nation to enact and substantiate it. If the 'nation' in question happens, like Britain in the 1980s, to be an eclipsed world power – no longer a great imperial aggressor, no longer a significant colonial leader, no longer a dominant industrial or economic force – then what basis remains for a particular, quantifiable 'national' consciousness? If the political and economic character of the 'nation' owes more to its participation in larger political and economic units – the EEC, NATO, American foreign policy, the multinational capitalist economy, the International Monetary Fund – then what sense does it make to continue talking about a specific, isolable 'national' identity?

All that seems left to the disappointed or reformed British nationalist is an emotion of 'patriotism', which can evidently be distinguished from the politics of nationalism, and is capable of surviving such losses and transformations as the demise of Empire and the descent from world eminence relatively undamaged and unscathed. Patriotism is associated with 'poetry', with emotion, with the heart, with tears; 'nationalism' with 'mindless' aggression, with 'tub-thumping' jingoistic assertiveness. In a review of the subsequent widely celebrated film version of *Henry V*,[21] Tom Hutchinson in the *Mail on Sunday* later proposed the same distinction: 'the film . . . touches the heart of emotion rather than the instinct for patriotism'.[22] But in the earlier review of the stage production, patriotism is indissolubly linked with the past. The plangency of patriotic feeling here derives from what Tom Nairn calls 'the glamour of backwardness': a nostalgia, a craving, unappeasable hunger for that which is irretrievably lost. Yet that loss may be regarded also as neither complete nor inconsolable, since the utterances of a 'patriotic poet' such as William Shakespeare (or Noel Coward) can transcend the absence and negation of history, and suffuse the soul with – not exactly a new fulfilment, but at least a new longing, a new mixing of memory and desire. Militaristic violence, inseparable from the historical actuality of nationalism, is strangely appeased in this flood of remembrance,[23] strangely pacified by 'the merciful perspective of history'. The British patriot, now no longer a nationalist, looks back regretfully, with resigned sadness, to his 'finest hour' in 1940, or the 'unlikely' victory of his ancestors at Agincourt; but, as re-awakened memories, these scenes of historical violence, recollected in tranquillity, acquire a power to comfort and console.

The patriotic emotion is anchored in the past. Inspired by the 'valour' 'gallantry' and 'courage' displayed by the manly deeds of a warrior race, and immortalized in the words of the 'old masters' (represented here by the in-this-context-unfortunately-named 'Shake-spear' and 'Coward'), patriotism paradoxically expresses itself in gestures of weakness, in a 'surrender' to tears. The binary polarization of gender implicit in this construction is evident in the feminity shared by those cast, respectively, as tear-jerker and tear-jerked (Penelope Keith and the Queen Mother); and the contradictory quality of the patriotic emotion itself manifested in the male observer's luxurious relishing of a weakness discovered in the contemplation of strength – like D. H. Lawrence, the writer here enjoys feeling his 'manhood cast Down in the flood of remembrance' as he 'weeps like a child for the past'.[24]

The patriotic emotion is anchored in the past, and besieged, embattled in the present. The England that surrounds Jack Tinker gives him no cause for patriotic celebration: it is rather a scene of bitter social conflict and class-antagonism, an England of transport and coalfield strikes. The English patriot does not see his emotional conviction rooted in the actuality of the nation that surrounds him, which seems systematically to negate his ideal national image. The patriotic emotion searches past and future for a habitable space, nostalgically embracing the glamour of backwardness, and optimistically extrapolating a projected landscape of hope. Elsewhere in the review Tinker quotes some lines from Noel Coward's *Cavalcade*, which exactly encapsulate that contradictory emotion:

> Let's drink to the spirit of gallantry and courage that made a strange Heaven out of unbelievable Hell, and let's drink to the Hope, that one day this country of ours, which we love so much, will find dignity and greatness and peace again.

The authentic accent of what might anachronistically be described as a 'postmodern' patriotism can in fact be located in what we think of as the very heart of the traditional discourse of British nationalism: it is even there in that notorious speech attributed to John of Gaunt in Shakespeare's *Richard II*, which in turn provided subsequent ages with a basic vocabulary of patriotic rhetoric.

> This royal throne of kings, this sceptred isle,
> This earth of majesty, this seat of Mars,
> This other Eden, demi-paradise,
> This fortress built by Nature for herself
> Against infection and the hand of war,
> This happy breed of men, this little world,
> This precious stone set in a silver sea

> Which serves it in the office of a wall
> Or as a moat defensive to a house
> Against the envy of less happier lands,
> This blessed plot, this earth, this realm, this England . . .
>
>   (*Richard II*, ii, i, 40–50)

It is natural to think of this fictionalized John of Gaunt as a great supporter of monarchical prerogative and royal power: certainly outside the play his famous patriotic speech has invariably been employed to endorse absolute authority, to support the autocratic will of many subsequent British kings and governments. Within the play of course this speech actually functions as a diatribe of criticism against the ruling monarch: Gaunt is not even depicting the England of the present, but expressing a nostalgic regret for an England which has long since vanished into the historical past. It is precisely because the England he sees before him – Richard's England – falls so far short of his idealized vision of what he believes England once was, that his poetic vision of national glory is so brightly and vividly imagined.

Gaunt's speech is not merely an appeal for strong leadership in the king, and it is certainly not a defence of the Renaissance doctrine of Divine Right and absolute royal authority. On the contrary, he imagines royal authority as inseparable from the power of the nobility; the golden age he longs for and regrets is that of a feudalism held together by the authority of a strong king *and* by the power of a strong aristocracy. The unacceptability of Richard's kingship consists, in Gaunt's eyes, in his modernizing programme of defeudalization, and his consequent slighting of the traditional aristocracy. It is ironic that so many subsequent appeals to English patriotism have been mounted on the basis of this elegant and barbaric statement of baronial self-interest, this celebration of a class that has scarcely earned the unqualified admiration of even the most conservative of thinkers. But as we shall see, this hypostatization of a sectional class-interest as the ideology of a 'nation' is a symptomatic element in the history of British patriotism.

John of Gaunt's image of England as a 'precious stone set in a silver sea' takes us to a margin, an edge, a border; to the south coast of Britain, and specifically to those white cliffs of Dover, over which, in Vera Lynn's wartime song, 'there'll be blue-birds . . . tomorrow, just you wait and see'. What more lyrical expression could there be of the patriotic hunger for an endlessly deferred fulfilment than that poignant expression of elegaic existentialism which, like John of Gaunt's speech, and Noel Coward's *Cavalcade*, attaches its emotion to the past and future as a way of confronting the absence and pain of the present? The iconic image that goes with the song is of course the famous white cliffs themselves, that long chalk escarpment which offers to the envy of less happier lands so characteristically 'English' a seascape.

The seaport of Dover, those famous white cliffs, and more generally the stretch of coastline from Southampton to the Thames estuary, occupy a peculiar and privileged place in the iconography and mythology of British nationalism. My initial reference to Vera Lynn invokes the Second World War, and specifically the period 1940–4 when France was under German occupation, and Britain in constant fear of an invasion. That 'rump' of England then felt (not for the first time) the vulnerability of exposure to another landmass, the threatening point of France that pokes aggressively towards southern Britain, intimately close in space (narrow enough to swim across) yet always mistrusted, perpetually perceived as alien, frequently feared. Of course in a war of aerial transport, long-range heavy bombers, guided missiles, that part of England was (though subject to shelling from the French coast) in many ways no more vulnerable than any other, its borders capable of being breached at any point. But it is those cliffs of the south coast that provide us with our most characteristic national image of vulnerability, exposure, openness to the peril of foreign invasion.

The mythological status of the white cliffs of Dover is far more ancient than 1940. In those legendary and mythological narratives that preceded the advent of modern historiography, Dover was actually what the anthropologist Malinowski called a 'spot of origins', a particular geographical location regarded by tradition as the source of a nation's genesis. Anthropologists have identified in the proliferation of such narratives a structural form which they term the 'myth of origin', a narrative which purports to explain the process of a nation's appearance in history. Medieval historians traced the ancestry of their various national populations and monarchies to the dispersal of the Trojan princes after the fall of Troy: Geoffrey of Monmouth claimed that the English were descended from Brutus, allegedly a descendant of Aeneas. In Holinshed there is a narrative describing the conquest of what was to become Britain by Brutus, whose companion Corineus succeeded in overthrowing the giant Gogmagog, the island's original inhabitant – 'by reason whereof the place was named long after, *The Fall or leape of Gogmagog*, but afterwards it was called *The Fall of Dover*'.[25] As John Turner has shown, such pseudo-historical narratives were retold in the Renaissance as morality fables, calculated to guide political conduct; but they were also retold as myths, designed to legitimize power: 'The black holes in time were to be occluded, the dangerous discontinuities of history papered over with myths that would confirm authority and marginalize the claims of political opposition'.[26] When James I in 1604 had himself proclaimed King of 'Great Britain', he was deliberately re-introducing an antiquarian geographical term in order to establish 'one single rule' over England and Scotland. The name itself was falsely derived from Brutus, and in 1605 James was celebrated in the Lord Mayor's show as the second Brutus who, in fulfilment of Merlin's ancient prophecy, would 'reunite what the original Brutus has put asunder'.[27]

The narratives of this 'mythical charter' enact a sequence of invasion, conquest, colonization and fragmenting. Dover is the point of entry, the aperture through which a new force of domination can enter the territory, settle it, and then – in a tragic political error – part it asunder. Reading through the political to the sexual, Britain is the female body, invaded by the colonizing male; the appropriate feminine resistance is over-thrown, and the country planted with fertile seed. The inevitable result of this process is however not unity, but parturition, splitting, division; not the formation of a single unified whole, but the multiplying of centrifugal energies. The myth imagines national origin as a cyclical process of invasion, unification, plantation, and division.

Precisely because in this myth Dover is the source of national identity, it is also the weakest point of the territory's physical defences. What one male can do to a female body, what one conqueror can do to a territory, another male, another conqueror, can repeat; and in every repetition the action is (in an important sense) identical. The fundamentally unitary nature of conquest/intercourse cuts sharply across powerful taboos based on binary oppositions of difference (legitimate/illegitimate, married/unmarried, pure/contaminated, good/evil); and thereby forms the basis of that male sexual jealousy which in turn butts onto xenophobic nationalism: that point where the linked elements of 'father' and 'fatherland' in the word 'patriotism' meet. Along the south coast England presents her white, chaste purity to the potential invader as a defensive repellant, but also as a temptation. 'Succeed where Napolean failed' urges an advertisement for the local South-East England tourist industry, the words emblazoned across an aerial photograph of the familiar iconic escarpment: 'spend a day in White Cliffs country'. The point where the nation's identity begins is also the point where it could most easily be violated or re-conquered.[28]

A key scene of Shakespeare's *Henry V* (II, ii) is set on that coastline, historically at Southampton (though usefully, for my purposes, the Folio text of the play misprints Southampton as 'Dover'). Henry and his nobles have here reached the 'extreme verge' of their territorial confine, a point of no return. Everything has been staked on the success of the French adventure; at the end of the scene Henry affirms, rhetorically but accurately, that his authority as monarch depends on victory: 'No King of England, if not King of France'. At this margin of the kingdom, which has the perilous quality of all territorial borders, the riskiest, most dangerous aspect of the whole enterprise – more subversive than the uneven odds at Agincourt – is encountered: internal dissension, mutiny within the ranks, self-betrayal. The periphery of England, that no-man's-land between England and France, marked by the sharp dividing line of the white cliffs, sanctified by the legendary myth of origins, is the point chosen for the enactment of a particular ritual: the cleansing of the English body politic by a sacrificial execution.

In the play-text Exeter defines the treachery of the conspirators simply as a hired murder, a contract killing undertaken for a French purse. On discovery however one of them, the Earl of Cambridge, hints at an ulterior motive:

> For me, the gold of France did not seduce,
> Although I did admit it as a motive
> The sooner to effect what I intended.
>
> (II, ii, 151–3)

In fact the three men arraigned here historically represented the cause of the deposed Richard II; the Earl of Cambridge's ulterior motive was that of re-establishing the legitimate dynasty toppled by the Lancastrians' usurpation. Ultimately they succeeded in forming the Yorkist power in the Wars of the Roses, in murdering Henry's son and in putting three kings on the English throne. The narrowing down of this complex constitutional problem to a simple focus on the question of political loyalty is a characteristic achievement of Henry's style of government, and of course a familiar mechanism of ideological coercion in times of war. Political dissent becomes treachery: internal difference is forced to collapse under the moral and ideological pressures of international conflict.[29]

Kenneth Branagh placed particular emphasis on his decision to reinstate sections of the play-text omitted from Laurence Olivier's film version, and in particular the whole of II, ii:

> I decided on including some significant scenes that Olivier's film, for obvious reasons, had left out: in particular, the conspirators' scene where Henry stage-manages a public cashiering of the bosom friends who have been revealed as traitors. The violence and extremism of Henry's behaviour and its effect on a volatile war cabinet were elements that the Olivier version was not likely to spotlight.[30]

The general line of comparison here is that Olivier's film treatment was severely constrained by its wartime context of production: as a patriotic celebration of Britain's military strength and resolve, sponsored by the Ministry of Information, indissolubly linked both psychologically and strategically with the projected (and of course successful) Allied invasion of occupied France, the film was unlikely to place any emphasis on internal treachery, or to foreground qualities in Henry's character and behaviour that might be read as unpleasantly 'violent' or 'extreme'.

Both film versions establish this scene by adapting the device of Shakespeare's Chorus. In the Olivier version, a painting of the white cliffs of Southampton/Dover frames an unmistakably theatrical set, the prow of a stage ship where Henry and his nobles receive the sacrament before embarking. The overtly theatrical quality of the scene relates it closely to the reconstructed Elizabethan stage on which all the earlier scenes have been played. In the Branagh version Derek Jacobi as Chorus appears on a cliff-top (white, of course) from which he delivers the prologue to act II. The sequence of directions reads:

The Chorus is standing on a grassy cliff edge, looking out to sea.
He turns to took at the camera.

CHORUS
The French, advised by good intelligence
    Of this most 'dreadful' preparation . . .

He turns to look towards the cliff top and we cut closer to the
traitors who have now appeared, passing through frame as their
names are mentioned.

CHORUS
One, Richard Earl of Cambridge . . .

As he walks away along the cliff edge, wrapping his scarf around
him against the cold sea air, beyond him we see the dramatic
white cliffs of the English coastline.[31]

Once the dramatic action is resumed, the Chorus disappears (though
in the original theatrical production he frequently remained on
stage), and the 'traitor scene' is established firmly in a naturalistic
'hostelry'.[32] The action is also played naturalistically, with a consistent emphasis on individual emotion. The key issue here is personal
rather than political; the emphasis falls on the shocking treachery of
Henry's friends, particularly his 'bed-fellow' the Earl of Cambridge.
At one point Henry throws Cambridge over a table with an almost
sexual intensity, violently enacting the pain of personal betrayal.[33]
The conspirators confess only their guilt: Cambridge's lines about
an alternative motive are cut.
    The main interest of the scene as presented here consists in a
dramatization of the psychological stresses and strains of such a
critical situation, as experienced in Henry's character. The dominant
device of close-up is used here, as throughout the film, to register the
psychological costs of authority. Branagh's intention may have been
to foreground the violence and extremism of Henry's behaviour: but
the naturalistic medium ensures that the nature of the spectator's
engagement with the action is one of individual identification.
Branagh's use (above) of theatrical metaphors – 'stage-manages',
'spotlight' – actually draws attention to the *anti-theatrical* medium
of filmic naturalism, in which very little space is left for the spectator

to reflect on the nature of the dramatic medium itself. No one could gather from this scene, any more than from Olivier's version of the same scene, that there is implicit in the dramatic text a subtext related to the critical question of legitimacy. Branagh has conspired with the character of Henry himself to obliterate the play's momentary exposure of a stress-point in the unity of the commonwealth. In this way the possibility of political dissent can be completely occluded, both within and through the text, since all political opposition is converted on this ideological terrain to civil treachery and personal betrayal.

The key difference between the two film versions seems to me to reside in their respective adaptations of Shakespeare's Chorus. I have argued earlier that Olivier's adaptation of the Chorus, and his initial setting of the production-text within a reconstructed Elizabethan theatre, put into circulation some of the 'radical and subversive potentiality of Shakespeare's play . . . to foreground the artificiality of its dramatic devices'. Branagh's adaptation of the Chorus is equally inventive and in many ways effective. The device of beginning with the Chorus in an empty film studio and opening set doors on to the dramatic action is an ingenious updating of Olivier's mock Globe theatre. Though the Chorus is sometimes shown to be involved in the action (e.g. at the siege of Harfleur), he more characteristically appears as an alienation-effect, emerging surprisingly from behind a tree after the execution of Bardolph, or appearing to block out the final scene of diplomatic reconciliation in the French court, where he delivers that sharply undercutting prophecy which calls into question Henry's political achievement. But the radical departure from Olivier's use of this device rests in the fact that, although the Chorus becomes involved in the action, the action never strays on to the territory of the Chorus. At one point in the original Royal Shakespeare Company stage production, Henry and the Chorus, in a brilliant *coup de théâtre*, almost bumped into one another, miming a surprised double-take of near-recognition: with a shock of delight we saw the fictional world of the dramatic action suddenly enter the fictionalizing activity of the Chorus. But in the film the naturalism of the action itself is never compromised in this way, despite the self-reflexive interventions of the intrusive choric witness.

It is abundantly clear, despite its radical features, in what relation Olivier's film stood to the nationalistic ideology of its time. But where does the Branagh film stand in relation to contemporary patriotic and nationalist ideologies? The original (1984) stage production, directed by Adrian Noble, in which Branagh played the king, became known as the 'post-Falklands' *Henry V*. That suggests of course a prevailing mood of revulsion against war, against imperialistic shows of strength, against militaristic patriotism. The film can easily be read in line with this view: it was 'made for a generation with the Indo-China war and the Falklands behind it and is wary of calls to arms', according to Philip French.[34] Branagh has 'stripped the veneer of jingoism from the play and shown war in its true horror';[35] the film 'emphasises the horror and futility of battle'.[36]

But the term 'post-Falklands' may not be quite as simple as that. 'Post' (as in 'postmodernism') does not always translate easily as 'anti' or 'counter': and it could well be that along with the obvious political advantages accruing to the power victorious in a military conflict ('No Prime Minister of Britain, if not Empress of South Georgia'), the Falklands war bequeathed to British culture a decidedly ambiguous interest in war, not entirely unconnected with the characteristic emotions of patriotism. Certainly many of the post-Falklands cultural productions, such as Charles Wood's play *Tumbledown*,[37] betray a fascination with the experience of combat, with soldierly camaraderie, with the anguish of extreme suffering, with the psychological stresses of military leadership. Branagh's approach to the character of *Henry V*[38] was certainly to some degree founded on exactly such a fascination with the moral and emotional complexities made available in the theatre of war. His notorious consultation of Prince Charles,[39] by way of research into the isolation of office and the loneliness of command, indicates a readiness to refer directly and attend sympathetically to the contemporary experience of monarchical power. In the stage production he played the character of Henry so as to disclose those emotional complexities, to reveal weakness as well as strength, self-suppression as well as self-aggrandisement, personal loss as well as national victory. In that production the Brechtian device of the Chorus was able to offer a counterpoise to this open though ambivalent admiration for the heroic individual: in the relatively naturalistic medium of the film, and of course under Branagh's own direction, there is no such system of checks and balances to subvert the invitation to empathic identification with the psychology of power.

Again, if we compare the very different social roles of Olivier and Branagh, we would expect very different perspectives on the play to emerge. The one was almost a natural product of the English *ancien régime*, his manly shoulders practically designed for the touch of the regal sword; the other aggressively constructs his own social persona as the tough and ambitious boy from working-class Belfast, determined to make it in the competitive market-place of the British theatre, as impatient with traditional institutions and fossilized establishments as the young shock-troops of the Thatcherite Stock Exchange. Now it is quite evident that Branagh's studious and systematic campaign of self-publicity, a strategy he obviously considers necessary to the fulfilment of his artistic ambitions, engages with the naturalistic medium of the film to provoke a structural parallelism between actor and hero.[40] This theme runs through all the reviews of the fiim. In deciding to make it, Branagh 'took on much the same odds as Henry did at Agincourt';[41] he 'has marshalled his forces as well as Henry led his army'.[42] 'Clearly he has some sort of affinity with the part of King Henry, but it does not seem an actorly affinity. Branagh too talks like a winner, and *Henry V* offers him better than any other play in the repertoire what might be called a yuppy dynamic, a mythology of success and self-definition rather than struggle.'[43]

A structural parallel is also perceived between the 'band of brothers' with whose help Henry achieves such extraordinary success, and the team of actors assembled by Branagh to make the film. Here in the reviews we encounter a series of metaphors which oddly and unselfconsciously link theatrical and militaristic vocabularies. 'Before shooting started, Branagh, like Henry, addressed his troops, his happy few, saying he wanted to make it a "company picture".'[44] 'There is already something of the spirit of Henry's happy few in the cast and crew behind the camera . . . every member of this film unit would go to the wall for Kenneth Branagh.'[45] 'The actors . . . beamed like the happy few, ready to cry God for Kenneth.'[46]

Even odder is a tendency, quite in the spirit of that great tradition of public school patriotism which identified hand grenades with cricket balls, to express the relationship between theatre and heroic combat in metaphors of sport. Branagh himself dubbed his team 'the English all-stars', and several critics quipped along the same hearty and sporting lines: 'Branagh has fielded the first XV.'[47] 'This is how Englishmen play their football, so it seems a perfectly natural style in which to wage their wars.'[48] 'The English take Harfleur with the help of one horse and the first XI.'[49] Alexander Walker described Branagh as resembling 'a rugby forward who collects a bloody nose on the battlefield'.[50] We do not have to search for long among these testaments of reception to observe the repressed spirit of patriotic emotion returning in these attenuated forms.

Lastly there is the crucial relationship between this film as a cultural product and the kind of cultural pattern being forged by Branagh in his entrepreneurial interventions into the theatrical economy. He stands for a reaction against the established national institutions of theatre, such as the Royal Shakespeare Company, and for the development of a privatized theatrical economy, with organizations like his own Renaissance Theatre Company supported by private and corporate sponsorship. Those who also approve of such developments are filled with passions of admiration when they contemplate Branagh's audacity, energy, ambition, nerve, determination, etc., etc., right through the whole vocabulary of self-help and entrepreneurial capitalism. 'Branagh's blitzkrieg left the profession breathless at his nerve, his energy and his disregard for the obstacles.'[51] 'The cream of our classical talent and an army of extras, horses and stunt-men . . . was in itself a saga of nail-biting crises surmounted by his calm certainty of what he wants to do, and unshakeable confidence in being able to do it.'[52] Emma Thompson, who married Branagh and who plays Katherine in the film, embraces the same free-market vocabulary of risk and initiative, linked with the heroic language of war: 'These are the warrior years. These are the times to take the risks and do the big things we might not have the courage or energy for later on.'[53] Some critics offered a clearer-sighted analysis, whether prompted by enthusiasm or reservation: Richard Corliss in *The Times* called Branagh 'an icon of Thatcherite initiative', and Adam Mars-Jones in *The Independent* proposed an exact model for the cultural dialectics involved: 'The real chemistry is not between actor and part, but between the idea of the star as entrepreneur and the idea of the king as a self-made man.'[54] Clearly the myth enacted in this film is capable of signifying at this level, perhaps even more readily than at the level of national culture and politics.

The emotion of patriotism and the politics of nationalism always involve, in any given historical situation, attachment to a particular sectional group, or class, or 'team', or army, which can be seen as bearing or leading the national destiny. At the same time in every historical situation there is a larger, more pluralistic and multiple, more complex and contradictory national collective which any sectarian nationalist ideology must ignore, deny, or suppress. The most natural context for this operation to be successfully conducted is that of war: and we have seen in the dramatization of Henry V's policy how it can be done. We also know from our own experience of the Falklands war that it is possible for a government voted into power by forty per cent of the population, and an army voted into power by nobody, to become self-appointed bearers of the entire nation's moral consciousness.

Raphael Samuel suggests that in contemporary Britain patriotic and nationalist feeling has sought and found a new home in the concept of the individual:

> Orwell wrote in 1940 that the 'privateness' of English life was one of the secrets of its strength . . . his account anticipates some major themes in post-war British life, in particular the break-up, or erosion, of corporate loyalties, and the increasingly home-centred character of British social life. Patriotism, on the face of it, is one of the victims of those developments. Yet it may be that, denied expression in the public sphere, it is finding subliminal support in the semiotics of everyday life.
>
> . . . Individualism also has more solid material supports. The spread of home ownership, the sale of council houses, and the inflation of house prices has renewed the importance of family wealth and given a whole new terrain to Lockean notions of private property. The revival of small businesses – a feature of British as of other post-industrial societies – is multiplying the number of home-based or family-run concerns, while the dispersal of employment shows signs of reunifying work and home. Ideologically, public spirit is much less highly regarded than it was in the 1930s and 1940s. On both Left and Right of the political spectrum, self-expression is treated as the highest good, individual rights as sacrosanct, and the enlargement of personal freedom – or its protection – the ideal object of policy. Government, for its part, has built a whole platform out of freedom of choice, making, or attempting to make, health, insurance, pensions, and schooling matters of individual responsibility, and turning non-intervention into the highest of statesmanly tasks.

As Margaret Thatcher put it in one of her best-remembered maxims: 'There is no society, only men and women and families.'[55]

Branagh's film version of *Henry V* is very clearly a product of this new age of individualism, and it is in this respect that it differs so sharply from the play-text of the 1590s and the Olivier film of the 1940s. Denied a home in nationalist politics, the emotional resources of patriotism gravitate inexorably towards their true heartland in the individualism of the new entrepreneur, whose conquest of new economic and artistic worlds continually endorses the cultural and ideological power of the old.

Kenneth Branagh did not, however, become constituted as such an individual subject, this 'icon of Thatcherite initiative', without a complex process of cultural negotiation. The film also has another history, through which can be traced the possibilities of its being read otherwise. Branagh is himself, as a product of working-class Protestant Belfast, a compatriot of Captain MacMorris, as well as a fellow-countryman of William Shakespeare, heir to the mantle of Lord Olivier, and a loyal subject of Prince Charles's mother. MacMorris's question 'what ish my nation?' (III, ii, 125) would at certain stages of his life, if now no longer, have been capable of provoking in him an existential anxiety parallel to the confused and exasperated anger voiced by Shakespeare's Irish Captain. When in 1970 his family, horrified by the growth of political violence in the province, moved permanently to England (where his father had already been working for some years) Branagh felt, according to the testimony of his 'autobiography', 'like a stranger . . . in a very strange land'.[56] This initial condition of alienation was resolved only by the assumption of 'dual nationality' in a divided self: 'After a year or so I'd managed to become English at school and Irish at home'.[57] He lived, he acknowledges, a 'double life',[58] perpetually conscious of a deep cultural difference masked by apparent assimilation and ethnic homogeneity.

Branagh's formative childhood experience was thus enacted on a highly significant marginal space of 'British' culture, close to another of those territorial borders on which the contradictions of a nationalist ideology become acutely visible. Born a British citizen, within the borders of the 'United' Kingdom, Branagh inherited a particular Irish sub-culture, that of a large working-class extended family on the edge of the Belfast docks. He was also heir, however, to the questionable advantages of that 'British' culture of self-improvement and meritocratic social mobility which took him eventually to RADA, the RSC and Kensington Palace. These social contradictions of divided culture and fragmented nationality can be read immediately from the brash, ambitious, self-mocking, self-important, painfully unstable discourse of Branagh's premature 'autobiography', a project in itself designed to consolidate a coherent social identity out of a fissured and contradictory social experience. They can also be read from the film, which, despite its totalizing attempt to relocate the problems of national identity and international conflict within the charismatic individual, occasionally uncovers and discloses surprising depths of cultural anxiety.

This anxiety can be traced in a symptomatic moment of textual 'excess', a point where the filmic narrative discloses an ideological 'stress-point' by delivering an emotional affect which remains unexplained by the contingent dramatic circumstances. As the miraculous victory of Agincourt becomes apparent, Captain Fluellen (played by Ian Holm) reminds Henry of the heroic deeds of his ancestor Edward, 'the Black Prince of Wales'. Fluellen offers a Celtic rereading of Anglo-Norman history, celebrating the heroic deeds of Welsh men-at-arms at Crecy, and appropriating Edward himself as an honorary Welshman. Branagh's screenplay interprets this exchange as follows.

Fluellen
. . . I do believe your Majesty takes no scorn to wear the leek upon Saint Davy's day.

The power of the Welshman's simple feeling is too much for the King who speaks the following through tears which he cannot prevent. He is near collapse.

Henry v
I wear it for a memorable honour;
For I am Welsh, you know, good countryman.

The King breaks down, and the two men hug each other.[59]

Such cinematic surges of emotional intensity are of course ambiguous in their effects, and can be read in many ways. Here there are readily available psychological explanations: this is the bitter price of heroism and military success; the post-orgasmic melancholy of the victor, satiated on violence; or the human cost of successful rule. Branagh's Henry also sheds tears at the hanging of Bardolph, the screenplay emphasizing the 'enormous cost' to the King of this necessary exercise of impartial justice.[60] More generally, the film's capacity to reduce its participants and observers to tears is frequently cited as a measure of its authenticity: after the shooting of Agincourt, Branagh 'went home exhausted and somehow defeated, and for no good reason burst into tears';[61] and Prince Charles is reputed to have been similarly 'reduced to tears' at a special preview.[62] The demonstrative parading of open grief may at first sight appear subversive of the values of tough masculinity, the rigid suppression of emotion required for the serious business of warfare. But it should be clear from the sodden royal handkerchief with which we began, that these tears are closer to those rituals of mourning (such as the militaristic memorial service of 'Remembrance Day'), which are rather a liturgical collusion with the ideology of patriotic war than an emotional interrogation of its values.

The moment in the film of extreme emotional exchange between Fluellen and Henry is in fact quite different from these examples. Neither the film-text nor the screenplay can adequately explain its intensity, its excessive superabundance of significance. And that leaking out of embarrassingly public grief seems to me to locate a fault-line in the film's hegemony: for the sudden burst of reciprocal grief is linked by the dialogue with questions of national identity. As we observe the dramatization of an English king and a Welsh soldier plangently embracing in a symbolic ritual of national unity, we also catch a momentary glimpse of an Irishman and a Scot weeping over the historical devastations of British imperialism. Can we not then read through the film's imagery of post-Agincourt 'carnage and wreckage'[63] the smoking ruins of that battlefield that is Ulster? And can we not catch in those verminous men and women 'pillaging the bodies of the dead'[64] a fleeting glimpse of the young Kenneth Branagh, joining in the looting of a bombed-out Belfast supermarket?[65] The iconic image of the dead boy carried by Henry throughout this sequence, in turn carries in this respect richer and deeper psychological reverberations than I have space to explore.

One of the most interesting details of Branagh's *Henry V* does not appear in the film (and is not therefore in the published screenplay,

which is a record of the final edited version, not a screenplay from
which the film was developed). When shooting the scene where the
Chorus strides the white cliffs of Southampton/Dover (filmed in fact
at Beachy Head, which is of course exactly midway between the
two), Branagh tried to use the same location for another sequence:

> We tried unsuccessfully to get another shot which I had felt at
> one stage could open the movie – a pan across the French coast-
> line eventually taking in the white cliffs of England and ending
> on the contemplative face of yours truly. The whole thing was
> accompanied by the hollow crown soliloquy from *Richard II*,
> which seemed to express something of the message of our *Henry
> V*. The shot did not work, and I decided to drop the Richard
> anyway. It simply didn't belong.[66]

Who, in that strangely elliptical and impersonal phrase, is 'yours
truly'? The actor or the role? English Harry or Irish Ken? The
doubling of identities is paralleled by a corresponding spatial ambivalence: that camera-pan simultaneously offers a depiction of the
point of view of King Henry, firmly established on his own territory,
contemplatively surveying the enemy coast; and delivers an external
view of the 'English' coast as it would be seen by an enemy, an
invader – or an immigrant. Prompted by the echoing words of
Richard II, a king ousted from his own territory by the usurper
whose heir now literally occupies its commanding heights, and by
the semiotic value latent in Branagh's 'dual identity', the spectator
presented with this filmic moment would have had ample opportunity to appreciate the position of an internal *émigré*, whose status
within the nation is in some way questionable; the paradox of belonging and alienation, the cultural anxiety of the internal *émigré*
about to establish his own territorial rights by violently overthrowing another's.

What would this sequence, if included in the film, have signified;
and what are the underlying reasons for its exclusion? The speech in
question from *Richard II* (iii, ii, 144–77) is as we have seen a
penetrating interrogation of the realities of power.

In the projected additional scene of Branagh's film, Richard's
challenging interrogation is placed exactly on the sharp white line of
a territorial border. Located there, the insistent questioning of the
speech goes beyond an expression of melancholy resignation at the

emptiness of power (the kind of thing calculated to set Prince
Charles clutching for the royal nose-rag), to an earnest meditation
on the nature of the peripheral delineations by which such spaces of
hollowness are bound and contained. If we read that border as
simultaneously the south coast of England and the border between
Ulster and Eire, we can grasp the paradox of definition and arbitrari-
ness, of clear geographical division and constructed geopolitical
disposition, which belongs to all territorial borders, especially those
between an imperialist and a colonized nation. Travelling back to
that mythical spot of origins, which is also a possible point of exit
(Beachy Head is a favourite haunt of suicides), some of the fundamental questions of British national identity can at last be posed.
Does a geographical boundary such as the English Channel prescribe mutual hostility and reciprocal violence between the neigh-
bouring nations?

> the contending kingdoms
> Of France and England, whose very shores look pale
> With envy of each other's happiness,
> May cease their hatred
>
> (*Henry V*, v, ii, 377–9)

The inclusion of that speech from *Richard II*, significantly poised on
the edge of England, could have hollowed out an illuminating space
between actor and character: a disclosure which could have expressed
these cultural contradictions even more eloquently, if the film
had found a means of including Shakespeare's reference to Essex,
returning from Ireland, 'bringing Rebellion broached on his sword'.
Meanwhile, as the film cameras whirred on the summit of Beachy
Head, constructing a sequence destined to become a hollow absence
in the film-text, far below and out to sea, other kinds of machinery
were simultaneously hollowing out a link between 'the contending
kingdoms', that 'Chunnel' which when completed will rob the white
cliffs of much of their centuries-old symbolism. For once Britain is
physically a part of Europe, the ideological stress on ancient national
mythologies wil be enormously intensified. The interesting combination, on the part of Britain's Tory government, of pro-European
commitment and chauvinistic resistance to European union, testifies
to the problems facing British national ideology. The government's
insistence on the private funding of what is self-evidently a public

construction project (leading to an endless series of financial crises), and the anxieties frequently expressed about what kinds of contamination may enter the realm once a major transport artery is plugged deep into its vitals (those who applaud the demolition of the Berlin Wall tend, when contemplating the Chunnel, towards extravagant fantasies of invasion by terrorists and rabid animals), indicate deep ideological ambivalences towards the destruction of a 'natural' boundary. Some residual reverence for the acculturated sanctity of the south coast even underlies reasonable conservationist anxieties about the fate of the white cliffs themselves; focusing as they do in particular on a spot some distance from the site of the tunnel itself, but legitimated by its very name as a space of that England (of which, according to the words of another popular wartime song, there will always be one) to be conserved: Shakespeare Cliff, near Dover.

Chapter Eight

Recycling History

1951 was the year in which the post-war Labour government fostered a 'Festival of Britain', intended as a celebration and promotion of British culture coinciding with the centenary of the Great Exhibition of 1851. The purpose underlying the Festival was that of demonstrating the success of the nation's post-war recovery and reconstruction under a Labour administration: to display, in the words of a Board of Trade committee, Britain's 'moral, cultural, spiritual and material' recovery from the destruction and demoralization of war:

> The main thrust of the Festival was towards advertising British achievements in science, technology and design . . . but the Festival was a significant cultural phenomenon, both in its conception and its reception. It is interesting to see how literary its treatment was, for the theme, in the words of the official guide, was 'The Autobiography of a Nation'. Those responsible for arranging the various sections of the shows were officially known as script writers, with the exhibition on the South Bank (the centre-piece, but by no means the only piece) divided into chapters of the 'island story'. The literary approach was essentially didactic and propagandist. This was to be 'a challenge to the sloughs of the present and a shaft of confidence cast forth against the future', said the official guide, falling back on the language of the King James' Bible.[1]

The Festival has been described as, to an extent, a continuity from the machinery of war-time propaganda: 'Both in its approach and its selection of personnel, the Festival of Britain betrayed its origins in the efforts and experience of the Ministry of Information and CEMA in wartime, when the idea of theme exhibitions with a confident message was first put into practice.'[2] CEMA, the Council for the

Encouragement of Music and the Arts, had been established in 1940 and became the Arts Council in 1946; as an instrument of state patronage its importance had been growing, and it was allocated an extra £400,000 to spend on the Festival itself. But despite the centralized planning, the project was able to build on a very broad basis of national support obviously created by the socializing influences of the war. A broad and active popular participation, familiar enough in traditional rituals such as coronations, jubilees and royal weddings, testified encouragingly to a degree of progress in the direction of a new democratic culture.

In cultural terms, however, the Festival now appears as an end to post-war potentialities for progressive change, an anticipation of Winston Churchill's Conservative election victory at the end of the year, rather than a symptom of a developing socialist national consciousness. Michael Frayn argued that the Festival testified to the hegemony of a radical middle class, which favoured Labour's programme for achieving social justice provided it was not permitted to change the fundamental basis of British society:

> With the exception of Herbert Morrison, who was responsible to the Cabinet for the Festival and who had very little to do with the actual form it took, there was almost no one of working-class background concerned in planning the Festival, and nothing about the results to suggest that the working classes were anything more than the lovable human but essentially inert objects of benevolent administration. In fact Festival Britain was the Britain of the radical middle classes – the do-gooders; the readers of the *New Statesman*, the *Guardian*, and the *Observer*; the signers of petitions; the backbone of the BBC.[3]

Naturally then this particular 'Autobiography of a Nation' involved, at least in cultural terms, an attempt to establish links with the past rather than a progressive vision of future change. The paradox is visible in the Jacobean language used by the official guide to express future aspiration; the Festival seemed to embody more strongly reactionary hopes for re-establishing of past glories, than a genuinely socialist vision of historical progress. Desmond Shaw-Taylor, music critic of the *New Statesman*, articulated precisely (though quite unconsciously) the contradiction between reactionary aspirations and the harsh economic and social problems those aspirations would leave untouched, using the Shakespeare myth as the proper language of an idealist's vision violated by a sordid contemporary reality:

> I feel as though our Philistine old Albion, so solid and beefy, has turned overnight into Prospero's insubstantial isle; an impression fostered by the strange glamour and glitter of the South Bank. But not for long is Anglo-Saxon reality to be held at bay. Lured on by the novelty and freshness and colour, I drop into one of the Festival restaurants, . . . and then, ah then, I am soon back in familiar old England. Not indeed in the fine old England of beef sirloins and saddles of mutton, but in our latter-day, take-it-or-leave-it England of lukewarm tomato soup and custard with a skin on the top.[4]

The return to power of Churchill, Shakespearean orator and leader of the 'band of brothers' which saved Britain in her hour of peril, was a fulfilment of those reactionary dreams, visible here in tense contradiction with the progressive hopes of the Labour government's last cultural intervention.

It was therefore entirely predictable that once again 'Shakespeare' should be mobilized to serve the cultural aims of this nationalistic but ostensibly broadly populist and democratic celebration. At this time, before the founding of the Royal Shakespeare Company in 1960, the Shakespeare Memorial Theatre was responsible for running an annual summer season of Shakespeare performances known as the Stratford Summer Festival. As its contribution to the Festival of Britain the Memorial Theatre staged a cycle of the English Histories, the *Richard II-Henry V* tetralogy, integrated into a unified chronological sequence of performances. The ideological context informing the production was the patriotic tradition discussed in the previous chapter, explicitly proclaimed by J. Dover Wilson in an essay called 'Shakespeare and English History as the Elizabethans understood it', contributed to a commemorative volume.[5]

The production represented, Dover Wilson argues, a uniquely successful alliance of criticism and theatre. Both institutions were responsible for distorting and misinterpreting Shakespeare: but an effective collaboration of the two would stand a better chance of discovering and fulfilling Shakespeare's 'purposes'. Those 'purposes' found their appropriate medium in the integrated cycle of historical plays, the perfect discourse for an articulation of the Tudor myth. 'Tudor history was entirely, even superstitiously, monarchical . . . its principal theme was the origin and glorification of the Tudor dynasty.'[6] With unshakeable assurance Dover Wilson asserts that Tudor historiography was entirely monarchical and loyalist; and that Shakespeare shared a common purpose with its propagandist motivations. A quotation from G. M. Trevelyan's *History of England* (1926) is employed to demonstrate that only a superstitious and ritualistic monarchism could have sustained the power of the Tudors, who evidently ruled by consent rather than force: 'English king-worship', said Trevelyan, 'was the secret of a family and spirit of an age.' This 'brilliant generalisation of our greatest living historian' proves to Dover Wilson 'the amazing fact that the strongest government this country has ever known had literally nothing to back it up – no standing army, no bureaucracy, no police . . . nothing but the adoration of the people'.[7] Tudor 'Englishmen' looked back over the period of civil wars and rejoiced in the monarchy which had delivered them from the curse providentially imposed for the deposition of Richard II: 'a monarchy divinely-ordained, absolute, unchallenged, and entirely popular'.[8] The chief intellectual faith of the age was social order, the great intellectual anxiety fear of social disturbance. Shakespeare's tetralogy follows the pattern of Halle's *Union*, and was inspired by the same philosophy of history: the usurpation of Henry IV produced a divinely-initiated chaos, an ever-present possibility to the thoughtful Elizabethan, anxious about the succession and unable to conceive of any society but a strong monarchy: 'All that is fundamental, the very stuff of Shakespeare's thought, as it was bound to be in an age when absolute monarchy, legitimacy, and the "divinity that doth hedge a king" seemed the only pillars of the social system.'[9]

The advantage of producing the plays in connected succession was, for Dover Wilson, that the pattern of orthodox Tudor constitutional theory becomes unmistakably clear in dramatic terms as it had already been clarified in criticism and scholarship; and the characterizations and perspectives produced by a connected historical narrative would secure more firmly the plays' orthodox moral position. Integration does not complicate the plays' potentiality for generating meaning, but reduces it; the larger and more complex structure does not, paradoxically, open out the plurality of significances, but rather constricts them to a fixed, pre-determined frame of reference. There is no possibility, for example, within the whole tetralogy, for an individual actor to develop a role like that of Hotspur or Falstaff to a point where it might introduce a dangerous imbalance into the orthodox moral pattern. Dramatic production of the whole sequence, properly handled, produces, according to Dover Wilson, results identical to those of genuine scholarship and true criticism, by ensuring correct measure and proportion, by eliminating bias and distortion: Bolingbroke and Prince Hal *must* be seen as sympathetic heroes, while Richard II, Hotspur and Falstaff *must* be condemned as forces dangerous to the state:

> As for the notion already glanced at, a notion entertained by many famous critics, that Henry V was a prig and a cad, I make bold to assert that anything so absurd could never have crossed the minds of either Shakespeare or his audience. To them Henry Monmouth was the ideal representative of order and security . . . They knew by experience that England's only safeguard against internal strife and 'the envy of less happier lands' was a Prince who, with the sceptre firmly in his grasp, could be the adored leader of a united and harmonious commonwealth, in which noble, merchant, yeoman and peasant worked together for the good of the whole. Such a Prince was their own Queen Elizabeth; such a Prince was Shakespeare's Henry of Monmouth.[10]

Dover Wilson describes his contribution to this volume, modestly and disingenuously, as an attempt to 'supplement with scholarship' the 'findings of the stage'. In fact the production was built on foundations of a pre-existent scholarly and critical orthodoxy, explicitly proclaimed by the Memorial Theatre's Director, Anthony Quayle:

> . . . it seemed to us that the great epic theme of the Histories had become obscured through years of presenting the plays singly, and many false interpretations had grown up, and come to be accepted, through star actors giving almost too persuasive and dominant performances of parts which the author intended to be by no means so sympathetic. Successful theatrical practice over a great number of years had stealthily built a mountain of misrepresentation and surrounded it with a fog of ignorance. This

was the producers' belief as we worked on the plays, and our purpose in presenting the History Cycle was to rediscover and try to reveal the author's true intentions.[11]

Not surprisingly, the author's true intentions were discovered to be identical with those of Dover Wilson, Tillyard and Wilson Knight: a demonstrative celebration of orthodox Tudor historical thought in which a rigid moral pattern secures a correct apportioning of the audience's 'sympathy': Hal is unquestionably a prodigal prince, ideal king and epic hero; Hotspur simply a hero manqué, Falstaff 'frankly vicious' and ripe for rejection without remorse.

The necessary 'unity' of the productions, as historical chronicle and moralistic parable, prescribed for the producers other kinds of unity: one of which seems to be a genuinely radical shift away from the nineteenth-century tradition of spectacular theatre towards a more open dramatic style based on the physical space of the Elizabethan Theatre. The set was designed by Tanya Moiseiwitsch to resemble an Elizabethan stage. Anthony Quayle writes:

> The next greatest problem was to devise a single setting which could serve all four plays, for to have invented different settings for each play would have destroyed that very unity for which we were striving, that unity which Shakespeare's own Globe preserved so well. The set had to be capable of embracing court and tavern, shire and city, indoor and out-of-door; it had to be the lists at Coventry and the quay-side at Southampton; it had to house the rebels in their barn before the battle of Shrewsbury, and the dying Bolingbroke in the Jerusalem chamber; and, since this list must have an end, it had to suggest the 'wooden O' of *Henry V*.[12]

The set was constructed behind the proscenium arch, and centred around a large wooden structure with a double-door entrance at stage level, a railed platform above, and flights of stairs leading down on each side. A throne stood by the proscenium arch as a permanent feature; otherwise props and hangings were introduced to suggest different locations – a palace, a garden, an inn, a battle-field. Behind the central structure was a cyclorama, illuminated to simulate sky for exterior locations, darkened or covered by hangings for indoor scenes. Despite the obvious modifications, the set's resemblance to an Elizabethan stage is readily apparent, and was evidently accepted as such by a range of critical judgments. The volume quotes one from the *Sunday Times*, which suggests that this production improved on the Elizabethan theatre:

> This year at Stratford (for the first time as far as I know) there has been a real attempt to stage the history plays as Shakespeare intended them to be staged, while avoiding any painful sense of pedantic archaism. Tanya Moiseiwitsch's permanent set was not a reconstruction of the Globe Theatre, but an improvement on it. By using steps up to a wide gallery, with doors opening out underneath it, the set had all the variety of Upper, Lower and Inner Stage which the plays demand, but without the limitation of movement between which was obviously an undesirable feature of the Globe.[13]

T. A. Jackson writing in the *Daily Worker* offered the same proposition with enthusiastic acceptance:

> Let me say at once that the performance was very fine. The stage setting reproduced admirably the lay-out of the stage of Shakespeare's day and so made possible all the pageantry business without any of that over lavish gorgeousness deemed imperative on the flat stage of Beerbohm Tree and Henry Irving. The pageantry and grouping were well-designed and perfectly rehearsed; the actors played as a team – nobody trying to steal the picture from anybody else.[14]

To this critic of the left the production combined a number of favourable features: a noticeable taming-down of the gorgeous pageantry previously regarded as inseparable from Shakespeare's histories in performance; the construction of an emblematic rather than an illusionistic set, with the flexibility and openness of the Elizabethan stage; the prevalance of ensemble performance over the star system. In their context these initiatives were obviously to a degree progressive, and they certainly throw light on the subsequent development of the RSC, which was clearly, in a limited sense, a force of progressive cultural change.[15] Perhaps this production was mobilizing a new Shakespeare: the appropriate contribution to a cultural festival which was, at least theoretically, based upon the popular successes of the Labour government in laying the foundations for a potentially progressive and democratic national unity.

The apparently radical initiative embodied in the set – the one aspect of the production, apart from Redgrave's expressionistic acting, to receive serious criticism – proves on closer inspection to have been too firmly meshed in the institutional and ideological character of the Theatre itself, and too strictly controlled by the orthodoxy which formed the production's intellectual credentials, to progress very far towards a radical new Shakespeare. The permanent set was conceived as an inclusive element in an overall 'continuity', an ideology of unified totality, which posed impervious barriers to the liberation of Shakespearean performance:

> Continuity is the essence of the presentation, and three con-
> ditions are necessary to achieve it. First, a controlling director
> who can fit the four productions into his conception. Then a
> permanent set which remains unchanged throughout, to give us
> the illusion of unity of place. Thirdly a set of actors who can carry
> from play to play those roles which overlap: and this not just in
> the major roles, Bolingbroke, Hal, Falstaff, but no less in the
> subsidiary parts, Northumberland, Westmorland, Lady Percy,
> and the characters from low life.[16]

The first requirement flows naturally from the play's ideological basis: a 'controlling director' committed to an orthodox critical interpretation would police the production, ensuring a consistent loyalty and adherence to a predetermined ideological pattern. The second stipulation reveals that the function of the permanent set was dependent on an uncritical commitment to illusionistic dramatic representation; which was also the distinctive character of the acting, as the illustrative still photographs and the unperturbed pleasure of the theatre critics quoted in this volume both illustrate; and of the costumes and armour, reflecting an attempt at illusionistic historical reconstruction. The third point testifies to the dominance of nat-uralism over the theatrical freedom of Elizabethan dramatic con-ventions: though minor parts were doubled, and Redgrave assigned several star characters, the major roles were sustained by consistent castings, thus naturalizing an actor in a particular part.

The distance between the style of this production and the radical potentialities of the Elizabethan theatre is now more visible, and can be used to measure accurately the production's conservative character. The stage set was much more illusionistic than an Elizabethan stage: distinguishing place and time by artificial lighting and by extensive embellishment and decoration (in the final scene of *Henry V*, the whole stage was transformed by elaborate hangings and canopies into a naturalistic interior representing the French court).[17] In the Elizabethan theatre time and place had to be signalled by convention, so that both would always remain flexible and relative, and the audience would always sustain an awareness of the constructed artifice of the proceedings, would never be seduced into the oblivion of empathetic illusion. Though an audience accustomed to the pageant and panoply of pre-war Shakespeare productions would doubtless find the stage forbidding and austere, there was no encouragement to the audience to recognize it as a stage, the conventionally signified site of a simulated reality. The Shakespeare Memorial Theatre could not but remain a nineteenth-century theatre, with a proscenium-arch stage which consituted the performance as a partitioned representation of reality, and the audience as remote and passive observers 'reading', rather than experiencing or participating in the performance. The Elizabethan stage depended on an entirely different relationship between actors and audience, with the spectators crowded on three (possibly four) sides, their visible and tangible presence exerting a far more distinct pressure on the nature of the production.[18]

The 1951 Festival production was thus able to hand the Dover Wilson/Tillyard/Wilson Knight version of Tudor ideology wholesale, to a passive audience, as a complete and unquestionable totality stripped of all its internal contradictions and constitutive tensions. As the stage becomes more naturalistic, it becomes more authoritarian and more effective in allowing ideology a free and unhampered passage to the spectator. As the stage becomes more illusionistic, it permits less space for the collaborative creation of meaning natural to the Elizabethan theatre. As the audience is further removed from the action, it becomes a passive consumer of a fixed ideology, rather than an active constituency intensely involved in a complex process of reciprocal communication in which ideologies can be interrogated, contradictions made visible, conventions subverted and orthodoxies exposed.

Jane Howell's 1983 production[19] of the 'first tetralogy' of English

History plays – *Henry VI Parts One, Two and Three*, and *Richard III* – can be taken as a striking example of the radical potentialities of Shakespeare in performance (particularly striking in the context of an overwhelmingly orthodox series such as the *BBC-TV Shakespeare*). The radical energies of the drama were released in part by a conscious attempt to reconstruct some of the physical characteristics of Elizabethan and pre-Tudor theatre: not by using a reconstructed model of a Renaissance playhouse, which would not adapt to film treatment, but by devising a set, a production style and an acting convention which would perform some of the functions of the Elizabethan theatre without denying the contemporaneity of the performance. We have considered the aesthetic and ideological effects of a production designed to convey historical authenticity, both by its echoes of the Elizabethan stage and its effort to construct a historically convincing simulacrum of fifteenth-century reality. The privileging of historical authenticity, in Shakespeare's time a progressive force, has become in our own century a conservative one: while the emergent class of Tudor England sought a vision of real historical process to challenge Christian providentialism, for us that positivistic science of history has become pre-eminently the history of our own ruling class. In terms of dramatic production, the locking of a play into a definite and finished historical period by costume, *mise en scène* and acting styles can now be seen as a systematic resistance to change rather than a recognition of its inevitability; and we must require of historical drama the potentiality for alienating and reflecting on its own constructed reality as well as the embodiment, in that constructed reality, of a historiographical interpretation.

Jane Howell's production needs to be considered in juxtaposition with the BBC's version of the second tetralogy, broadcast in 1978 and 1979, a relationship of contrast which I have discussed more thoroughly elsewhere.[20] The *Richard II-Henry V* cycle was directed by David Giles under the producership of Cedric Messina: the productions are a fair sample of the orthodox, establishment Shakespeare, endemic to the BBC-TV series. The decision of Cedric Messina to make the English histories a basic constituent of the first two 'seasons' was correctly diagnosed by an American reviewer as an act of chauvinism, locating the *BBC-TV Shakespeare* in that nationalistic tradition already described.

In the first two 'seasons' (1978–9) . . . there has been a clear emphasis on English history – almost half the plays. . . . Cedric Messina, the originator of the series and the producer of the first two seasons . . . thinks the histories, from *Richard II* up to *Henry V*, are 'the highest achievement of Shakespeare's art. . . . It seems to me, with a lot of hindsight, that these histories are a sort of "Curse of the House of Atreus in English" . . . *Richard II, 1* and *2 Henry IV*, and *Henry V* . . . work out a cycle of guilt, retribution and expiation for the murder of *Richard II*. The BBC productions are very conscious of the continuities of this cycle'.[21]

The overall conception of these plays is correctly diagnosed here as the conventional Tillyard doctrine of providential order violated by usurpation, providential retribution punishing the guilty. The traditionalist line was confirmed and supported by right-wing theoretician Paul Johnson, who contributed an associated broadcast:

According to the orthodox Tudor view of history, the deposition of the rightful and anointed king, Richard II, was a crime against God, which thereafter had to be expiated by the nation in a series of bloody struggles . . . Shakespeare found in the tragic circumstances of Richard II's life a very clear illustration of the general principle that the rule of law was the only barrier against anarchy. Every man in society, in his proper place and degree, had rights and duties . . . Hierarchy was ordained by divine justice and human law.[22]

Television production obviously made much more readily available the possibilities for organizing the plays into an integrated historical narrative:

It was decided that the English histories, from *Richard II* through the *Henry IV*'s, *V* and *VI* to *Richard III*, would be presented in chronological order so that some day in the not too distant future, the eight plays that form this sequence will be able to be seen in their historical order, a unique record of the chronicled history of that time.[23]

Messina's global ambition was fulfilled, but not as he originally envisaged its realization: far from securing a uniformity and continuity of style for the whole cycle, the BBC permitted Jane Howell to mount a production which thoroughly subverted the ideological stability of the earlier versions. The second tetralogy emerges from this production as a constituent element in an inclusive and integrated dramatic totality, illustrating the violation of natural social 'order' by the deposition of a legitimate king. The plays are produced in 'classic drama' style with predominantly naturalistic devices of acting, *mise en scène* and filming. Actors are identified wholly with their roles, growing old in them; settings are more naturalistic than conventionalized; camera movements and angles always 'straightforward', with no 'arty-craft' shooting.

In the case of Jane Howell's production of the first historical tetralogy, the director's whole conception of the Shakespearean history play diverges strikingly from that propounded by Cedric Messina and evidently accepted by David Giles. Where Messina saw the history plays conventionally as orthodox Tudor historiography, and the director employed dramatic techniques which allow that ideology a free and unhampered passage to the spectator, Jane Howell takes a more complex view of the first tetralogy as, simultaneously, a serious attempt at historical interpretation, and as a drama with a peculiarly modern relevance and contemporary application. The director's conception of the plays emphasized their revelation of historical change: not the 'mutability' which operates within a framework of universal order, nor the meaningless flux of metaphysical historicism; but the collision of institutions and ideologies within a specific historical formation – in this case the dialectic of chivalry dissolving from a precarious code of social order into ruthless competition for power: a historical situation which cannot be identified with, but can indirectly suggest analogies with the present:

> . . . the code of the people had been for a long time a belief in chivalry; in the first play one starts to see the death of chivalry, which was epitomised in Henry V . . . When times change people don't realise it for an awfully long time, and so one still has the remnants of chivalry in many ways in *Part Two* . . . with Gloucester's death anarchy is loosed . . . You're into a time of change in which there is no code except survival of the fittest . . . what interests me is that I think we are today in that sort of state, in a time of change.[24]

At the same time there was no intention of sealing the plays firmly into a remote historical period visible only as colourful pageant: by securing a link with perennial traditions of popular entertainment, the production team hoped to synthesize the historical and the contemporary into a single complex dimension capable of generating multiplicity of meaning. The set designer, Oliver Bayldon, recorded that the set was based on an adventure playground in Fulham: '. . . it really was very medieval: it had nooses and cross beams and a bit like a tower: . . .' With a power station looming in the background the location suggested 'equally images of modernity and shadows of medieval castle'. 'We talked about medieval scale and the idea of a circus . . . then the mystery play's stages became the towers we now have. . . . We'd talked about Northern Ireland and Beirut and South America, warlords and factions, and I'd been trying to make it as modern as possible, yet at the same time not modern in such a way that it distracts.'[25]

Howell's ambition was partially to respect those specific characteristics inscribed in the play by the material conditions of its original production: the plays could be made to function as they originally did only by restoring them to a similar physical environment:

> . . . because I knew Shakespeare had written for a company, and you can sense in the plays that there's a lot of doubling, you just know that his company was fifteen or perhaps it was augmented to twenty-five, so there must have been a lot of doubling again, I felt: Go back to the original rules. It just seemed practically *and* artistically a good idea. I was very concerned with obeying the original rules of the play. I think if you're going to do a play you'd better know how it was done originally . . . because it will only work on a certain sort of structure.[26]

Howell evidently managed to establish for the production something like an Elizabethan *ensemble*, very different from the star-system operating in the earlier production of the second tetralogy:

> With this sequence of four plays Howell has once again, as is both her habit and her policy, brought together a group of actors many of whom she has worked with before . . . who form her unofficial repertory company.[27]

Like an Elizabethan stage, the set was deliberately designed as non-representational and unlocalized: Sir Philip Sidney would have bitterly resented the arbitrary flexibility of a single space designated as a court, a castle, a garden, a battlefield, purely by signalled convention. The combination of a non-illusionistic set and actors doubling roles prevents any possibility of a complete 'suspension of disbelief' on the part of the audience. The acting styles too, though enormously varied, were based on a rejection of Stanislavskian method:

> Shakespeare you have to say and allow to affect you rather than seeking to justify the lines. A lot of the work is to say, 'Look, what is the line, what is the intellectual sense, *play* the intellectual sense, stop mucking about with the emotions, follow the intellect'. You have to go that way round rather than doing all this method nonsense – which none of my lot do anyway – of getting yourself in a state and then going on to play it.[28]

Evidently the producer Jonathan Miller's personal influence over this production was minimal, and one can gather probable reasons for this. Asked in an interview how one should stage battle-scenes for the TV screen, he replied that any form of stylization or theatrical presentation would have to be compatible with the irrepressible realism of the camera's mode of perception; various devices could be employed, but 'one would hesitate to use them in the really important plays . . . since they seem to take place in the less good plays, the introduction of electronic gimmickry could be an aid to covering up a second-rate play . . .'[22] The producer's withdrawal of interest from these self-evidently 'second-rate' plays obviously created a space for the creative intervention of a genuinely radical director. She solved the problem of battle-scenes simply by using film techniques, montage and rapid cutting. The climactic battle of *Henry VI Part One* was 'carefully scored as a transition in terms of style', beginning with a self-evidently theatrical, staged fight, filmed in long-shots; modulating into a filmic 'montage of very quick details . . . tight, fast and hard'; and returning to the naturalist/theatrical mode for a static close-up vision of Talbot's death. The director's willingness to embrace the theatrical, to mix conventions and to violate naturalism enabled her to make strikingly effective television of material declared by the Executive Producer to be practically unscreenable. A theatricalized historical pageant presents the spectator with a dramatizing of history in which the history is less prominent than the dramatization; a filmic montage conveys by a 'theatre of cruelty' assault on the senses the bloody savagery of a historic civil war, applicable to any war in any time and place; and the ideology of chivalry is interrogated from a liberal-individualist perspective by the intense *personalizing* of Talbot's dying speech, naturalistically played and filmed in a moving and gory close-up.

This production illustrates very effectively how the theatrical style hinted at by the 1951 production could be pushed much further towards a radical reproduction of Shakespeare's historiography. The set was completely non-illusionistic, looking both modern and Elizabethan and pretending to be neither. Costumes were a mixture of the historical and the emblematic. Acting styles varied, but with a general avoidance of straight-forward naturalism: the alienating device of direct address to camera was used extensively. Jonathan Miller is quoted as arguing that it would be impossible to mix the conventions of television with those of an Elizabethan theatre – hopeless to try recreating the 'wooden O' within the 'electronic square'.[30] His primary concern here was, as always, to defend television naturalism: but he makes a persuasive point about television's elimination of the audience. How could the live audience of an Elizabethan play be contained within the television screen's frame? Jane Howell solved this problem simply: by constituting members of the cast, as frequently as possible, as an active and participating audience, bringing the vitality and changeableness of that audience to the customary blankness of the television screen.

Here then are two examples of 'history in performance', both in their way experimental, both attempting to establish a continuity with the Elizabethan theatre. One is fundamentally conservative, the other radical and progressive.

To express in a concise formula the distinctions between the divergent kinds of drama produced by these different versions of Shakespeare's history plays, we could do worse than adopt Brecht's distinction between 'Theatre for Pleasure' and 'Theatre for Instruction', between the drama of empathy and the drama of 'alienation'.

The dramatic theatre's spectator says: Yes, I have felt like that too – Just like me – it's only natural – It'll never change – The sufferings of this man appal me, because they are inescapable –

That's great art; it all seems the most obvious thing in the world
– I weep when they weep, I laugh when they laugh.

The epic theatre's spectator says: I'd never have thought it –
That's not the way – That's extraordinary, hardly believable – It's
got to stop – The sufferings of this man appal me, because they
are unnecessary – That's great art: nothing obvious in it – I laugh
when they weep, I weep when they laugh.[31]

The Elizabethan theatre was not a theatre of illusion. In fact it
was rather a theatre of alienation, in the sense familiarized by the
dramatic theory and practice of Brecht. A theatre audience watching a modern-dress production of a Shakespeare play in one of
our 'national' theatres, though conscious of some tension between
language and visual style, will assume that the play is addressed
primarily to the present. A television audience watching David
Giles's BBC production of *Henry IV*, which operates entirely in the
conventions of television naturalism (in terms of which a studio set,
for example, appears naturalized and not instantly recognizable
as a wooden construction) will gather that the play is about the
fifteenth century. Both audiences are responding to, and have their
perceptions constituted by, aesthetic conventions of an illusionistic
kind, which insist on the *reality* of the illusion they convey,
naturalize their own fictionality. But the Elizabethan stage, as earlier
discussions have indicated, was neither naturalist not illusionistic.
Modern costume was a neutral accompaniment of a familiar
modern environment and a contemporary, though highly specialized, language: it did not distract the audience from appreciating
the historical world signified in a particular style of poetry, such as
the language of chivalry in *Richard II*. Moreover, the stage being
unlocalized, times could be distinguished or identified as easily as
places; if, as Sidney complained, you could have Asia on one side of
the stage and Africa on another, so on the same stage the fifteenth
century could co-exist with the present: a chivalric medieval prince
could meet a band of sixteenth-century soldiers led by a figure from
immemorial carnival. But co-existence is not confusion in a theatre
of alienation: the distinctions between times and places can be held
as easily as the distinction between actor and role, between visible
object and signified fiction, between empathic identification and
detached objective interest.

History on the Elizabethan stage was not merely a mirror of the contemporary world, nor was it simply a historical reconstruction of the past. A historical play in the Elizabethan theatre was (like all Elizabethan plays) a complex montage capable of connecting and distinguishing very diverse realities, past and present time, near and remote space, subjective consciousness and exterior world. The past could be perceived as past, not to be confused with the present, and yet capable of relevance to the present by the exercise of the curious metaphorical imagination typical of Renaissance thought. Henry V was not in any sense identifiable with the Earl of Essex: but the two cases could be brought into interesting analogical connection. Shakespeare's relationship with the past was one of knowledge through difference.

Conclusion:
Politics of Culture

A definite relationship has been proposed between the originating moment of a text's production and the subsequent history of its reproduction. Those formal and ideological characteristics and capacities inserted into it by the specific determinations and liberties bearing on its initial construction, are all that the activity of reproduction has to work on – although of course that operation can only be conducted within the context of specific political assumptions and a distinct ideological problematic. Shakespeare's English history plays have been considered in the light of two determining contexts: the historiographical and the dramatic, both of which prescribed the exact nature and balance of determinacy and freedom registered in the cultural product itself. The primary determinant was the political, cultural and ideological hegemony of the state itself, which rigidly and strictly prescribed, by patronage, legal interference, bureaucratic control and censorship, the limited spaces of cultural production, both in historiography and in drama. It is not at all surprising then that the ideological framework of Shakespeare's historiography should resemble that of Halle's *Union of the Noble and Illustrious Houses*, beginning with the baronial crisis of 1398 and ending with Henry VII's victory at Bosworth. The dramatic form of the plays was also, self-evidently, thoroughly compatible with the requirements of the Tudor state, imposed through practical controls over the organization of the acting profession, the licensing of companies, the censorship of plays.

Although the state could prescribe and police the spaces of cultural discourse, it could not, ultimately, guarantee or thoroughly determine what was produced in them. There were forces of liberty as well as forces of oppression at work within these allocated sites of cultural struggle, just as there were competing ideologies and contradictory forces at work in the society as a whole. In historiographical terms the plays enact a radical shift from the monarchist framework of the Tudor myth to a problematic of secular and positivist historiography, which was clearly, regarded with hindsight, an emergent cultural discourse of the future. In dramatic terms the plays enact a dialectical conflict of meanings arising from their own ambivalent status as exploratory acts of free performance, based on the fixed determinacy of written historiographical materials, and about to become themselves, by the economic mechanisms of their historical context, literary works of a comparable kind. In that space between deterministic literary historiography and popular comic-romantic historical fiction, the plays interrogate not only the determinism of the old providential mythology, but the new determinism of positivist historiography with its equally strict limitations on imaginative reconstruction of the past. Those discrete and alternative positions of intelligbility discoverable in literary/dramatic works such as Shakespeare's English history plays, are not constructed simply from the ideological characters of individual readings: they are present as potentialities within the historically determined structure of the plays.

By defining as precisely as possible the historical character of the space which produces a cultural discourse, primarily in terms of the political and ideological pressures informing its constitutive activity, it becomes possible to assign the conflicting forces of ideological competition to their respective origins; and furthermore to define and evaluate a text's political position *vis-à-vis* the forces of progress and reaction in a given historical moment. The separable historiographical discourses visible in Shakespeare's English history plays can thus be assigned to their different historical provenances. The providential monarchism of Tudor ideology, propagandist instrument of the sovereign state's hegemony, is very clearly exposed in *Richard II* as a constricting frame protecting a dissolving social formation. That structure is interrogated by the discourse of secular humanist historiography, which discloses the actual social contracts underlying the ideology of absolute monarchy, diagnoses their vulnerability, and proposes a Machiavellian process of political change to replace the apologetic providentialism of orthodox Tudor history. The historical location of such an ideology can be focused in the career of a statesman like Bacon: a new state bureaucracy, drawn from upwardly mobile members of lower social classes, prepared to operate within the framework of the old monarchy but with new political methods. Both these historiographical traditions

are contained and placed within a theoretical framework comparable
to the discoveries of the 'new historians': an empirical sociology of
historical formations which is to be distinctly associated with the
bourgeois and progressive gentry classes. This theoretical problematic is probably close to Shakespeare's own ideological position,
as the bare facts of his later life can be made to testify.[1] It is however
principally in opposition to this ideology that a fourth cultural force
is brought into play in *Henry IV Part One:* a utopian comic
historiography associated with the liberating practices of popular
drama in a theatre of alienation, which poses an entirely different,
entirely radical and oppositional method of conceiving the past; a
form of historical fiction which is, in the terms of this argument, no
less important as an activity of historical reconstruction than the
proto-modern historiography in which our own society finds its
image. The radical energies of this discourse were rooted both
in the popular saturnalian traditions of social celebration, and in
the historical character of the drama itself as it appeared on the
Elizabethan stage. The importance of the relationship between the
historiographical and dramatic dimensions of the enterprise, is that
it becomes possible, by respecting a historically-determined cultural
'identity', to define this discourse as the dominant element of the
drama: and to locate its ideology more firmly in oppositional than in
orthodox tendencies of political thought.

It is via the strategic interrelating of different discourses that the
plays speak of their own time, the later sixteenth century. They do
not address the present directly, by universalist historical generali-
zation or contemporary political allegory: but implicitly, by their
structural organization of ideologies and by the peculiar character
of a historiography embodied in dramatic form. The decline of
feudalism in the fourteenth and fifteenth centuries released many
different social forces to new kinds of liberty and new patterns of
oppression: first the feudal barons themselves, who made the nation
their battleground throughout the fifteenth century; then the new
centralizing monarchy, the bureaucracy and professions invigorated
by broader education and greater social mobility, the emergent bourgeoisie seeking greater economic freedoms, the people released
from feudal bondage to the new servitude of wage-slavery. In this
transitional period of the sixteenth century, between the dissolution
of feudalism and the final establishment of a proto-capitalist state,
much more was in the balance than the centralizing propaganda of

the Tudors could ever admit. These competing social forces produced the competing ideologies of Renaissance historiography: the plays reflect on those ideologies, and thereby indirectly on the social forces themselves. Feudalism is seen as a society of the past, containing within itself contradictory possibilities for an unstable absolute monarchy and a powerful social contract of crown and nobility. Absolute monarchy is not seen as a necessary constitutional pattern of the past or the present, not seen as inseparable from 'kingship'; but rather as a policy forced on monarchs in different historical situations when the social contract breaks down, a policy which has anarchic and socially disruptive results. Having disclosed this historical truth, the plays mobilize and reflect on other discourses associated with both the emergent bourgeoisie and the people; and they conclude, in *Henry IV Part Two*, with a vision of popular oppositional energies subdued to the emergent priorities of the imminently hegemonic discourse of determinist historiography. There is no necessity for simple readings of the plays as mirrors of Elizabethan society, for direct identification of those fifteenth-century monarchs with Elizabeth I, or of Falstaff with the progressive gentry or bourgeoisie; and by distinguishing clearly between past and present, the plays in effect discourage such reductive identification. The conflicts and contradictions of Shakespeare's contemporary society are mediated through the play of discourses and meanings generated by the drama, and become visible only when those discourses are historically analyzed. Thus it is no 'sentimentalizing' of Falstaff to argue that the 'rejection' signals in Shakespeare's historiographical vision a profoundly regrettable ideological closure. Nor is it to attribute to Shakespeare any prophetic anticipation of the ultimate victory of bourgeois society: though in subsequent history these plays were to discover significances not fully available to their writer or their audience.

By deploying cultural discourses which represent the ideologies of different social classes, the plays make themselves available for reactionary *or* progressive reproduction. The particular constellating of ideologies derived from the monarchy, the progressive nobility and gentry, and the bourgeoisie, suggests why Shakespeare's historical drama should have become uniquely significant to our own society, since it was precisely those groups which in the aftermath of the Revolution established the future pattern of British society's historical development. To an extent then, Shakespeare is the great

poet of British bourgeois society: not for all time, but for that
historical formation's particular age.

Yet, as my later chapters have shown, conservative reproduction
transmits an ideology, not a true vision: the plays also contain the
potentiality for radical and progressive reproduction, on account of
their historical origins in a period before the shape of bourgeois
culture was fully and definitely formed. There is a reactionary
'Shakespeare', constructed and designed to hold that culture together. There is also a 'free Shakespeare', potentially a force for
destabilising that culture and pushing it towards social transformation, a force inseparable from the nature of drama itself. It would be
unthinkable to close this discussion of history and theatre, which
proposes drama as a model for political change, without quoting the
words of the working dramatist and marxist thinker who fought all
his life to establish that relationship, in theory and in practice:

> No, we cry from the lower benches in our discontent
> Enough! That will not do. Have you really
> Not yet heard it is now common knowledge
> That this net was knotted and cast by men?
> Today everywhere, from the hundred-storeyed cities
> Over the seas, cross-ploughed by teaming liners
> To the loneliest villages, the word has spread
> That mankind's fate is man alone. Therefore
> We now ask you, the actors
> Of our time – a time of overthrow and of boundless mastery
> Of all nature, even men's own – at last
> To change yourselves and show us mankind's world
> As it really is: made by men and open to alteration.
>
> (Bertolt Brecht, 1935)[2]

Notes

Introduction

1. E. M. W. Tillyard, *The Elizabethan World Picture* (London: Chatto and Windus, 1943), and *Shakespeare's History Plays* (London: Chatto and Windus, 1944).
2. Irving Ribner, *The English History Play in the Age of Shakespeare* (Princeton: Princeton University Press, 1957), p. 12.
3. H. A. Kelly, *Divine Providence in the England of Shakespeare's Histories* (Cambridge, MA: Harvard University Press, 1970).
4. *Ibid.*, p. 36.
5. See for example Lily B. Campbell, *Shakespeare's Histories: Mirrors of Elizabethan Policy* (San Marino, CA: Huntingdon Library, 1947), pp. 59–60.
6. See Moody E. Prior, *The Drama of Power* (Evanston, IL: Northwestern University Press, 1973).
7. J. G. A. Pocock, *The Ancient Constitution and the Feudal Law* (Cambridge: Cambridge University Press, 1957), p. 1.
8. See F. Smith Fussner, *The Historical Revolution* (London: Routledge, 1962).
9. Sir John Davies, 'Dedications' to *Irish Reports* (*Les Reports des Cases et Matters en Ley, Resolves at Adjudges en les Courts del Roy en Ireland*) (Dublin: John Frankton, 1615).
10. Pocock, *Ancient Constitution*, p. 10.
11. Anne Barton, 'The King Disguised: Shakespeare's *Henry V* and the Comical History', in Joseph G. Price (ed.), *The Triple Bond* (University Park, PA: Pennsylvania State University Press, 1975).
12. Barton, 'The King Disguised', p. 97, quoting from Maurice Keen, *The Outlaws of Mediaeval Legend* (London: Routledge, 1961).
13. Barton, 'The King Disguised', p. 111.
14. *Ibid.*, p. 116.

Chapter One

1. David M. Bergeran, *Shakespeare: A Study and Research Guide* (London: Macmillan, 1975), p. 56.
2. See Alvin B. Kernan, '*The Henriad*: Shakespeare's Major History Plays', in Alvin B. Kernan (ed.), *Modern Shakespeare's Criticism*. (San Diego, CA: Harcourt Brace, Jovanovich, 1970), pp. 245–75.
3. See G. Wilson Knight, *The Olive and the Sword* (Oxford: Oxford University Press, 1944); J. Dover Wilson, *The Fortunes of Falstaff* (Cambridge: Cambridge University Press, 1964), and D. A. Traversi, *Shakespeare from 'Richard II' to 'Henry V'* (London: Hollis and Carter, 1957). The *New Shakespeare* edition, by Arthur Quiller-Couch and John Dover Wilson, was published in 1926, and reissued in revised form in 1953. See Introduction, note 6 for Lily B. Campbell.
4. E. M. W. Tillyard, *Shakespeare's History Plays* (London: Chatto and Windus, 1944, reprinted 1980), p. 21.
5. Tillyard, *Shakespeare's History Plays*, p. 23.
6. *Ibid.*, pp. 319–21.
7. *Ibid.*, p. 291.
8. *Ibid.*, p. 299.
9. *Ibid.*, p. 302.
10. *Ibid.*, pp. 298–9.
11. *Ibid.*, p. 263.
12. *Ibid.*, p. 269.
13. *Ibid.*, pp. 276–7.
14. Jonathan Dollimore and Alan Sinfield, 'History and Ideology: the instance of *Henry V*', John Drakakis (ed.), in *Alternative Shakespeares* (London: Methuen, 1986), pp. 208–10.
15. See Karl Marx, *Critique of Hegel's Philosophy of Right*, in Karl Marx and Frederick Engels, *Collected Works*, vol. 2 (London: Lawrence and Wishart, 1975).
16. See A. P. Rossiter, *Angel with Horns and Other Shakespeare Lectures*, edited by Graham Storey (London: Longmans, Green, 1961); and Robert Ornstein, *A Kingdom for a Stage* (Cambridge, MA: Harvard University Press, 1972). For Irving Ribner, see Introduction, note 3.
17. Ornstein, *A Kingdom for a Stage*, p. 27.
18. Wilbur Sanders, *The Dramatist and the Received Idea* (Cambridge: Cambridge University Press, 1968), and Moody E. Prior, *The Drama of Power* (Evanston, IL: Northwestern University Press, 1973).
19. John Wilders, *The Lost Garden* (London: Macmillan, 1978), p. 9.
20. See for example Michel Foucault, *Language, Counter-memory, Practice*, edited by Donald Bouchard (Oxford: Blackwell, 1977); Michel Foucault *Power/Knowledge*, edited by Colin Gordon (Brighton:

Harvester, 1980); Louis Althusser, *For Marx* (*Pour Marx*, Paris, 1966), translated by Ben Brewster (Harmondsworth: Penguin, 1969).

21. See Stephen Greenblatt, *Shakespearean Negotiations* (Oxford: Oxford University Press, 1988), and *Learning to Curse* (London: Routledge, 1990).

22. 'Invisible Bullets', in Alan Sinfield and Jonathan Dollimore (eds), *Political Shakespeare* (Manchester: Manchester University Press, 1985), pp. 18–47. Also in Greenblatt, *Shakespearean Negotiations*.

23. Leonard Tennenhouse, *Power on Display* (London: Methuen, 1986), p. 83.

24. Tony Bennett, *Formalism and Marxism* (London: Methuen, 1979), pp. 147–8.

25. Tony Bennett, 'Text and History', in Peter Widdowson (ed.), *Re-Reading English* (London: Methuen, 1982), p. 227.

26. See Peter Widdowson, '"Literary Value" and the Reconstruction of Criticism', *Literature and History*, vol. 6 (Autumn 1980), pp. 138–50; Catherine Belsey, 'Re-reading the Great Tradition', in Widdowson (ed.), *Re-Reading English*: Alan Sinfield, 'Four Ways with a Reactionary Text', and Peter Stallybrass, 'Re-thinking Text and History', *Literature/Teaching/Politics*, no. 2 (1983), pp. 96–107.

27. Stallybrass, 'Re-thinking Text and History', *passim*.

28. See Catherine Belsey, 'Literature, History, Politics', *Literature and History*, vol. 9 (Spring 1983), pp. 19–20; Peter Brooker, 'Post-structuralism, Reading and the Crisis in English', in Widdowson, *Re-reading English*, pp. 65–7; Stallybrass, 'Re-thinking Text and History', pp. 96–7.

29. Bennett, 'Text and History', pp. 229; 234.

30. Belsey, 'Literature, History, Politics', p. 23.

31. See, for example, Irene Dash, *Wooing, Wedding and Power: Women in Shakespeare* (New York: Columbia University Press, 1981), and Marianne Novy, *Love's Argument: Gender Relations in Shakespeare* (Chapel Hill, IN and London: University of North Carolina Press, 1984).

32. See, for example, Kathleen McLuskie, 'The Patriarchal Bard: feminist criticism and Shakespeare (*King Lear* and *Measure for Measure*)', in Sinfield and Dollimore (eds), *Political Shakespeare*, pp. 88–108; Peter Erickson, *Patriarchal Structures in Shakespeare's Drama* (Berkeley and London: University of California Press, 1985).

33. See Juliet Dusinberre, *Shakespeare and the Nature of Women* (London: Macmillan, 1975); Kathleen McLuskie, *Renaissance Dramatists* (Hemel Hempstead: Harvester Wheatsheaf, 1989); Lisa Jardine, *Still Harping on Daughters: Women and Drama in the Age of Shakespeare* (Brighton: Harvester, 1983); Catherine Belsey, *The Subject of Tragedy:*

Identity and Difference in Renaissance Drama (London: Methuen, 1985).

34. For representative samples of work by Julia Kristeva, Hélène Cixous and Luce Irigaray, see Elaine Marks and Isabelle de Courtivron (eds) *New French Feminisms* (Brighton: Harvester, 1981).

35. 'It is, for example, a little disappointing that feminist criticism has continued to follow traditional assumptions about the established hierarchy *within* the canon, privileging the tragedies above all, then the middle comedies and the problem plays . . . I regret that feminist criticism has so far neglected the earliest plays (apart from the fairly inevitable promotion of *The Taming of the Shrew* and the history plays). Ann Thompson, ' "The warrant of womanhood": Shakespeare and feminist criticism', in Graham Holderness (ed.) *The Shakespeare Myth* (Manchester: Manchester University Press, 1988), p. 85.

36. See, for example, Carol Thomas Neeley, 'Constructing the Subject: Feminist Practice and the New Renaissance Discourses', *English Literary Renaissance*, no. 18 (1988), pp. 5–18.

37. See Valerie Wayne (ed.), *The Matter of Difference: Materialist Feminist Criticism of Shakespeare* (Hemel Hempstead: Harvester Wheatsheaf, 1991).

38. Belsey, 'Literature, History, Politics', p. 26.

39. Jeremy Hawthorne, *Identity and Relationship* (London: Lawrence and Wishart, 1973).

40. Linda Bamber, *Comic Women, Tragic Men: a study of gender and genre in Shakespeare* (Stanford: Stanford University Press, 1982), and Coppélia Kahn, *Man's Estate: masculine identity in Shakespeare* (Berkeley: University of California Press, 1981).

41. Bamber, *Comic Women, Tragic Men*, p. 137.

42. *Ibid.*

43. *Ibid.*

44. *Ibid.* p. 141.

45. Kahn, *Man's Estate*, p. 47.

46. Greenblatt, *Learning to Curse*, p. 3.

47. See Walter Cohen, 'Political criticism of Shakespeare', and Don E. Wayne, 'Power, politics and the Shakespearean text: recent criticism in England and the United States', in Jean E. Howard and Marion F. O'Connor (eds), *Shakespeare Reproduced* (London: Methuen, 1987); and Graham Holderness, 'Production, Reproduction, performance; marxism, history, theatre', in Francis Barker, Peter Hulme and Margaret Iverson (eds), *Uses of History: Marxism, postmodernism and the Renaissance* (Manchester: Manchester University Press, 1991).

48. Jonathan Dollimore, 'Shakespeare, Cultural materialism and the New Historicism', in Sinfield and Dollimore (eds), *Political Shakespeare*, p. 2.

49. Jean-François Lyotard, *The Postmodern Condition: a report on knowledge* (*La Condition Postmoderne*, Paris, 1979), translated by Geoff Bennington and Brian Massumi (Manchester: Manchester University Press, 1984).
50. Catherine Belsey, 'Making Histories Then and Now: Shakespeare from *Richard II* to *Henry V*', in Francis Barker, Peter Hulme and Margaret Iverson (eds), *Uses of History: Marxism, postmodernism and the Renaissance* (Manchester: Manchester University Press, 1991).
51. See Fredric Jameson, 'Postmodernism, or the Cultural Logic of Late Capitalism', *New Left Review*, no. 146 (1984), pp. 53–92, and 'Postmodernism and Consumer Society', in Hal Foster (ed.), *Postmodern Culture* (London: Pluto Press, 1985); Terry Eagleton, 'Capitalism, Modernism and Postmodernism', *New Left Review*, no. 152 (1985), pp. 60–73.
52. Karl Marx, 'The Eighteenth Brumaire of Louis Bonaparte', *Die Revolution* (New York: 1852).

Chapter Two

1. E. M. W. Tillyard, *Shakespeare's History Plays* (London: Chatto and Windus, 1944), p. 244.
2. Peter Ure (ed.), *The Arden Shakespeare: King Richard II* (London: Methuen, 1961), p. lxiv.
3. Raphael Holinshed, *Chronicles of England, Scotlande and Irelande* (London, 1577, 2nd edition 1587, facsimile reprint New York: AMS Press, 1965), vol. 2.
4. See Graham Holderness, Nick Potter and John Turner, *Shakespeare: the Play of History* (London: Macmillan, 1988), pp. 24–5.
5. Holinshed, *Chronicles*, vol. 2, pp. 774ff.
6. *Ibid.*, pp. 774–81.
7. *Ibid.*, p. 793.
8. *Ibid.*, p. 836.
9. *Ibid.*, p. 843.
10. Tillyard, *Shakespeare's History Plays*, pp. 257–9.
11. Derek Traversi, *Shakespeare from 'Richard II' to 'Henry V'* (London: Hollis and Carter, 1957), pp. 12–13.
12. See Henry C. Lea, *Superstititon and Force: Essays on the Wager of Battle* (Philadelphia: Lea, 1866), pp. 148ff.
13. See G. D. Squibb, *The High Court of Chivalry* (Oxford: Oxford University Press, 1959), pp. 22ff.
14. The action is a very precise focus of the conflict I am describing within feudal ideology. Although the whole combat ritual is based on the principles of feudal justice, the king had absolute right to terminate the

battle whenever he wished. The point is made in an ordinance on 'The Order of Battle in the Court of Chivalry' (now in *The Black Book of the Admiralty*, Rolls Series, pp. 325–6), which was presented to Richard II on the occasion of his coronation. The author and presenter of the ordinance – a circumstance not without historical irony – was his uncle, Thomas of Woodstock, Duke of Gloucester.

15. As we learn later from the development of pastoral imagery in the 'garden-scene' (III, iv) (with its ironical counterpoint to Richard's method of 'farming the realm' – see note 17 below), this image of England is actually ideological – it conceals and suppresses real political tensions in a medium of courtly pastoral. For an extended discussion of the politics of pastoral *genre* in *Richard II*, see Graham Holderness, Nick Potter and John Turner, *Shakespeare: the Play of History* (London: Macmillan, 1988), pp. 33–40.

16. See Chapter Four, pp. 71–3, for the development of this image in *Henry IV Part One*.

17. 'Farming the realm' involved the transference of a portion of the royal revenues – i.e. taxes levied from nobles and commons – to an individual in exchange for sums of ready money. The phrase contrasts ironically with the pastorialism of Richard's earlier words (see note 15 above).

18. Gaunt uses the play on the word 'bond' frequently explored in Shakespeare, especially in *The Merchant of Venice*: originally under feudalism a social relationship, increasingly with the rise of capitalism an economic contract.

19. See J. G. Bellamy, *The Law of Treason in the Later Middle Ages* (Oxford: Oxford University Press, 1970), p. 10.

20. See Walter Pater, 'Shakespeare's English Kings', in *Appreciations* (London: Macmillan 1889).

Chapter Three

1. The notion of 'historical consciousness' is explored more fully in Graham Holderness, Nick Potter and John Turner, *The Play of History* (London: Macmillan, 1988).

2. Bamber, *Comic Women, Tragic Men*, p. 139.

3. Christopher Hill, *The World Turned Upside Down* (Harmondsworth: Penguin, 1972).

4. Lawrence Stone, *The Family, Sex and Marriage 1500–1800*, abridged edition (Harmondsworth: Penguin, 1979).

5. Catherine Belsey, *The Subject of Tragedy: Identity and Difference in Renaissance Drama* (London: Methuen, 1985).

6. Juliet Dusinberre, *Shakespeare and the Nature of Women* (London: Macmillan, 1985).

Chapter Four

1. See Ure (ed.), *King Richard II*, pp. xiii–xviii for the facts of the case; and for an extensive discussion, Annabel Patterson, *Shakespeare and the Popular Voice* (Oxford: Blackwell, 1989).
2. Ure (ed.), *King Richard II*, p. 158.
3. Zdenek Stribrny, 'Henry V and History', in Michael Quinn (ed.), '*Henry V*': *a Collection of Critical Essays* (Nashville and London: Aurora Publishing, 1969), p. 187.
4. J. H. Walter, *The Arden Shakespeare: King Henry V* (London: Methuen, 1954), pp. xiv–xxi.
5. See Holinshed, *Chronicles*, vol. 3, p. 65.
6. William Hazlitt, 'Henry V', in *Characters of Shakespeare's Plays* (London; privately printed, 1817).
7. Hazlitt, 'Henry V, p. 158.
8. Walter (ed.), *King Henry V*, pp. xiv–xvii.
9. Holinshed, *Chronicles*, vol. 3, p. 104.
10. Walter Benjamin, *Understanding Brecht* (London: New Left Books, 1977), p. 4.
11. Herbert Arthur Evans (ed.), *The Life of King Henry V* (London: Methuen, 1903), p. 147.
12. See Robert Lacey, *Robert, Earl of Essex* (London: Weidenfeld and Nicolson, 1971), and Patterson, *Shakespeare and the Popular Voice*.

Chapter Five

1. L. G. Salingar, 'The Social Setting', in Boris Ford (ed.), *The Age of Shakespeare* (Harmondsworth: Penguin, 1955), pp. 16–17.
2. See E. K. Chambers, *The English Folk-Play* (Oxford: Clarendon Press, 1933).
3. See Richard Southern, 'The Technique of Play Presentation', in Norman Sanders (et. al., (eds.)), *The Revels History of Drama in English*, vol. 2, 1500–1576 (London: Methuen, 1980), p. 69ff.
4. *Ibid.*, p. 6.
5. *Ibid.*, pp. 7ff.
6. *Ibid.*, p. 24.
7. See Andrew Gurr, *The Shakespearean Stage 1574–1642*, 2nd. edition (Cambridge: Cambridge University Press, 1980), p. 28, and M. C. Bradbrook, *The Rise of the Common Player* (Cambridge: Cambridge University Press, 1962), p. 37.
8. E. K. Chambers, *The Elizabethan Stage* (Oxford: Oxford University Press, 1923), vol. 4, p. 270.
9. Chambers, *Elizabethan Stage*, vol. 2, p. 86.

10. Chambers, *Elizabethan Stage*, vol. 2, pp. 87–8.
11. Gurr, *Shakespearean Stage*, p. 31.
12. Bradbrook, *Common Player*, pp. 39–40.
13. Gurr, *Shakespearean Stage*, p. 6.
14. *Ibid.*, p. 22.
15. *Ibid.*, p. 4.
16. To identify precisely where this 'break' occurs is a difficult project, and a theoretical debate of some current importance. The striking variations between different Elizabethan printed texts, masked by modern editorial procedures, indicate a different relationship between performance and publication. Some of the so-called 'bad Quarto' texts will shortly be published in new editions by Harvester Wheatsheaf under the series title *Shakespeare Originals*, edited by Graham Holderness and Bryan Loughrey. See also Margreta de Grazia, *Shakespeare Verbatim* (Oxford: Oxford University Press, 1991).
17. Gurr, *Shakespearean Stage*, p. 113.
18. Philip Sidney, *A Defence of Poetry* (1595), edited by Jan van Dorsten (Oxford: Oxford University Press, 1966), p. 65.
19. John Russell Brown, *Free Shakespeare* (London: Heinemann, 1974), pp. 111–12.

Chapter Six

1. J. G. Frazer, *The Golden Bough*, Part VI: *The Scapegoat* (London: Macmillan, 1925), p. 306.
2. See E. K. Chambers, *The Mediaeval Stage* (Oxford: Oxford University Press, 1903), pp. 95–6.
3. Frazer, *Scapegoat*, pp. 306–8.
4. *Ibid.*, p. 308.
5. *Ibid.*, p. 329.
6. Chambers, *Mediaeval Stage*, p. 145.
7. Phillip Stubbes, *Anatomy of Abuses in England* (1583), edited by Frederick J. Furnivall (London: New Shakespeare Society, 1877), p. 149.
8. See C. L. Barber, *Shakespeare's Festive Comedy* (Princeton, N.J.: Princeton University Press, 1959), and Robert Weimann, *Shakespeare and the Popular Tradition in the Theatre*, edited by Robert Schwarz (Baltimore: Johns Hopkins University Press, 1978), pp. 15ff.
9. Mikhail Bakhtin, *Rabelais and his World*, translated by Helen Iswolsky (Cambridge, MA.: CIT Press, 1968). This work was first published in the USSR in 1965, though written in 1940.
10. Bakhtin, *Rabelais*, pp. 5–6.
11. *Ibid.*, p. 81.

12. See Barber, *Festive Comedy*, pp. 50–1.
13. See A. L. Morton, *The English Utopia* (London: Lawrence and Wishart, 1978).
14. Bakhtin, *Rabelais*, pp. 9; 24.
15. *Ibid.*, p. 19.
16. *Ibid.*, p. 24.
17. *Ibid.*
18. *Ibid.*, pp. 33–4.
19. J. Dover Wilson, *The Fortunes of Falstaff* (Cambridge: Cambridge University Press, 1964), pp. 5ff.
20. Bakhtin, *Rabelais*, p. 24.
21. Dover Wilson, *Fortunes of Falstaff*, pp. 5ff.
22. *Ibid.*, p. 7.
23. *Ibid.*, p. 22.
24. *Ibid.*, p. 25.
25. *Ibid.*, p. 128.
26. *Ibid.*
27. Barber, *Festive Comedy*, p. 195. See above, pp. 7–8 for Tillyard on the Prince.
28. *Ibid.*, pp. 195.
29. *Ibid.*, p. 226.
30. *Ibid.*, pp. 213–4.
31. *Ibid.*, p. 216.
32. A. R. Humphreys (ed.), *The Arden Shakespeare: Henry IV Part One* (London: Methuen, 1960), p. lvi.
33. *Ibid.*
34. *Ibid.*, p. lvii.
35. A. R. Humphreys (ed.), *The Arden Shakespeare: Henry IV Part Two* (London: Methuen, 1960), pp. lx–lxi.
36. J. F. Danby, *Shakespeare's Doctrine of Nature* (London: Methuen, 1961), pp. 83–4.
37. Elliot Krieger, *A Marxist Study of Shakespeare's Comedies* (London: Macmillan, 1979), p. 133.
38. Rosemary Jackson, *Fantasy: the Literature of Subversion* (London: Methuen, 1981), p. 14.
39. Cf. Daniel Seltzer, 'Prince Hal and Tragic Style', *Shakespeare Survey*, vol. 30 (1977), p. 24.
40. Cf. A. C. Bradley, 'The Rejection of Falstaff', *Oxford Lectures on Poetry* (London: Macmillan, 1959).
41. Dover Wilson, *Fortunes of Falstaff*, p. 33.
42. Humphreys (ed.), *Henry IV Part One*, p. xliv.
43. *Ibid.*, p. xlix.
44. Michael Drayton, Anthony Munday, Richard Hathaway and Robert

Wilson. See Barton, 'The King Disguised', p. 107. The play can be found in C. F. Tucker Brooke (ed.), *The Shakespeare Apocrypha* (Oxford: Oxford University Press, 1918).

45. See Andrew Gurr, *The Shakespearean Stage 1574–1642*, 2nd edition (Cambridge: Cambridge University Press, 1980), pp. 117; 119.
46. Thomas Heywood, *King Edward IV* (1600) (London: Shakespeare Society, 1842), p. 93.
47. Falstaff speaks 'in King Cambyses' vein', i.e. in the style of Thomas Preston's *Lamentable Tragedie, mixed full of pleasant mirth, containing the Life of Cambises, King of Percia* (1569), or rather in a style recalling the successors of that vein of high-flown dramatic rant, Kyd and Green. The rhetorician Lyly is also parodied by the use of 'euphuism' – 'the affectation of recondite learning, trite quotations, rhetorical questions, verbal antitheses and alliterations' – see Humphreys, *Henry IV Part One*, p. 78.
48. J. Dover Wilson (ed.), *The First Part of the History of Henry IV* (Cambridge: Cambridge Univesity Press, 1946), p. 186.
49. Dover Wilson, *Fortunes of Falstaff*, p. 120.

Chapter Seven

1. G. Wilson Knight, *The Olive and the Sword* (Oxford: Oxford University Press, 1944). The first version was published as a pamphlet *This Sceptered Isle* in 1940. For details of the stage production, see G. Wilson Knight, *Shakespearean Production* (London: Faber, 1964).
2. 'Cato', *Guilty Men* (London: Gollancz, 1940), p. 48.
3. Angus Calder, *The Peoples' War 1939–45* (London: Cape, 1965).
4. *Ibid.*, p. 17.
5. Henry Pelling, *Britain in the Second World War* (London: Collins, 1970).
6. Knight, *Olive and Sword*, p. 1.
7. *Ibid.*
8. *Ibid.*, p. 2
9. *Ibid.*, p. 4.
10. *Ibid.*, p. 5.
11. *Ibid.*, p. 16.
12. *Ibid.*, p. 89.
13. *Ibid.*, pp. 29; 32.
14. *Ibid.*, p. 37.
15. G. Wilson Knight, in C. Woolf and J. Moorcroft Wilson (eds), *Authors Take Sides on the Falklands* (London, 1982).
16. See Clayton C. Hutton, *The Making of 'Henry V'* (London: Hutton, 1944).

17. See, for example, Frederick Aicken, 'Shakespeare on the Screen', *Screen Education* (Sept–Oct., 1963), p. 33, and J. Blumenthal, '*Macbeth* into *Throne of Blood*', *Sight and Sound*, 34 (1965), p. 191.
18. See for example Michael Balcon and E. Lindgren, *20 Years of British Film, 1925–45* (London: Falcon Press, 1947), and Blumenthal, '*Macbeth*', pp. 191 and 195n.
19. Laurence Olivier, quoted in Roger Manvell, *Shakespeare and the Film* (London: Dent, 1975), p. 56.
20. Jack Tinker, *Daily Mail*, 29 March 1984; reprinted in *London Theatre Record*, IV, 7 (1984), p. 270.
21. *Henry V*, directed by Kenneth Branagh, produced by Bruce Sharman (1989); based on a 1984 production of the Royal Shakespeare Company, directed by Adrian Noble. My description 'widely celebrated' can be measured in the press reviews quoted later in this chapter; and see also the *Shakespeare on Film Newsletter*, 14, 2, which cites in support of Robert F. Wilson's positive evaluation ('*Henry V*/Branagh's and Olivier's Choruses') a celebratory 'Chorus of critics' (pp. 1–2). Branagh received Academy Award nominations as best actor and best director.
22. Tom Hutchinson, *Mail on Sunday*, 8 October 1989.
23. The phrase derives from D. H. Lawrence's poem 'Piano' (see note 24), but occurs in the stage directions of Branagh's *Henry V* screenplay: see K. Branagh, *Henry V by William Shakespeare: a Screen Adaptation* (London: Chatto & Windus, 1989), p. 32.
24. D. H. Lawrence, 'Piano', in K. Sagar (ed.), *Selected Poems of D. H. Lawrence* (Harmondsworth: Penguin, 1972), p. 21.
25. Holinshed, *Chronicles*, vol. 1, p. 443.
26. J. Turner, '*King Lear*', in G. Holderness, N. Potter and J. Turner, *Shakespeare: the Play of History* (London: Macmillan, 1988), p. 92. See also T. Hawkes, 'Lear's map: a general survey', *Deutsche Shakespeare-Gesellschaft-West Jahrbuch* (1989), pp. 36–7.
27. Turner, in Holderness, Potter, and Turner (1988), p. 93.
28. cf. Seamus Heaney's poem 'Act of Union', where a sexual relationship is linked metaphorically with the political connection of Britain and Ireland, colonizer and colonized: 'I grow older/Conceding your half-independent shore/Within whose borders now my legacy/Culminates inexorably.'
29. See K. P. Wentersdorf, 'The conspiracy of silence in *Henry V*', *Shakespeare Quarterly*, vol. 27 (1976), pp. 264–87 and G. Holderness, '*Henry V*' in Holderness, Potter, and Turner (1988), pp. 70–2.
30. Branagh, *Henry V* (1989), p. 12.
31. *Ibid.*, pp. 35–6.
32. *Ibid.*, p. 36.

33. *Ibid.* See stage directions, p. 40; illustration, p. 41.
34. P. French, *Observer*, 8 October 1989.
35. A. Mars-Jones, *The Independent*, 5 October, 1989.
36. C. Tookey, *Sunday Telegraph*, 8 October 1989.
37. Charles Wood, *Tumbledown* (Harmondsworth: Penguin, 1987).
38. Kenneth Branagh discusses his approach to the stage role of Henry V in Philip Brockbank (ed.), *Players of Shakespeare* (Cambridge: Cambridge University Press, 1985), and in his autobiography, *Beginning* (London: Chatto & Windus, 1989), pp. 137–9.
39. See Branagh, *Beginning*, pp. 141–4.
40. See Michael Quinn, 'Celebrity and the semiotics of acting', *New Theatre Quarterly*, VI, 22 (1990), pp. 154–161.
41. P. Lewis, *Sunday Times*, 10 September 1989.
42. P. French, *Observer*, 8 October 1989.
43. A. Mars-Jones, *The Independent*, 5 October 1989.
44. P. Lewis, *Sunday Telegraph*, 24–30 September 1989.
45. B. Bamigboye, *Daily Mail*, 18 November 1989.
46. P. Lewis, *Sunday Times*, 10 September 1989.
47. Ian Johnstone, *Sunday Times*, 8 October 1989.
48. A. Lane, *The Independent*, 30 September 1989.
49. A. Bilson, *Sunday Correspondent*, 8 October 1989.
50. A. Walker, in the *London Evening Standard*, 25 May 1989. Branagh himself ironically traced the roots of his career to a conjuncture of drama and sport: at school he was made captain of both rugby and football teams, 'I suspect for my innate sense of drama – I loved shouting theatrically butch encouragement to "my lads"' (Branagh, *Beginning*, p. 28).
51. P. Lewis, *Sunday Times*, 10 September 1989.
52. P. Lewis, *Sunday Telegraph*, 24–30 September 1989.
53. Quoted by P. Lewis, *Sunday Telegraph*, 24–30 September 1989.
54. R. Corliss, *The Times*, 13 November 1989, and A. Mars-Jones, *The Independent*, 5 October 1989.
55. Raphael Samuel, 'Introduction: exciting to be English', in Raphael Samuel (ed.), *Patriotism: the Making and Unmaking of National Identity*, vol. 1, *History and Politics* (London: Routledge, 1989), pp. xli–xlii; xxxix–xl.
56. Branagh, *Beginning*, p. 22.
57. Ibid., p. 23.
58. Ibid., p. 24.
59. Branagh, *Henry V*, p. 111.
60. Ibid., pp. 71–4.
61. Quoted by P. Lewis, *Sunday Times*, 10 September 1989.
62. H. Davenport, *Daily Telegraph,* 5 October 1989.

63. Branagh, *Henry V*, p. 113.
64. *Ibid.*
65. See Branagh, *Beginning*, p.20.
66. *Ibid.*, p. 239.

Chapter Eight

1. Robert Hewison, *In Anger: Culture and the Cold War, 1945–60* (London: Weidenfeld and Nicolson, 1981), pp. 48–9.
2. Hewison, *In Anger*, p. 49.
3. Michael Frayn in Michael Sissons and Philip French, *The Age of Austerity* (London: Hodder and Stoughton, 1963).
4. Quoted in Robert Hewison, *In Anger*, p. 55.
5. J. Dover Wilson and T. C. Worsley, *Shakespeare's Histories at Stratford 1951* (London: Max Reinhardt, 1952).
6. *Ibid.*, p. 7.
7. *Ibid.*, p. 8.
8. *Ibid.*, p. 9.
9. *Ibid.*, p. 9.
10. *Ibid.*, p. 22.
11. Anthony Quayle, 'Foreword' to Wilson and Worsley, *Shakespeare's Histories*, pp. xviii–ix.
12. *Ibid.*, p. ix.
13. Rosemary Anne Sissons, quoted in Wilson and Worsley, *Shakespeare's Histories*, p. 55.
14. T. A. Jackson, quoted in Wilson and Worsley, *Shakespeare's Histories*, pp. 65.
15. See Alan Sinfield, 'Royal Shakespeare', in Jonathan Dollimore and Alan Sinfield (eds), *Political Shakespeare* (Manchester: Manchester University Press, 1985).
16. T. C. Worsley in Wilson and Worsley, *Shakespeare's Histories*, p. 31.
17. *Ibid.*, photograph facing p. 10.
18. Buzz Goodbody's attempts to radicalize Shakespeare productions at Stratford's The Other Place involved changing the relations between actors and audience in this direction. See Dympna Callaghan, 'Buzz Goodbody: Directing for Change', in Jean I. Marsden (ed.), *The Appropriation of Shakespeare: Post-Renaissance Reconstructions of the Works and the Myth* (Hemel Hempstead: Harvester Wheatsheaf, 1991).
19. Directed by Jane Howell as part of the BBC/Time–Life Shakespeare series, under the producership of Jonathan Miller. Broadcast 1983.
20. See Graham Holderness, 'Radical Potentiality and Institutional Closure: Shakespeare in film and television', in Dollimore and Sinfield

(eds), *Political Shakespeare*, and (with Christopher McCullough), 'Boxing the Bard: the cultural politics of television Shakespeare'. *Red Letters*, no. 18 (1986), pp. 23–33.

21. Maurice Charney, 'Shakespearean Anglophobia: the BBC–TV series and American Audiences', *Shakespeare Quarterly*, vol. 31 (1980), p. 292.
22. Paul Johnson, '*Richard II*', in Roger Sales (ed.), *Shakespeare in Perspective* (London: BBC/Ariel Books, 1983), pp. 33–5.
23. Cedric Messina, 'Preface' to *The BBC-TV Shakespeare: 'Richard II'* (London: BBC/Ariel Books, 1978), pp. 7–8.
24. Jane Howell, quoted in Henry Fenwick, 'The Production', in *The BBC-TV Shakespeare Series: 'Henry VI, Part One'* (London: BBC/ Ariel Books, 1983), pp. 22–3.
25. *Ibid.*, p. 24.
26. *Ibid.*, p. 29.
27. Fenwick in *BBC-TV 'Henry VI Part One'*, p. 25.
28. Howell quoted by Fenwick in *BBC-TV 'Henry VI Part One'*, p. 24.
29. Ann Pasternak Slater, 'An Interview with Jonathan Miller', *Quarto*, vol. 10 (September 1980), p. 9.
30. Slater, 'Interview with Miller', p. 9. See also Jonathan Miller interviewed in Graham Holderness (ed.), *The Shakespeare Myth* (Manchester: Manchester University Press, 1988).
31. John Willett (ed.), *Brecht on Theatre* (London: Methuen, 1964), p. 71.

Conclusion

1. See Edward Bond, *Bingo* (London: Eyre Methuen, 1974).
2. Bertolt Brecht, *Poems*, edited by John Willett and Ralph Manheim (London: Eyre Methuen, 1975), p. 234.

Bibliography

Aicken, Frederick, 'Shakespeare on the screen', *Screen Education* (Sept–Oct., 1963), pp. 32–7.

Althusser, Louis, *For Marx* (*Pour Marx*, Paris, 1966), translated by Ben Brewster (Harmondsworth: Penguin, 1969).

Bakhtin, Mikhail, *Rabelais and his World*, translated by Helen Iswolsky (Cambridge, MA: CIT Press, 1968).

Balcon, Michael, and E. Lindgren, *20 Years of British Film, 1925–45* (London: Falcon Press, 1947).

Bamber, Linda, *Comic Women, Tragic Men: A study of gender and genre in Shakespeare* (Stanford: Stanford University Press, 1982).

Barber, C. L., *Shakespeare's Festive Comedy: A study of dramatic form and its relation to social custom* (Princeton, NJ: Princeton University Press, 1959).

Barber, C. L., 'The Family in Shakespeare's development: tragedy and sacredness', in Kahn, Coppélia and Schwarz, Murray M. (eds), *Representing Shakespeare: new psychoanalytic essays* (Baltimore: Johns Hopkins University Press, 1980).

Barton, Anne, 'The King Disguised: Shakespeare's *Henry V* and the comical history', in Price, Joseph G. (ed.), *The Triple Bond* (University Park, PA: Pennsylvania State University Press, 1975).

Bellamy J. G., *The Law of Treason in the Later Middle Ages* (Oxford: Oxford University Press, 1970).

Belsey, Catherine, 'Re-reading the Great Tradition', in Widdowson, Peter (ed.), *Re-Reading English* (London: Methuen, 1982).

Belsey, Catherine, 'Literature, history, politics', *Literature and History*, vol. (Spring 1983), pp. 17–27.

Belsey, Catherine, *The Subject of Tragedy: Identity and difference in renaissance drama* (London: Methuen, 1985).

Belsey, Catherine, 'Making Histories Then and Now: Shakespeare from *Richard II* to *Henry V*', in Barker, Francis, Hulme, Peter and Iverson, Margaret (eds), *Uses of History: Marxism, postmodernism and the Renaissance* (Manchester: Manchester University Press, 1991).

Benjamin, Walter, *Understanding Brecht* (London: New Left Books, 1977).

Bennett, Tony, *Formalism and Marxism* (London: Methuen, 1979).

Bennett, Tony, 'Text and history', in Widdowson, Peter (ed.), *Re-Reading English* (London: Methuen, 1982).

Berger, Harry J., Jr., 'Psychoanalysing the Shakespeare text', in Parker, Patricia and Hartman, Geoffrey (eds), *Shakespeare and the Question of Theory* (New York and London: Methuen, 1985).

Bergeran, David M., *Shakespeare: A study and research guide* (London: Macmillan, 1975).

Blumenthal, J., '*Macbeth* into *Throne of Blood*', *Sight and Sound*, 34 (1965), pp. 190–5.

Bond, Edward, *Bingo* (London: Eyre Methuen, 1974).

Bradbrook, Muriel, *The Rise of the Common Player* (Cambridge: Cambridge University Press, 1962).

Bradley, A. C., 'The rejection of Falstaff', *Oxford Lectures on Poetry* (London: Macmillan, 1959).

Branagh, Kenneth, *Beginning* (London: Chatto and Windus, 1989).

Branagh, Kenneth, *Henry V by William Shakespeare: A screen adaptation* (London: Chatto and Windus, 1989).

Brecht, Bertolt, *Poems*, edited by John Willett and Ralph Manheim (London: Eyre Methuen, 1975).

Bristol, Michael D., *Carnival and Theatre: Plebian culture and the structure of authority in renaissance England* (London and New York: Methuen, 1985).

Brockbank, Philip (ed.), *Players of Shakespeare* (Cambridge: Cambridge University Press, 1985).

Brooker, Peter, 'Post-structuralism, reading and the crisis in English', in Widdowson, Peter (ed.), *Re-Reading English* (London: Methuen, 1982).

Brown, John Russell, *Free Shakespeare* (London: Heinemann, 1974).

Campbell, Lily B., *Shakespeare's Histories: Mirrors of Elizabethan policy* (San Marino CA: Huntingdon Library, 1947).

Calder, Angus, *The Peoples' War 1939–45* (London: Cape, 1969).

'Cato', *Guilty Men* (London: Gollancz, 1940).

Certain Homilies Appointed to be read in Churches in the time of Queen Elizabeth (London; SPCK, 1908).

Chambers, E. K., *The Mediaeval Stage* (Oxford: Oxford University Press, 1903).

Chambers, E. K., *The Elizabethan Stage* (Oxford: Clarendon Press, 1923).

Chambers, E. K., *The English Folk-Play* (Oxford: Clarendon Press, 1933).

Charney, Maurice, 'Shakespearean Anglophobia: the BBC-TV series and American audiences', *Shakespeare Quarterly*, vol. 31 (1980), pp. 287–92.

Cohen, Walter, 'Political criticism of Shakespeare' in Howard, Jean E. and

O'Connor, Marion F. (eds), *Shakespeare Reproduced* (London and New York: Methuen, 1987).

Creton, Jean, *Archaeologia, vol. XX: Translation of a French metrical history of the deposition of King Richard II*, edited and translated by John Webb (London; Society of Antiquaries, 1819).

Danby, J. F., *Shakespeare's Doctrine of Nature* (London: Methuen, 1961).

Daniel, Samuel, *The Civil Wars*, edited by Laurence Michel (New Haven: Yale University Press, 1958).

Dash, Irene, *Wooing, Wedding and Power: Women in Shakespeare's plays* (New York: Columbia University Press, 1981).

Davies, Sir John, 'Dedications' to *Irish Reports* (*Les Reports des Cases et Matters en Ley, Resolves at Adjudges en les Courts del Roy en Ireland*) (Dublin: John Frankton, 1615).

Davies, Tony, 'Education, ideology and literature', *Red Letters*, no. 7 (n.d.), pp. 4–15.

Dekker, Thomas, *The Shoemaker's Holiday*, edited by D. J. Palmer (London: Ernest Benn, 1975).

Dollimore, Jonathan, 'Shakespeare, cultural materialism and the new historicism', in Dollimore, Jonathan and Sinfield, Alan (eds) *Political Shakespeare* (Manchester: Manchester University Press, 1985).

Dollimore, Jonathan, and Sinfield, Alan, 'History and ideology: the instance of *Henry V*', in Drakakis, John (ed.), *Alternative Shakespeares* (London: Methuen, 1986).

Doyle, Brian, 'Against the tyranny of the past', *Red Letters*, no. 10 (n.d.), pp. 23–33.

Dusinberre, Juliet, *Shakespeare and the Nature of Women* (London: Macmillan, 1975).

Drayton, Michael, Munday, Anthony, Hathaway, Richard and Wilson, Robert, 'The Fortunes of Sir John Oldcastle', in Brooke, C. F. Tucker (ed.), *The Shakespeare Apocrypha* (Oxford: Oxford University Press, 1918).

Eagleton, Terry, 'Capitalism, modernism and postmodernism', *New Left Review*, no. 152 (1985), pp. 60–73.

Erickson, Peter, *Patriarchal Structures in Shakespeare's Drama* (Berkeley and London: University of California Press, 1985).

Evans, Herbert Arthur, (ed.), *The Life of King Henry V* (London: Methuen, 1903).

Fenwick, Henry, 'The production', in *The BBC-TV Shakespeare Series: 'Henry VI, Part One'* (London: BBC/Ariel Books, 1983).

Ford, Boris (ed.), *The Age of Shakespeare* (Harmondsworth: Penguin, 1955).

Foucault, Michel, *Language, Counter-memory, Practice*, edited by Donald Bouchard (Oxford: Blackwell, 1977).

Foucault, Michel, *Power/Knowledge*, edited by Colin Gordon (Brighton: Harvester, 1980).

Frazer, J. G., *The Golden Bough*, Part VI: *The scapegoat* (London: Macmillan, 1925).

Fussner, F. Smith, *The Historical Revolution* (London: Routledge and Kegan Paul, 1962).

Girard, Rene, *Violence and the Sacred* (Baltimore: Johns Hopkins University Press, 1979).

Grady, Hugh, *The Modernist Shakespeare* (Oxford: Oxford University Press, 1991).

Grazia, Margreta de, *Shakespeare Verbatim* (Oxford: Oxford University Press, 1991).

Greenblatt, Stephen, 'Invisible bullets', in *Shakespearean Negotiations: The Circulation of social energy in Renaissance England* (Oxford: Oxford University Press, 1988).

Greenblatt, Stephen, *Learning to Curse: Essays in early modern culture* (London: Routledge, 1990).

Gurr, Andrew, *The Shakespearean Stage 1574–1642*, 2nd. edition (Cambridge: Cambridge University Press, 1980).

Halle, Edward, *The Union of the Two Noble and Illustre Families of Lancaster and York* (London; In officina R. Graftoni, 1548).

Hawkes, Terence, *Shakespeare's Talking Animals* (London: Methuen, 1977).

Hawkes, Terence, 'Lear's map: a general survey', *Deutsche Shakespeare-Gesellschaft-West Jahrbuch* (1989), pp. 134–47.

Hawthorne, Jeremy, *Identity and Relationship* (London: Lawrence and Wishart, 1973).

Hazlitt, William, 'Henry V', in *Characters of Shakespeare's Plays* (London; privately printed, 1817).

Heaney, Seamus, *North* (London: Faber, 1975).

Hewison, Robert, *In Anger: Culture and the Cold War, 1945–60* (London: Weidenfeld and Nicolson, 1981).

Heywood, Thomas, *King Edward IV* (1600) (London: Shakespeare Society, 1842).

Hill, Christopher, *The World Turned Upside Down* (Harmondsworth: Penguin, 1972).

Holderness, Graham, 'Radical potentiality and institutional closure: Shakespeare in film and television', in Dollimore, Jonathan and Sinfield, Alan (eds.), *Political Shakespeare* (Manchester: Manchester University Press, 1985).

Holderness, Graham with Christopher McCullough, 'Boxing the bard: the cultural politics of television Shakespeare', *Red Letters*, no. 18 (1986), pp. 23–33.

Holderness, Graham (ed.), *The Shakespeare Myth* (Manchester: Manchester University Press, 1988).

Holderness, Graham, Nick Potter and John Turner, *Shakespeare: the Play of History* (London: Macmillan, 1988).

Holderness, Graham, 'Production, reproduction, performance; marxism, history, theatre', in Barker, Francis, Hulme, Peter and Iverson, Margaret, *Uses of History: Marxism, postmodernism and the Renaissance* (Manchester: Manchester University Press, 1991).

Holderness, Graham (ed.), *Shakespeare's History Plays: A new casebook* (London: Macmillan, 1992).

Holinshed, Raphael, *Chronicles of England, Scotlande and Irelande* (London, 1577, 2nd edition 1587, facsimile reprint New York: AMS Press, 1965).

Howard, Jean E. and O'Connor, Marion F., *Shakespeare Reproduced* (London and New York: Methuen, 1987).

Humphreys, A. R. (ed.), *The Arden Shakespeare: Henry IV Part One* (London: Methuen, 1960).

Humphreys, A. R. (ed.), *The Arden Shakespeare: Henry IV Part Two* (London: Methuen, 1960).

Hutton, Clayton C., *The Making of 'Henry V'* (London: Hutton, 1944).

Jackson, Rosemary, *Fantasy: The literature of subversion* (London: Methuen, 1981).

Jameson, Fredric, 'Postmodernism, or the cultural logic of late capitalism', *New Left Review*, no. 146 (1984), pp. 53–92.

Jameson, Fredric, 'Postmodernism and consumer society', in Foster, Hal (ed.), *Postmodern Culture* (London: Pluto Press, 1985).

Jardine, Lisa, *Still Harping on Daughters: Women and drama in the age of Shakespeare* (Brighton: Harvester, 1983).

Johnson, Paul, '*Richard II*', in Sales, Roger (ed.), *Shakespeare in Perspective* (London: BBC/Ariel Books, 1983).

Kahn, Coppélia, *Man's Estate: masculine identity in Shakespeare* (Berkeley: University of California Press, 1981).

Kantorowicz, E. H., *The King's Two Bodies* (Princeton, NJ: Princeton University Press, 1957.

Keen, Maurice, *The Outlaws of Mediaeval Legend* (London: Routledge and Kegan Paul, 1961).

Kelly, Henry Ansagar, *Divine Providence in the England of Shakespeare's Histories* (Cambridge, MA: Harvard University Press, 1970).

Kernan, Alvin B., '*The Henriad*: Shakespeare's major history plays', in Kernan, Alvin B. (ed.), *Modern Shakespeare Criticism* (San Diego, CA: Harcourt Brace Jovanovich, 1970), pp. 245–75.

Knight, G. Wilson, *The Olive and the Sword* (Oxford: Oxford University Press, 1944).

Knight, G. Wilson, *Shakespearean Production* (London: Faber, 1964).

Krieger, Elliot, *A Marxist Study of Shakespeare's Comedies* (London: Macmillan, 1979).

Lacey, Robert, *Robert, Earl of Essex* (London: Weidenfeld and Nicolson, 1971).

Lawrence, D. H., *Selected Poems of D. H. Lawrence*, edited by K. Sagar (Harmondsworth: Penguin).

Lea, Henry C., *Superstititon and Force: Essays on the wager of battle* (Philadelphia: Lea, 1866).

Leavis, F. R., 'A retrospect', *Scrutiny*, XX (1963), pp. 1–20.

Longhurst, Derek, '"Not for all time, but for an age": an approach to Shakespeare Studies', in Widdowson, Peter, (ed.), *Re-Reading English* (London: Methuen, 1982).

Lyotard, Jean-François, *The Postmodern Condition: a report on knowledge* (*La Condition Postmoderne*, Paris, 1979), translated by Geoff Bennington and Brian Massumi (Manchester: Manchester University Press, 1984).

Manvell, Roger, *Shakespeare and the Film* (London: Dent, 1975).

Marks, Elaine and Isabelle de Courtivron (eds), *New French Feminisms* (Brighton: Harvester, 1981).

Marsden, Jean I. (ed.), *the Appropriation of Shakespeare: Post-Renaissance reconstructions of the works and the myth* (Hemel Hempstead: Harvester Wheatsheaf, 1991).

Marx, Karl, *Critique of Hegel's Philosophy of Right*, in Karl Marx and Frederick Engels, *Collected Works*, vol. 2 (London: Lawrence and Wishart, 1975).

Marx, Karl, 'The Eighteenth Brumaire of Louis Bonaparte', *Die Revolution* (New York; 1852).

McLuskie, Kathleen, 'The Patriarchal bard: feminist criticism and Shakespeare (*King Lear* and *Measure for Measure*)', in Dollimore, Jonathan and Sinfield, Alan, (eds), *Political Shakespeare* (Manchester: Manchester University Press, 1985).

McLuskie, Kathleen, *Renaissance Dramatists* (Hemel Hempstead: Harvester Wheatsheaf, 1989).

Messina, Cedric, 'Preface' to *The BBC-TV Shakespeare: 'Richard II'* (London: BBC/Ariel Books, 1978).

Montrose, Louis Adrian, 'Renaissance literary studies and the subject of history', *English Literary Renaissance*, no. 16 (1986), pp. 5–18.

Morton, A. L., *The English Utopia* (London; Lawrence and Wishart, 1978).

Mulhern, Francis, *The Moment of 'Scrutiny'* (London: New Left Books, 1979).

Nairn, Tom, *The Enchanted Glass: Britain and its monarchy* (London, Radius, 1988).

Neeley, Carol Thomas, 'Constructing the subject: Feminist practice and the new renaissance discourses', *English Literary Renaissance*, no. 18 (1988), pp. 5–18.

Novy, Marianne, *Love's Argument: Gender relations in Shakespeare* (Chapel Hill, IN: University of North Carolina Press, 1984).

Ornstein, Robert, *A Kingdom for a Stage: the achievement of Shakespeare's history plays* (Cambridge, MA: Harvard University Press, 1972).

Pater, Walter, 'Shakespeare's English Kings', in *Appreciations* (London: Macmillan, 1889).

Patterson, Annabel, *Shakespeare and the Popular Voice* (Oxford: Blackwell, 1990).

Peele, George, *King Edward I* (1593), edited by W. W. Greg (Oxford: Oxford University Press, 1911).

Pelling, Henry, *Britain in the Second World War* (London: Collins, 1970).

Pocock, J. G. A., *The Ancient Constitution and the Feudal Law* (Cambridge: Cambridge University Press, 1957).

Porter, Joseph A. *The Drama of Speech Acts: Shakespeare's Lancastrian tetralogy* (Berkeley: University of California Press, 1979).

Preston, Thomas, *A Lamentable Tragedie, mixed full of pleasant mirth, containing the Life of Cambises, King of Percia* (1569), Johnson, Carl Robert (ed.), (Salzburg: Universität Salzburg, 1975).

Prior, Moody E., *The Drama of Power* (Evanston, IL: Northwestern University Press, 1973).

Quinn, Michael, 'Celebrity and the semiotics of acting', *New Theatre Quarterly*, VI, 22 (1990), pp. 154–161.

Ribner, Irving, *The English History Play in the Age of Shakespeare* (Princeton, NI: Princeton University Press, 1957).

Rossiter, A. P., *Angel with Horns and other Shakespeare Lectures*, edited by Graham Storey (London: Longmans Green, 1961).

Ryan, Kiernan, *Shakespeare* (Hemel Hempstead: Harvester Wheatsheaf, 1989).

Saccio, Peter, *Shakespeare's English Kings: History, chronicle and drama* (London: Oxford University Press, 1977).

Salinger, L. G., 'The social setting', in Ford, Boris (ed.), *The Age of Shakespeare* (Harmondsworth: Penguin, 1955).

Samuel, Raphael (ed.), *Patriotism: The making and unmaking of national identity*, vol. 1, *History and Politics* (London: Routledge, 1989).

Sanders, Wilbur, *The Dramatist and the Received Idea* (Cambridge: Cambridge University Press, 1968).

Seltzer, Daniel, 'Prince Hal and tragic style'', *Shakespeare Survey*, vol. 30 (1977), pp. 13–34.

Sidney, Philip, *A Defence of Poetry* (1595), edited by Jan van Dorsten (Oxford: Oxford University Press, 1966).

Sinfield, Alan, 'Four ways with a reactionary text', in *Literature/Teaching/ Politics*, no. 2 (1983), pp. 81–95.

Sinfield, Alan, 'Royal Shakespeare ', in Dollimore, Jonathan and Sinfield, Alan (eds), *Political Shakespeare* (Manchester: Manchester University Press, 1985).

Sissons, Michael and Philip French (eds), *The Age of Austerity* (London: Hodder and Stoughton, 1963).

Southern, Richard, 'The technique of play presentation', in Sanders, Norman *et. al.* (eds.), *The Revels History of Drama in English*, vol. 2, 1500–1576 (London: Methuen, 1980).

Spelman, Henry, *Archaeologus* (London: Beale, 1626).

Squibb, G. D., *The High Court of Chivalry* (Oxford: Oxford University Press, 1959).

Slater, Ann Pasternak, 'An interview with Jonathan Miller', *Quarto*, vol. 10 (September 1980), pp. 9–12.

Stallybrass, Peter, 'Re-thinking text and history', in *Literature/Teaching/ Politics*, no. 2 (1983), pp. 96–107.

Stallybrass, Peter, and Allon White, *The Politics and Poetics of Transgression* (London: Methuen, 1990).

Stone, Lawrence, *The Family, Sex and Marriage 1500–1800*, abridged edition (Harmondsworth: Penguin, 1979).

Stow, John, *The Survey of London* (1633), Wheatley, H. B. (ed.), (London: Dent, 1956).

Stribrny, Zdenek, '*Henry V* and history', in Quinn, Michael (ed.), '*Henry V': a Collection of Critical Essays* (Nashville and London: Aurora Publishers, 1969).

Stubbes, Phillip, *Anatomy of Abuses in England* (1583), edited by Frederick J. Furnivall (London: New Shakespeare Society, 1877).

Tennenhouse, Leonard, *Power on Display* (London: Methuen, 1986).

Thompson, Ann, ' "The warrant of womanhood": Shakespeare and feminist criticism', in Holderness, Graham (ed.), *The Shakespeare Myth* (Manchester: Manchester University Press, 1988).

Tillyard, E. M. W., *The Elizabeth World Picture* (London: Chatto and Windus, 1943).

Tillyard, E. M. W. *Shakespeare's History Plays* (London: Chatto and Windus, 1944).

Traversi, D. A., *Shakespeare from 'Richard II' to 'Henry V'* (London: Hollis and Carter, 1957).

Trevelyan, G. M., *History of England* (London, 1926).

Ure, Peter (ed.). *The Arden Shakespeare: King Richard II* (London: Methuen, 1961).

Virgil, Polydore, *Anglica Historia*, edited by Denys Hay (London: Royal Historical Society, 1950).

Walter, J. H., *The Arden Shakespeare: King Henry V* (London: Methuen, 1954).

Wayne, Don E., 'Power, politics and the Shakespearean text: recent criticism in England and the United Staters', in Howard, Jean E. and O'Connor, Marion F. (eds), (London: Methuen, 1987).

Wayne Valerie, (ed.), *The Matter of Difference: Materialist feminist criticism of Shakespeare* (Hemel Hempstead: Harvester Wheatsheaf, 1991).

Weimann, Robert, *Shakespeare and the Popular Tradition in the Theatre*, translated by Robert Schwarz (Baltimore: Johns Hopkins University Press, 1978).

Wentersdorf, Karl P., 'The conspiracy of silence in *Henry V*', *Shakespeare Quarterly*, vol 27 (1976), pp. 264–87.

Widdowson, Peter, '"Literary value" and the reconstruction of criticism', *Literature and History*, vol. 6 (Autumn 1980), pp. 138–50.

Widdowson, Peter (ed.), *Re-Reading English* (London: Methuen, 1982).

Wilders, John, *The Lost Garden* (London: Macmillan, 1978).

Willett, John (ed.), *Brecht on Theatre* (New York: Eyre Methuen, 1964).

Wilson, J. Dover (ed.), *The First Part of the History of Henry IV* (Cambridge: Cambridge University Press, 1946).

Wilson, J. Dover and T. C. Worsley, *Shakespeare's Histories at Stratford 1951* (London: Max Reinhardt, 1952).

Wilson, J. Dover, *The Fortunes of Falstaff* (Cambridge: Cambridge University Press, 1964).

Wood, Charles, *Tumbledown* (Harmondsworth: Penguin, 1987).

Index